IMAGES
of America

JACKSON HEIGHTS

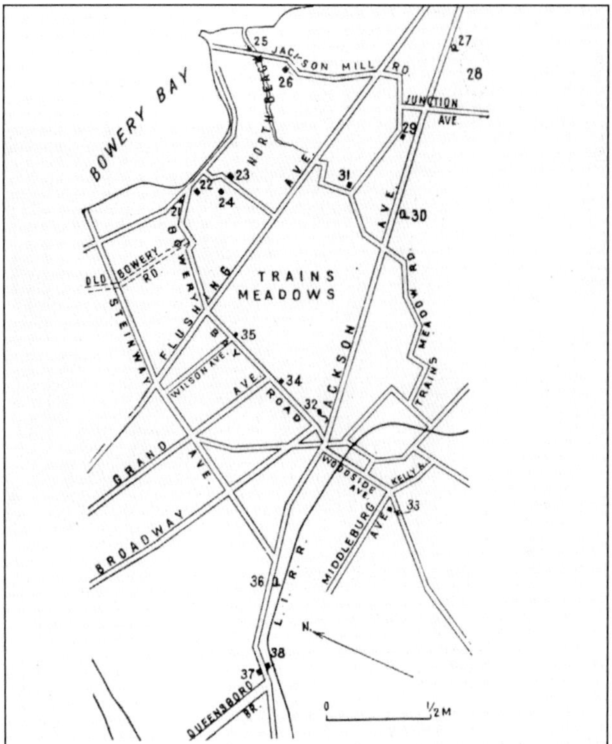

PLATE 29. BOWERY BAY AND WOODSIDE

21—Isaac Rapalye House. 22—Riker Homestead. 23—Luyster Cemetery. 24—Abraham R. Luyster House. 25—Site Wessels' Mill. 26—Farmhouse Abraham and Isaac Rapalye. 27—Five Mile Stone. 28—Site Fashion Race Course. 29—Daniel Rapalye House. 30—Four Mile Stone. 31—Duryea House. 32—Moore Family Cemetery. 33—J. M. Morrell House. 34—Cornelius Purdy House. 35—Riker House. 36—Two Mile Stone. 37—Millstone. 38—Site Skillman-Paynter House.

Map of Trains Meadow, 1909. In Colonial times, the area of Jackson Heights was known as Trains Meadow. This early-20th-century map depicts the old homesteads and the ancient byways that ran through them. The namesake of the neighborhood, Jackson Avenue, a toll road that followed Indian trails and was named after John C. Jackson in the 1850s, would become today's Northern Boulevard (Route 25A). To the north is Newtown, or modern-day Elmhurst, and beyond that is the Bowery Bay, which was renamed Flushing Bay so as not to be confused with the Bowery on the Lower East Side of Manhattan. This map, published in the book *Landmarks of New York* by Arthur Everett Peterson, lists the many homes belonging to some of the founding families of Queens, including Daniel Rapalye, Cornelius Purdy, and the Riker family. (Courtesy of the Queens Borough Public Library, Illustrations Collection–Woodside.)

On the Cover: "Nothing is so essential for the development of character as the environment of childhood. It is not enough that the child shall have the advantages of good parentage and proper home surroundings. There must be also the companionship of good playmates and an opportunity for the child to enjoy the outdoors. It is difficult to develop a sunny and independent nature in a child who is hedged in by the hard brick walls of the city. Life that gives the child an outlook on nature, with her ample spaces and fresh growing things, fits the child for any future. Without these the admonitions of parents and teachers fail of their intent." Text originally published in *Queensborough* magazine, September–October 1925. (Courtesy of the Queens Chamber of Commerce.)

IMAGES
of America

JACKSON HEIGHTS

Jason D. Antos and
Constantine E. Theodosiou
Foreword by council member
Daniel Dromm

ARCADIA
PUBLISHING

ISBN 978-0-7385-9833-8

Published by Arcadia Publishing
Charleston, South Carolina

Printed in the United States of America

Library of Congress Control Number: 2012949670

For all general information, please contact Arcadia Publishing:
Telephone 843-853-2070
Fax 843-853-0044
E-mail sales@arcadiapublishing.com
For customer service and orders:
Toll-Free 1-888-313-2665

Visit us on the Internet at www.arcadiapublishing.com

To our families, who inspired us to reach for the heights

Contents

Foreword

When the Queensboro Corporation developed Jackson Heights in the early part of the 20th century, a new model for urban living was created. The multiple-dwelling garden apartments that were eventually built offered stark alternatives to the congested environments New York City's residents were limited to at the time.

These cooperative apartment communities introduced a new concept in city living. The Jackson Heights of today is, in many respects, reflective of the Jackson Heights of long ago: new, experimental, and avant-garde.

Jackson Heights' true architectural marvel, however, is in its ability to promote a sense of community for middle-class families. The uniformity of the neighborhood block in Jackson Heights reminds us, among other things, of a shared responsibility to care for our trees, to collectively ensure the safety of our children, and to work together to strengthen the institutions that serve our communities directly. In many ways, it is the foundation of this principle that has also drawn people from nearly every corner of the world to coexist within the same zip code.

Today, Jackson Heights has become a snapshot of America. It is a place primarily made up of a thriving immigrant population whose cultures are stitched together because they all share similar struggles and common goals.

The neighborhood's acceptance of diversity is what drew me here as an activist to organize the lesbian, gay, bisexual, and transgender rights movement in the early 1990s and later encouraged me to run for public office.

The faces in Jackson Heights may be forever changing, but the spirit of it will always remain the same. New York City has been called "the greatest collection of villages in the world," and it is places like Jackson Heights that give New York its distinction among the greatest cities of the world.

—Council member Daniel Dromm (District 25)

ACKNOWLEDGEMENTS

The authors wish to thank the following individuals and organizations that helped with this project: our acquisitions editor Caitrin Cunningham for her guidance and patience, Al Clarke at the Queens County Topographical Bureau, the Queens Historical Society, the staff of The Archives (formerly the Long Island Division) at the Queens Borough Public Library, Ron Marzlock and Queens Chamber of Commerce executive director Jack Friedman, and community outreach liaison Jacqueline Donado. Special thanks go to city council member Daniel Dromm for agreeing to write the foreword. All photographs, unless otherwise noted, come from the collection of the authors.

INTRODUCTION

Jackson Heights . . . is one of the brightest spots during the past five years in the real estate horizon of Queens Borough.

—Walter I. Willis, editor
Queens Borough, New York City, 1910–1920 (1920)

It was the afterglow of Consolidation, the celebrated union between Manhattan and its neighboring counties in 1898. New York—now proudly known as Greater New York—was poised to become the financial epicenter of the world. Delighted at the prospect and what it could mean for the city, city officials were nevertheless hard pressed to house 3.4 million newly urbanized New Yorkers. Inspired by the city's sense of destiny (yet guided by the sweet scent of profit), land developers in the outer boroughs took their cue and sprang into action. This was a defining moment for the citizens of New York: By building on the last of the city's primeval landscape, these businessmen were ushering in, in actual terms, the new century's much-anticipated promise.

From the barren stretches of northern Queens, a suburban-styled cooperative development was destined to emerge. Scrupulously designed and executed, it was deemed a model of community planning. Its centerpiece, the garden apartment, brought a renowned British reformer's vision of sound and healthy living to fruition in the United States for the first time. But, amid this newfound splendor and sophistication comes the fact that this community was restricted. It was standing policy. Period ads stated it openly. Yet the spirit of democracy has since prevailed; today, the area claims to have the highest concentration of social and ethnic diversity in New York City and, by some accounts, the entire country.

This is Jackson Heights, an American story.

Unlike much of the rest of Queens, Jackson Heights owes its existence to real estate development that swept the entire borough early in the last century. The name refers to the area's main thoroughfare, Jackson Avenue (today's Northern Boulevard), named after he who first laid it out, John C. Jackson, and its slightly raised topography. Sporting "Heights" in the place-name also lent an air of social prestige, but there was more to Jackson Heights than investors making good on their money. A prominent business journal named *Queens Borough*, maintained that it was just as much "to make . . . an ideal community which would attract those who sought not only a home, but social and other advantages which go to make life worthwhile."

This rang true because of the transformation Queens underwent as a result of consolidation. The Queensboro Bridge's completion in 1909 in particular marked the start of groundbreaking changes: subway service to Manhattan's business centers, a vastly improved local infrastructure, and an industrial base set to expand along the East River. Queens was soon publicized as the city's premier "borough of homes" something that, to local chronicler Henry Isham Hazelton, its idle farmlands held the key:

> It is generally conceded that the midtown zone of Manhattan is the "all-day, twenty-four-hour business heart of New York City." With the transit lines which now operate eastward from Thirty-fourth Street, Forty-second Street, and Fifty-ninth Street, and other lines to be built in the future, it is inevitable that the industrial, commercial, and residential growth of New York City must be in Queens and that the time of travel has turned definitely eastward.
>
> Manhattan has reached a stage in its growth where further development only produces greater congestion and discomfort. Just a mile to the east are the thousands of acres of land in Queens, ripe for development. Here a vast area waits with open arms for the overcrowded millions of other boroughs.

Meanwhile, speculators were already drawn to Queens' possibilities. Among them was a syndicate of bankers and land agents led by Edward Archibald MacDougall, who from as early as 1906 eyed the substantial landholdings in the north central part of the borough. Roughly 350 acres in total, this was the Trains Meadows section of old Newtown village (between Woodside and Elmhurst, south of Northern Boulevard), whose history extended to the Dutch Colonial period. It briefly served as a British encampment before the Battle of Long Island, and later in the 19th century, it was where affluent New Yorkers kept country homes. The bucolic presence of the local racetrack and stables point to horse racing as a principal sporting event. Nearby marshlands were ideal for hunting snipe. But by 1910, all this hardly mattered. What did matter was the spirit of progress through the practice of development. Starting with the 128-acre Barclay-Dugro tract, the newly incorporated Queensboro Corporation spent $3.8 million (more than $44.1 million in 2012) to acquire the Trains Meadow territory, seen then as the largest land deal in city limits by a private entity. At Queensboro's behest, the city sealed off the Trains Meadows Road to lay down the necessary groundwork for the new Jackson Heights community. Speaking before an audience at the International Town, City and Regional Planning Conference 15 years later, MacDougall made this assessment:

> Twelve years ago the tract of land that comprises Jackson Heights was open farms . . . the equivalent of 100 city blocks, peacefully overlooking the northward moving skyline of Manhattan and traversed by a half dozen wagon roads. Today [in 1925] Jackson Heights, the property of the Queensboro Corporation, has 5 1/2 miles of paved roads, over $25,000,000 has been invested in the erection of 122 four and five story apartment buildings, besides many smaller houses, over $1,000,000 invested in the physical improvement of the property, more than 1,500 families have their homes here, and this year alone accommodations for 300 additional families will be ready, with a more intensive program . . . well under way.

Though its unfinished appearance before World War I might have looked uninviting to some, Jackson Heights managed to lure permanent residents. But to get to Manhattan, these "true pioneers" (a term coined by Jackson Heights author Daniel Karatzas) had to undergo a 90-minute-long streetcar commute to Hunter's Point in Long Island City for the Thirty-fourth Street ferry. As part of the Dual Subway System designed to serve the transportation needs of the outer boroughs, the Corona Extension (the elevated IRT Flushing Line) appeared in Jackson Heights in April 1917. For a nickel, residents were able to reach Grand Central Terminal in just 20 to 25 minutes, leading some to believe they had the best of both worlds: city life by day, a tranquil setting to come home to. MacDougall saw his area property values skyrocket.

Just who was Edward Archibald MacDougall? Clearly, he was a businessman of his time: shrewd, driven, cocksure; the kind who let his credentials speak for himself. Born in Brooklyn in 1874, MacDougall established himself as a developer in Brooklyn and Long Island City soon after completing his education. Early in his career, he had a hand in forging the residential section at Kissena Park in Flushing. He was a member of the Borough Planning Commission and, in time, became governor of the Real Estate Board of New York. Along the way, he was chaired the city's Bridges and Tunnels Committee, which gave him an insider's knowledge on the Corona Extension, and the Queensboro Chamber of Commerce, a post he found particularly useful when it came to Jackson Heights. As New York City subway historian Clifton Hood put it, MacDougall chose not to implement standard practices in place, having "conceived [Jackson Heights as] completely planned and largely self-contained." It paid off. According to AM *New York*, Jackson Heights is one of New York City's "hidden gems."

Though not opposed to building single-family homes, MacDougall preferred apartment complexes as the basis of construction throughout the community. This made for a compact neighborhood (albeit one that stood a better chance to be cost effective), but the symmetry and uniformity of the buildings presented a stately appearance. This said, MacDougall's crowning achievement was in realizing the garden apartment concept espoused in the late 19th century by the Garden Cities movement founder, Britain's Ebenezer Howard. Queensboro architect Andrew J. Thomas cleverly adjoined the courtyards of neighboring complexes to create the illusion of seamless interior garden space. Residents enjoyed splendid vistas and, more importantly, privacy: "Shielded from the street by the buildings and protected from the traffic noises and pedestrians' stares," asserts Hood, "these interior spaces became semi-private oases of light, air, [and] greenery."

Jackson Heights was hailed as the first garden apartment suburb in the nation, whose merit MacDougall hoped would be enhanced through what was termed "social cohesion." Queensboro introduced a cooperative ownership plan in 1919 that gave apartment dwellers the opportunity to be, in effect, homeowners. This innovation, revolutionary for its time, had Queens Chamber of Commerce secretary Walter Willis declare, "The 'Own-Your-Own-Home' desire can be fulfilled in the new apartment houses at Jackson Heights." Generous amenities included playgrounds, tennis courts, a community garden, and even a 12-hole golf course. Residents had access to a clubhouse known as "The Casino." Queensboro supported the formation of clubs, sports leagues, and children activities. It printed the *Jackson Heights News*, which kept tabs on local events and individual doings. It donated property for the erection of local churches. Yet with all this munificence came Queensboro's expectation that residents adhere to its "distinctive way of life," stressing social, economic, and cultural homogeneity. ("Jackson Heights . . . an association of home-loving people whose aim in life is to promote fellowship, happiness and good will" was how *Queens Borough* championed the move.) Clifton Hood found a graver reality to be the case, however:

> As a strong private corporation that intervened in all aspects of Jackson Heights, Queensboro wielded great power over the lives of its inhabitants. It used its power to protect Jackson Heights' property values and reputation for suburban exclusivity. Queensboro thus enforced middle-class standards of decorum by prohibiting residents from shaking their mops or brooms out of their windows or from drying their wash on their clotheslines.

More pointedly, the Queensboro Corporation screened prospective residents, requiring, for example, "acceptable" social and business references. In practice, Queensboro favored an Anglo-Saxon Protestant clientele and likewise denied access to Catholics, African Americans, and Jews in particular. To be sure, Jackson Heights was not the only place in New York City's limits to have similar restrictions, but within its domain, Queensboro applied these to its satisfaction. Our dismay notwithstanding, this rode on the momentum of the federal government's decision to limit the entry of certain immigrant groups after the First World War. Making this more disturbing was Queensboro's belief that this made sound business sense.

While the Roaring Twenties was the banner decade for Jackson Heights, the Great Depression unraveled many of its prior successes. During these leaner years, Queensboro witnessed three cooperative complexes fail. Apartments that cost $20,000 went unsold at $3,000. To stem his losses, MacDougall offered rentals for the first time, dashing any hope that his beloved community remain exclusive and suburban-like. By mid-decade, Queensboro opted to develop the land once reserved for nobler purposes. Some garden apartment dwellers continued to maintain their grounds on an individual basis (a testament to the popularity of the concept), but the garden apartment enclave that Queensboro nurtured for the better part of two decades was over. We can only surmise how Edward MacDougall took to all this. After spending the better part of four and a half decades in his chosen profession, he died in 1944.

By the late 1940s, when potential customers looked towards places like Long Island's Levittown to pursue the American dream (that is, an actual house to call home) the once renowned Jackson Heights cooperative fell out of favor. The Carlton fared so poorly in 1947 that Queensboro, now headed by A. Edward MacDougall, was compelled to offer solely rentals. In two years came the Greenbrier, the last cooperative Queensboro made public. It was the last gasp. At the same time, municipal incursions were on the uptick: area residents found themselves forced to hault the New York City Housing Authority in 1947 from erecting public housing in their midst. On a lighter note, the Queensboro Library opened its Jackson Heights branch in 1954.

Inevitably, grimmer city-bred forces would take their toll in the neighborhood. (Signified in the 1980s by the cruel play on the community name: "Crackson Heights.") Scars remain, but signs of resilience are evident. Thanks to the Jackson Heights Beautification Group, the venerable 36-block residential heart of the community is now a historic district, restoring a lost measure of dignity to the area. To the delight of gourmands, the Jackson Heights Greenmarket has become a local fixture; it is Queens' first year-round farmers market and its largest. For more than 50 years, the Jackson Heights Arts Club has sponsored artistic shows and instruction. With the Local Art Collaborative Exchange (LACE), musicians, photographers, poets, writers, as well as visual and performing artists, are given new venues. This engendered a high degree of social acceptance, as the strong presence of the local LGBT community attests. Galvanizing after the hate-inspired murder of model Julio Rivera in 1990, its annual Queens Pride parade expresses the triumph of individual freedom with considerable fanfare. From the 1950s through to the 1980s, Jackson Heights has been home for immigrants from different parts of Latin America, India, Pakistan, and Bangladesh. While such a heady mix of such social and cultural diversity would have taken Edward MacDougall and his Queensboro colleagues aback, a walk through Little India shows the concept of social cohesion indeed alive and well. Only now, it's more along more egalitarian lines.

One

A Neighborhood Is Born

It was nothing more than a wide-open canvas of rolling hills, small collect ponds, and dirt paths that led to the indiscriminately scattered farmhouses. There were only three main roads—Jackson Avenue (today's Northern Boulevard); Bowery Bay Road, which wound its way from Jackson Heights' western end to the northern terminus of North Beach and the Flushing Bay; and Trains Meadow Road. These ancient arteries were not paved but were dirt-covered, hard-packed surfaces conditioned by years of passing horseshoes and iron-rimmed wagon wheels. Before the coming of the Queensboro Bridge and Edward A. MacDougall's Queensboro Corporation, the area was known as Trains Meadow—although no trains ever crossed its terrain; the name is a corruption of the phrase "Long Drains Meadow," referring to channels that had been dug to drain the wetlands throughout the terrain. Of the dozens of marshes and brooks, some measuring six to eight feet wide and three or four feet deep, the largest was Sackhickniyeh Brook. At the turn of the 20th century, Queens had a population of 152,999, or two persons per acre. In Trains Meadow, which was located within the confines of Newtown, one of the oldest established territories in the borough, dwelled several families. The largest two were the Leverich and Barclay families. The namesake for Manhattan's Barclay Street, the Barclays built a racetrack along Northern Boulevard that ran between Seventy-second and Seventy-fourth Streets. Every season, people from Manhattan, Brooklyn, and Long Island ventured to the rural reaches of Trains Meadow to watch the races at Barclay's track.

In the days of the American Revolution, Queens was pro-British, and its towns, hamlets, and villages witnessed many events of the conflict. The summer of 1776 proved eventful for Jackson Heights. After the Battle of Long Island, the entire British army marched to Newtown. On August 31, an army of 4,000 British soldiers, led by Sir Henry Clinton, marched along Trains Meadow Road and set up camp near what became Northern Boulevard. During that same period, members of Gen. William Howe's British army set up an encampment at present-day Thirty-seventh Avenue and Seventy-third Street. Known as the Royal Highlanders, they stayed there for two weeks. On September 15, they journeyed across Newtown Creek to the Battle of Kip's Bay near midtown Manhattan and the East River.

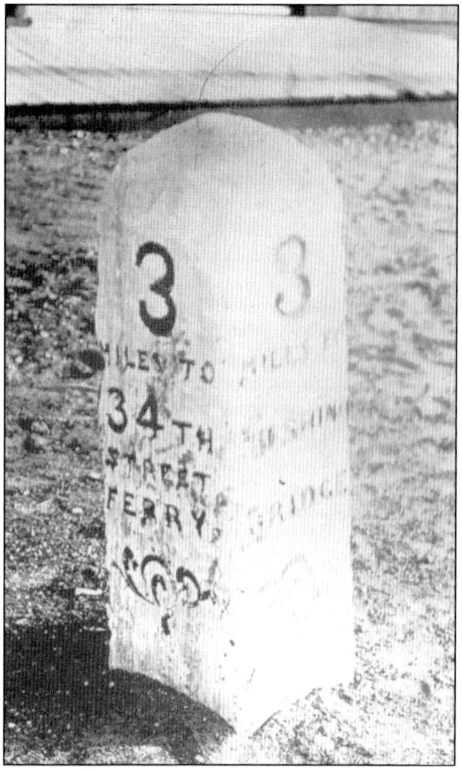

Counting the Miles. And so, the journey through the history of Jackson Heights begins. On April 16, 1858, the Hunter's Point, Newtown, and Flushing Turnpike Company was incorporated to build a road that would stretch from the East River in Long Island City to Flushing. Two Queens residents, John C. Jackson and his wife's cousin Alpheus P. Riker, were its president and treasurer, respectively. After just 15 months, on July 13, 1860, the road opened and was named Jackson Avenue in honor of the company's president, who supervised and championed this new route. During this time, Jackson placed stone mileposts along the road, a custom that he brought with him from his native England. These markers led the way through Trains Meadow, which would one day bear the name of the benefactor of the town's main thoroughfare.

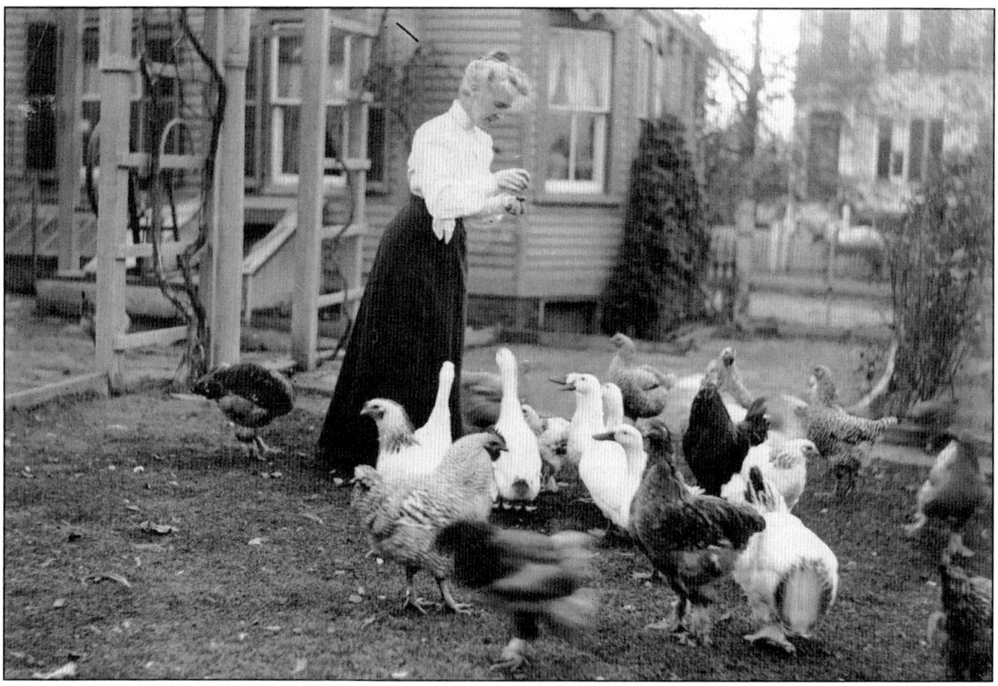

Feeding Time. In this never-before-published photograph from 1898, a Mrs. Fowler of Trains Meadow Road is seen feeding her chickens, roosters, and geese. This scene was typical in most neighborhoods throughout Queens the year that it became a borough of New York City.

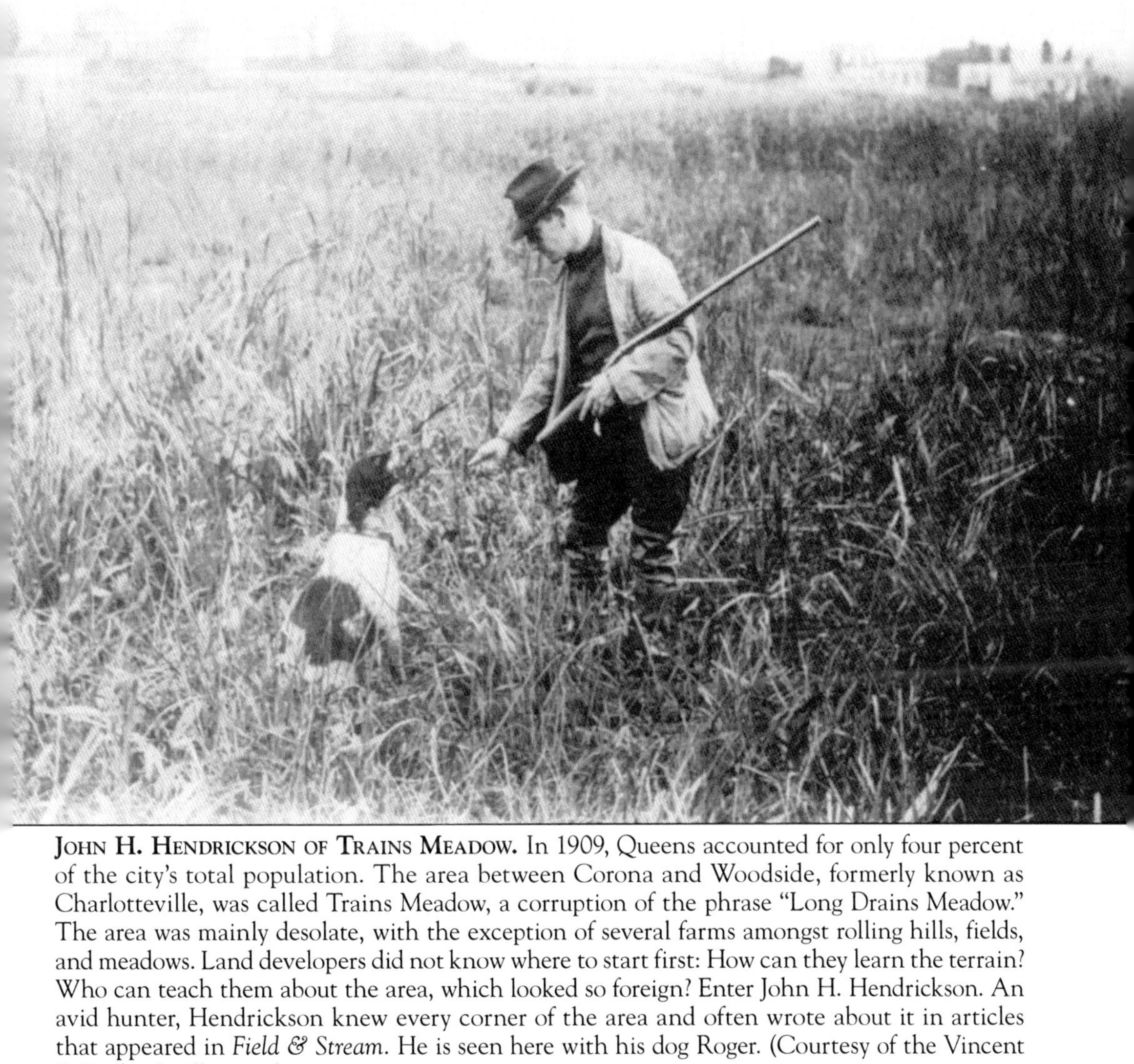

JOHN H. HENDRICKSON OF TRAINS MEADOW. In 1909, Queens accounted for only four percent of the city's total population. The area between Corona and Woodside, formerly known as Charlotteville, was called Trains Meadow, a corruption of the phrase "Long Drains Meadow." The area was mainly desolate, with the exception of several farms amongst rolling hills, fields, and meadows. Land developers did not know where to start first: How can they learn the terrain? Who can teach them about the area, which looked so foreign? Enter John H. Hendrickson. An avid hunter, Hendrickson knew every corner of the area and often wrote about it in articles that appeared in *Field & Stream*. He is seen here with his dog Roger. (Courtesy of the Vincent F. Seyfried collection.)

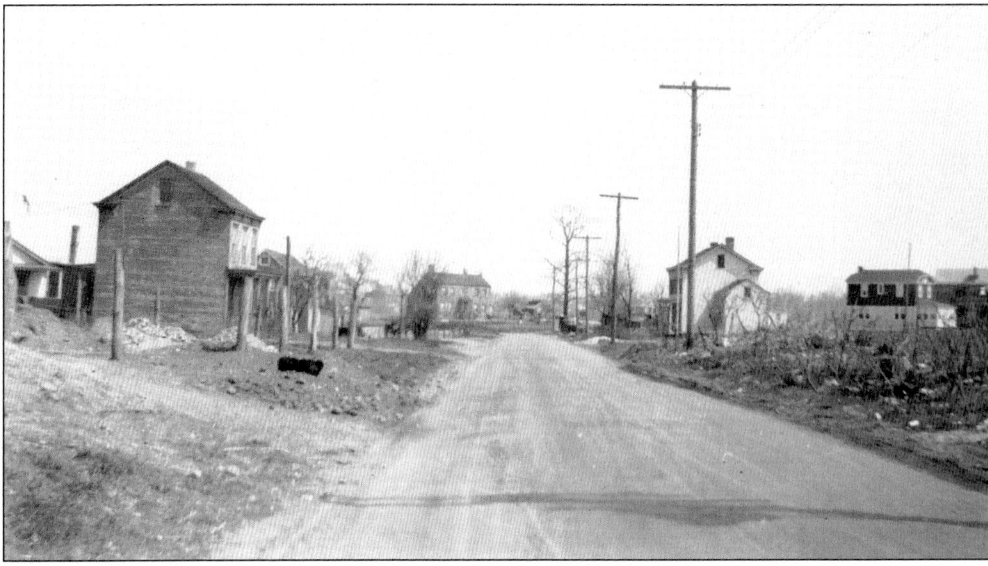

Trains Meadow Road. Trains Meadow Road was a continuation of the old Trains Meadow Lane, laid out as early as 1672 and one of the only main roads through the meadow. People first used it as a footpath but later widened it for carriages and wagons. This view looks northeast from Twenty-fourth Street (now Eighty-first Street) down Trains Meadow Road (now in the proximity of Thirty-first Avenue). (Courtesy of the Queens Borough Public Library, Long Island Division, Eugene L. Armbruster Photographs.)

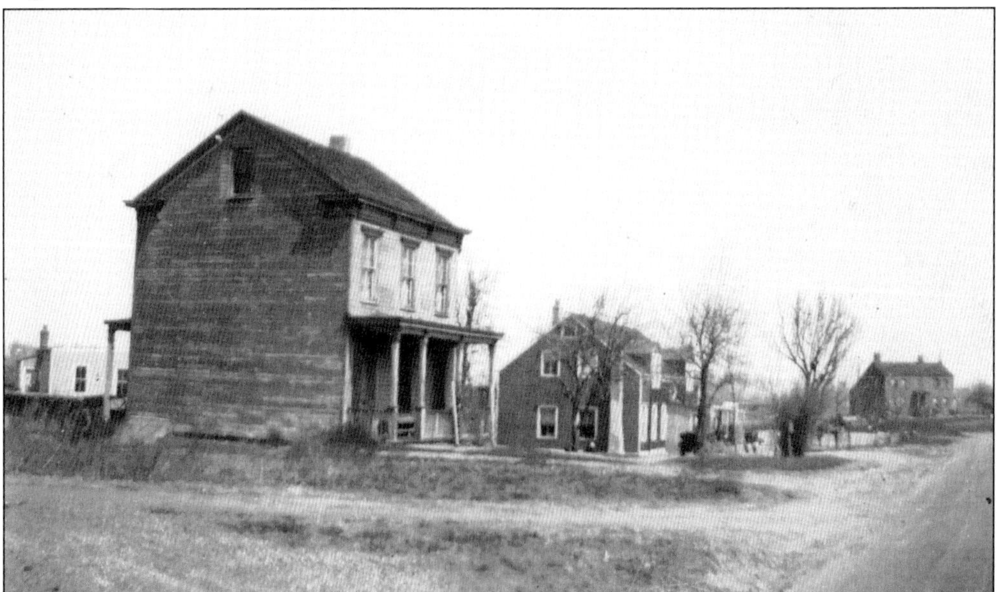

A Walking Tour. Moving down Trains Meadow Road, the first home encountered is the Stump family house on the left. Located at what was known then as the corner of Twenty-fourth Street and Trains Meadow Road, the current address of the home would be 8019 Thirty-first Avenue. The Stump house was one of the only structures that survived the initial development by the Queensboro Corporation. (Courtesy of the Queens Borough Public Library, Long Island Division, Eugene L. Armbruster Photographs.)

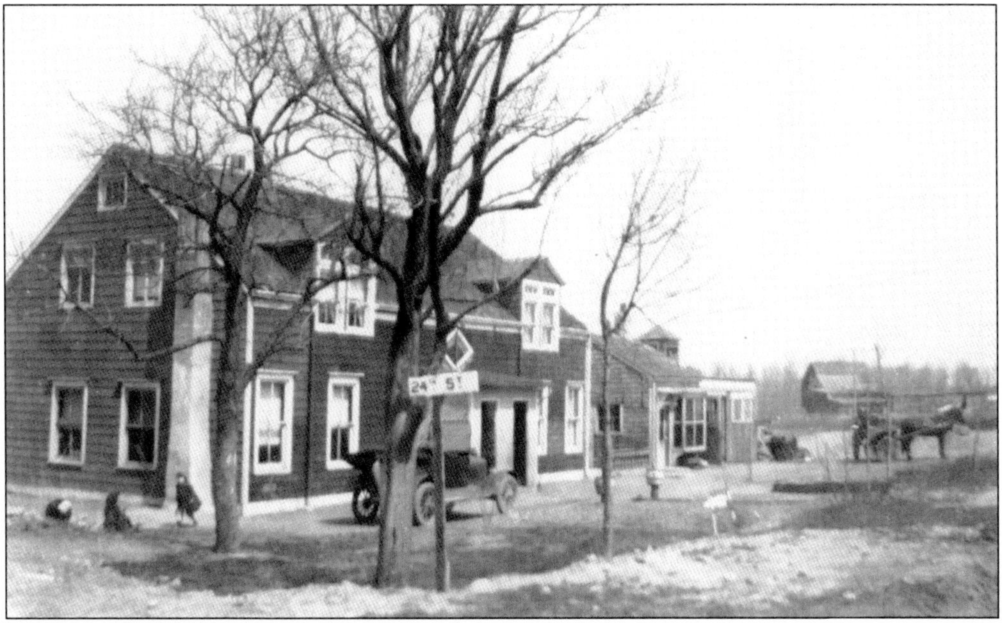

The Green House. The next stop after Stump's was the Green house, located just east of what is now Eighty-first Street. The Green families were one of many who sold their properties to the Queensboro Corporation, and thus the house was demolished during the development of Jackson Heights. (Courtesy of the Queens Borough Public Library, Long Island Division, Eugene L. Armbruster Photographs.)

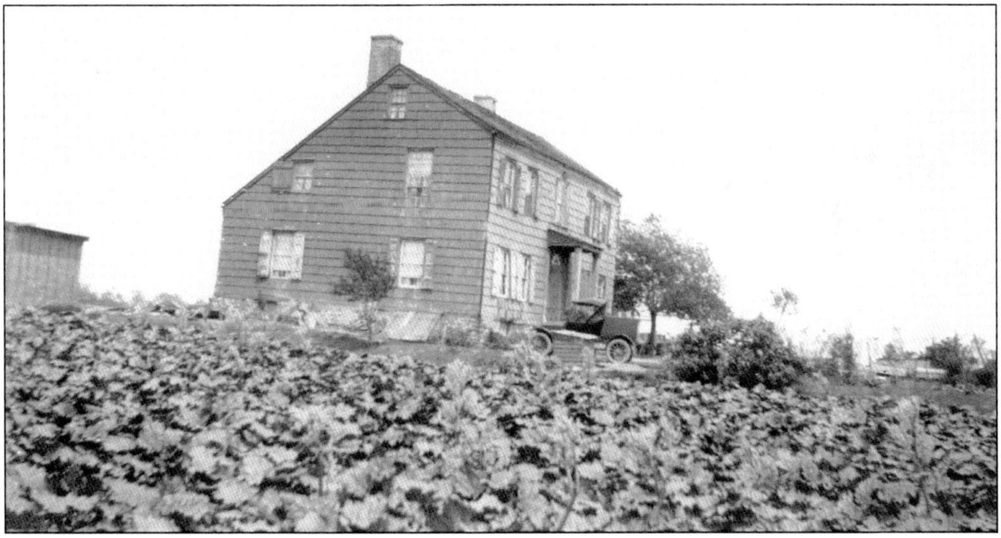

Hazard-Duryea House. Erected by Judge James Hazard, this homestead was located on the northeast corner of Trains Meadow Road (Thirty-first Avenue) and Poor Bowery Road (Eighty-second Street). Prior to the American Revolution, the Hazard family was one of the most prominent families in Newtown. It was Thomas Hazard who came from Wales in 1636 to the New World and would establish one of the founding families of Newtown. A judge of common pleas, Hazard died on April 25, 1765. The farm was later sold to John Duryea. More than 160 years later, it was demolished, in 1927. (Courtesy of the Queens Borough Public Library, Long Island Division, Eugene L. Armbruster Photographs.)

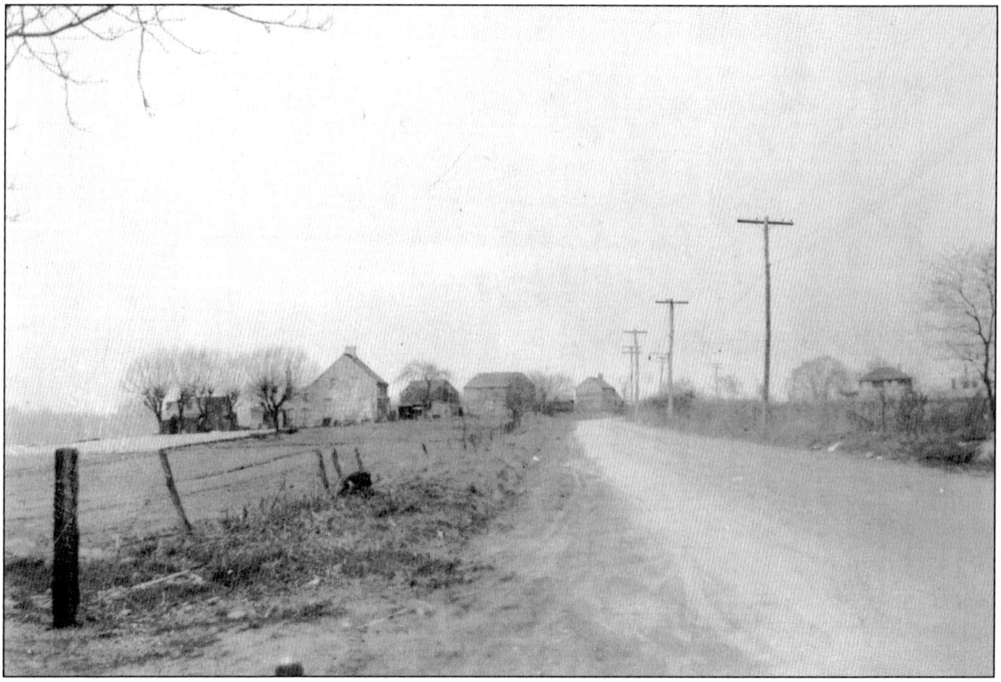

Opposite View. This view from the winter of 1924 looks southwest down Trains Meadow Road from Twenty-first Street (now Seventy-eighth Street). (Courtesy of the Queens Borough Public Library, Long Island Division, Eugene L. Armbruster Photographs.)

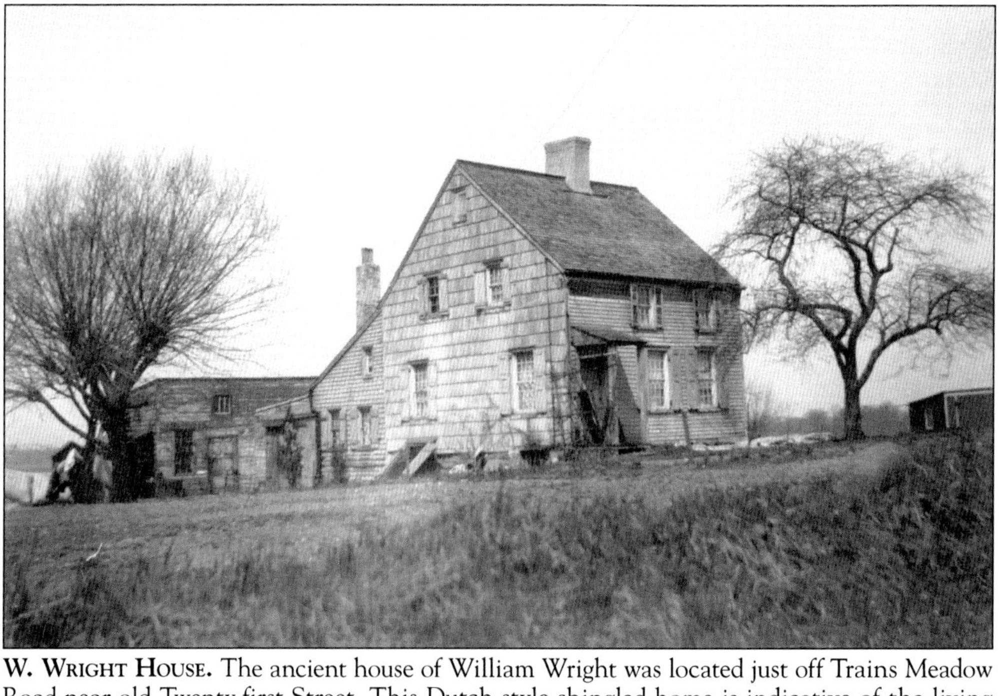

W. Wright House. The ancient house of William Wright was located just off Trains Meadow Road near old Twenty-first Street. This Dutch-style shingled home is indicative of the living conditions prior to the arrival of MacDougall. (Courtesy of the Queens Borough Public Library, Long Island Division, Eugene L. Armbruster Photographs.)

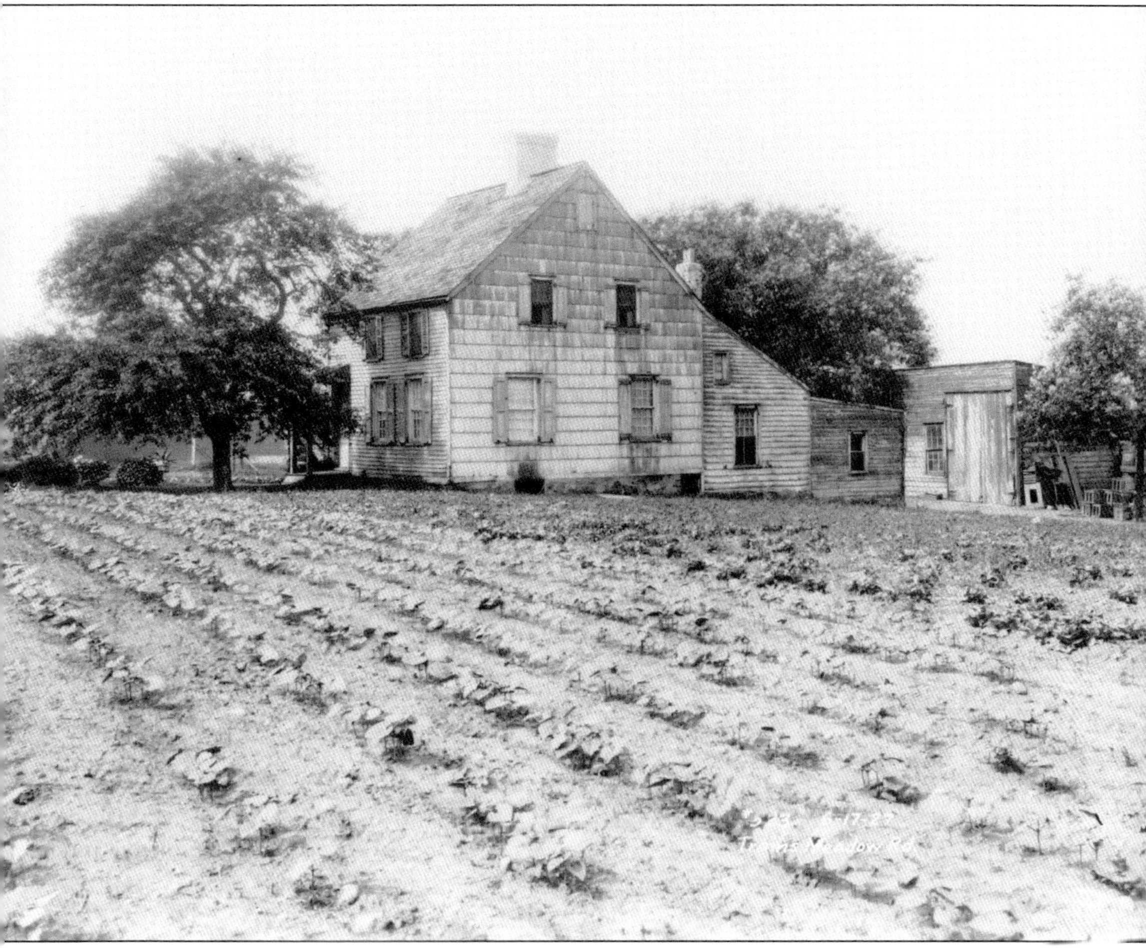

Harvesttime. In keeping with New York City mayor William J. Gaynor's remark about "the cornfields of Queens," this c. 1915 photograph offers a rare view of the Wright house during planting season. (Courtesy of the Queens Borough Public Library, Long Island Division, Eugene L. Armbruster Photographs.)

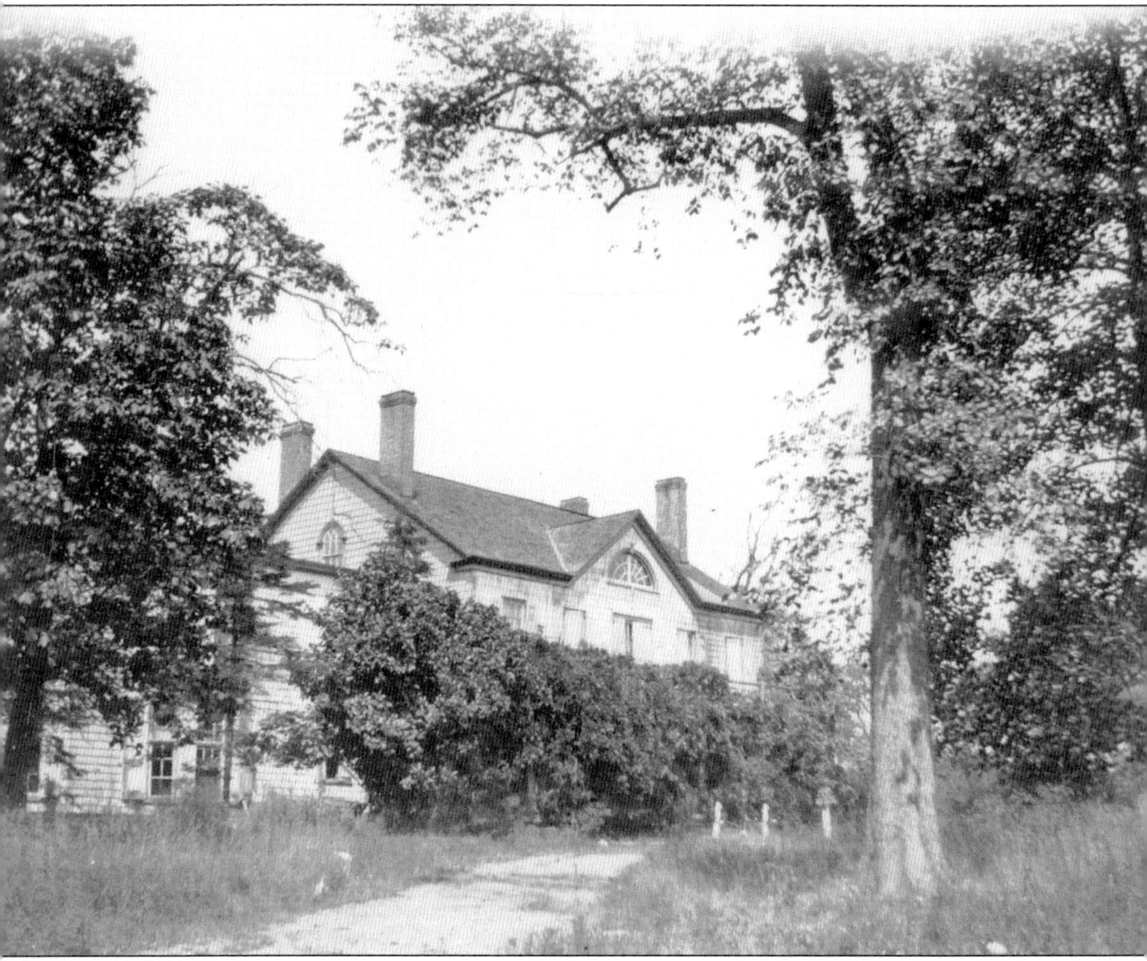

A Country Estate. Here, partially hidden behind the foliage, is another typical home along Trains Meadow Road. (Courtesy of the Queens Borough Public Library, Long Island Division, Eugene L. Armbruster Photographs.)

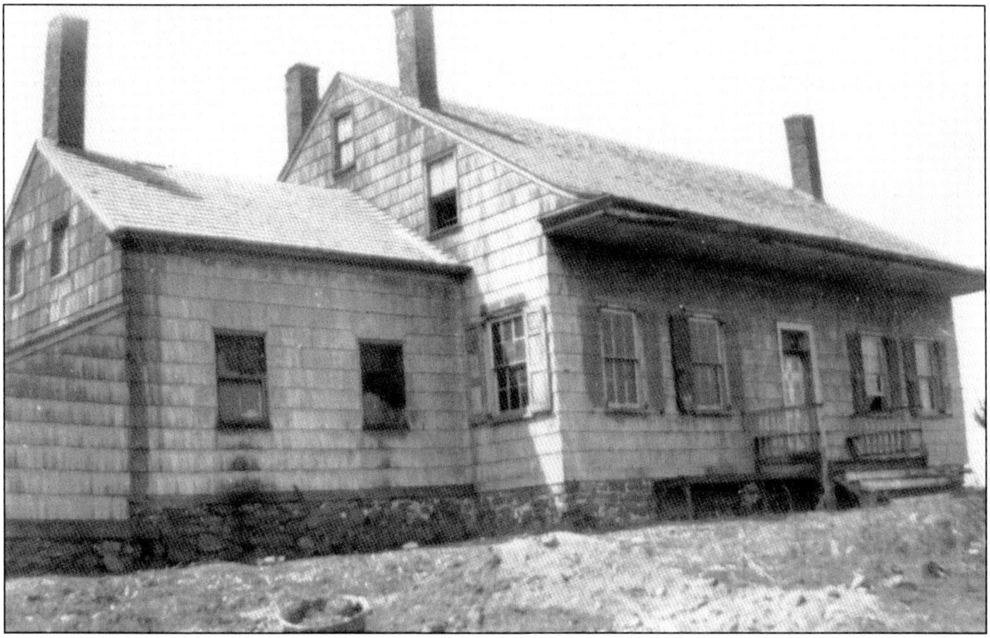

David Rapelye House. Located on the southeast corner of Thirty-second Avenue and Eighty-ninth Street, this shingle-roofed home of David Rapelye was built in 1737 and remained in his possession until 1776. It succumbed to demolition in May 1926. The structure featured a facade made up of 30-inch shingles and had a brick foundation. As one entered through the front door, he or she was immediately led into a central hallway. There were two rooms on either side located on the first and second floors. The Rapelye family is another old name found in the early history of Queens. The name comes from that of de Rapalie or Rapalje, who were French nobles. They were expelled from France in the 1500s because of their Protestant beliefs. (Courtesy of the Queens Borough Public Library, Long Island Division, Eugene L. Armbruster Photographs.)

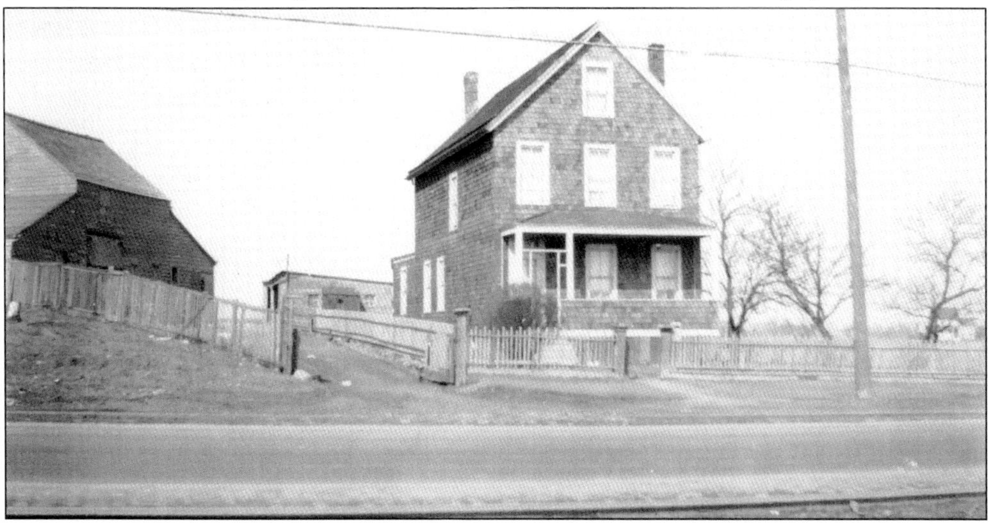

Fred Johnson House. Located at the northeast corner of Eighty-sixth Street and Northern Boulevard was the Fred Johnson house. This shingled structure sat on one of the many spreads purchased by the Queensboro Corporation as building in Jackson Heights progressed. (Courtesy of the Queens Borough Public Library, Long Island Division, Eugene L. Armbruster Photographs.)

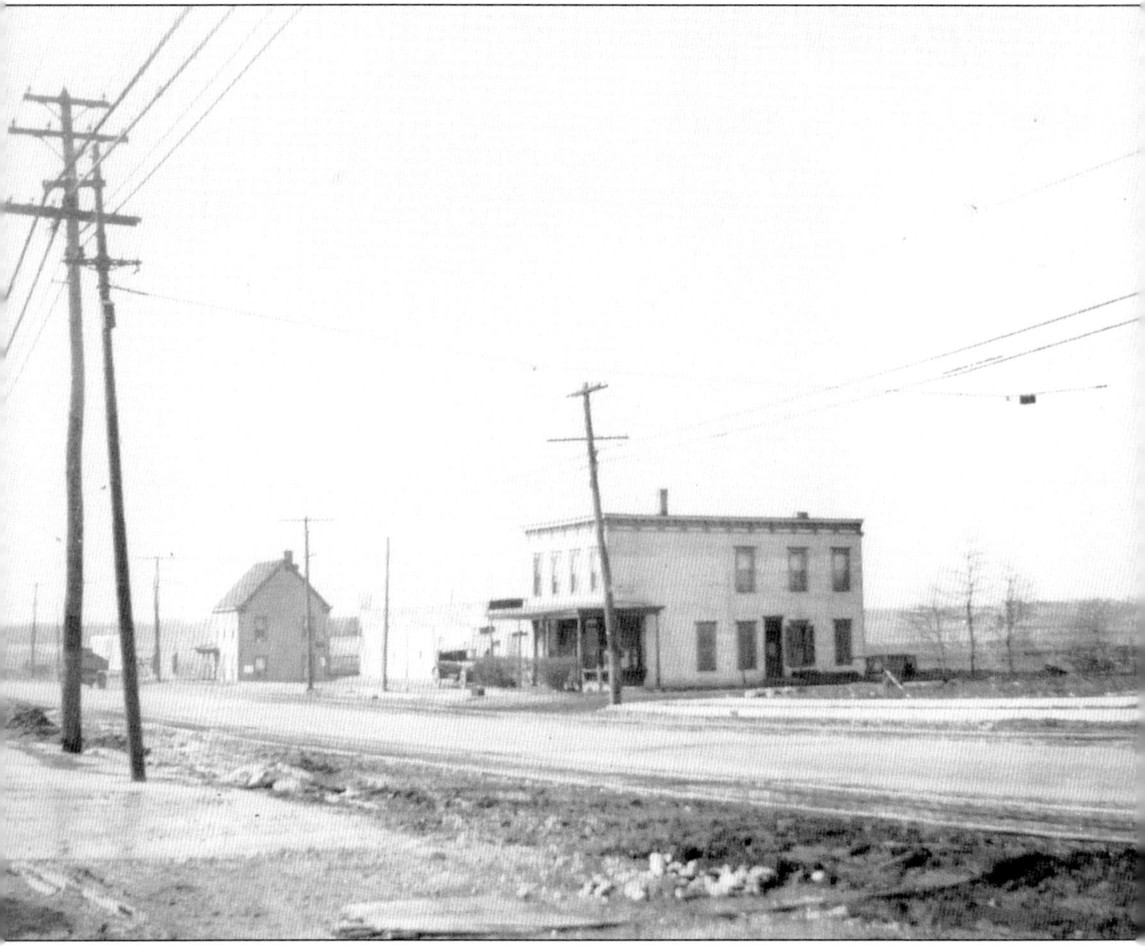

DESOLATE SURROUNDINGS. Before the coming of clothing boutiques, family pharmacies, and restaurants, most of Northern Boulevard was a stretch of auto repair shops, decaying saloons, homesteads, and inns that dated back to the days of the stagecoach. The J. Pack's Roadhouse and the Jackson Auto Garage between Seventy-seventh and Seventy-eighth Streets are seen here in their final days before widespread development took place. (Courtesy of the Queens Borough Public Library, Long Island Division, Eugene L. Armbruster Photographs.)

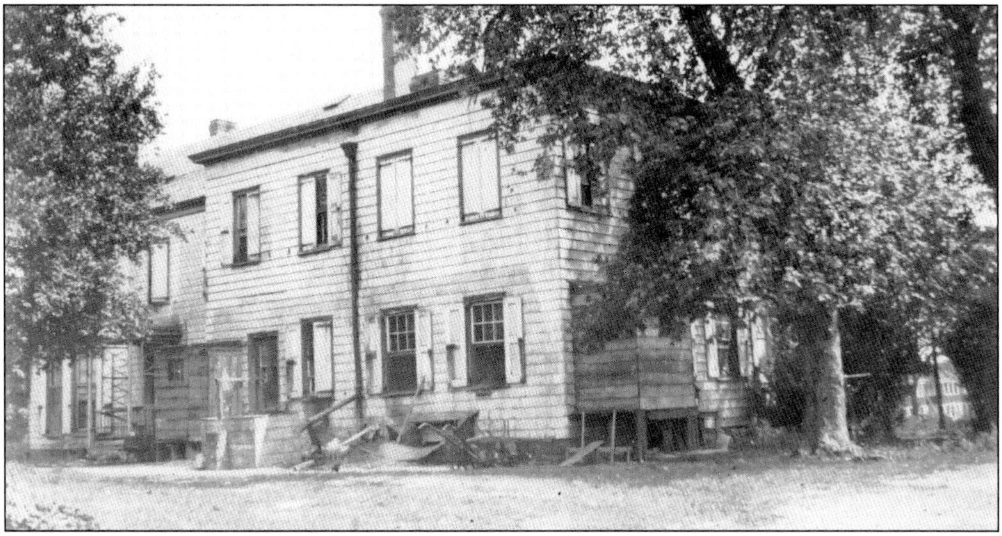

H. Leverich House. One of the largest landowners in Trains Meadow next to the Barclay and Dugro families was the Leveriches. The first family member to come to Queens was the Reverend William Leverich, who settled in Newtown, then known as Middleburg, in 1662. Here is a rear view of the house that belonged to Henry S. Leverich. The property was located north of Elmhurst Avenue, also known as Shell Road (now Thirty-seventh Avenue), on the east side of what is now Ninety-third Street. (Courtesy of the Queens Borough Public Library, Long Island Division, Eugene L. Armbruster Photographs.)

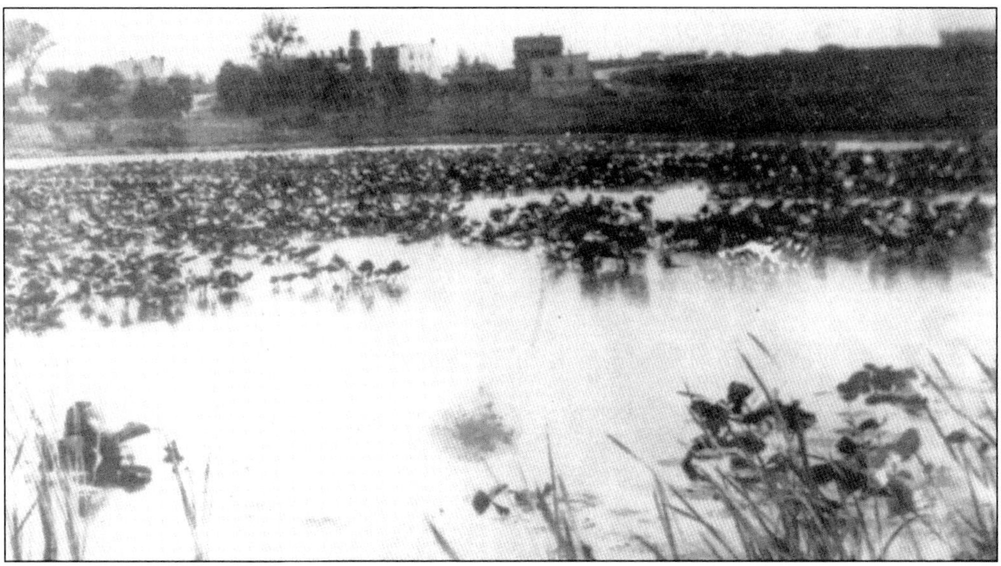

An Idyllic Scene. Known as "Bucko's Pond" or "the Duck Pond," this body of water lay on the western border of Jackson Heights near Woodside. Located just south of Northern Boulevard and stretching as far south as Thirty-fifth Avenue, the pond was owned by John O'Connor, who used it as an ice works facility. From west to east, it stretched from Sixty-fourth to Seventieth Streets. In the background, homes can be seen along Trains Meadow Road. Ponds like this are the reason for the area being named "Drains Meadow" because the water would collect like so. The area is now the location of the Brooklyn-Queens Expressway and New York Connecting Railway.

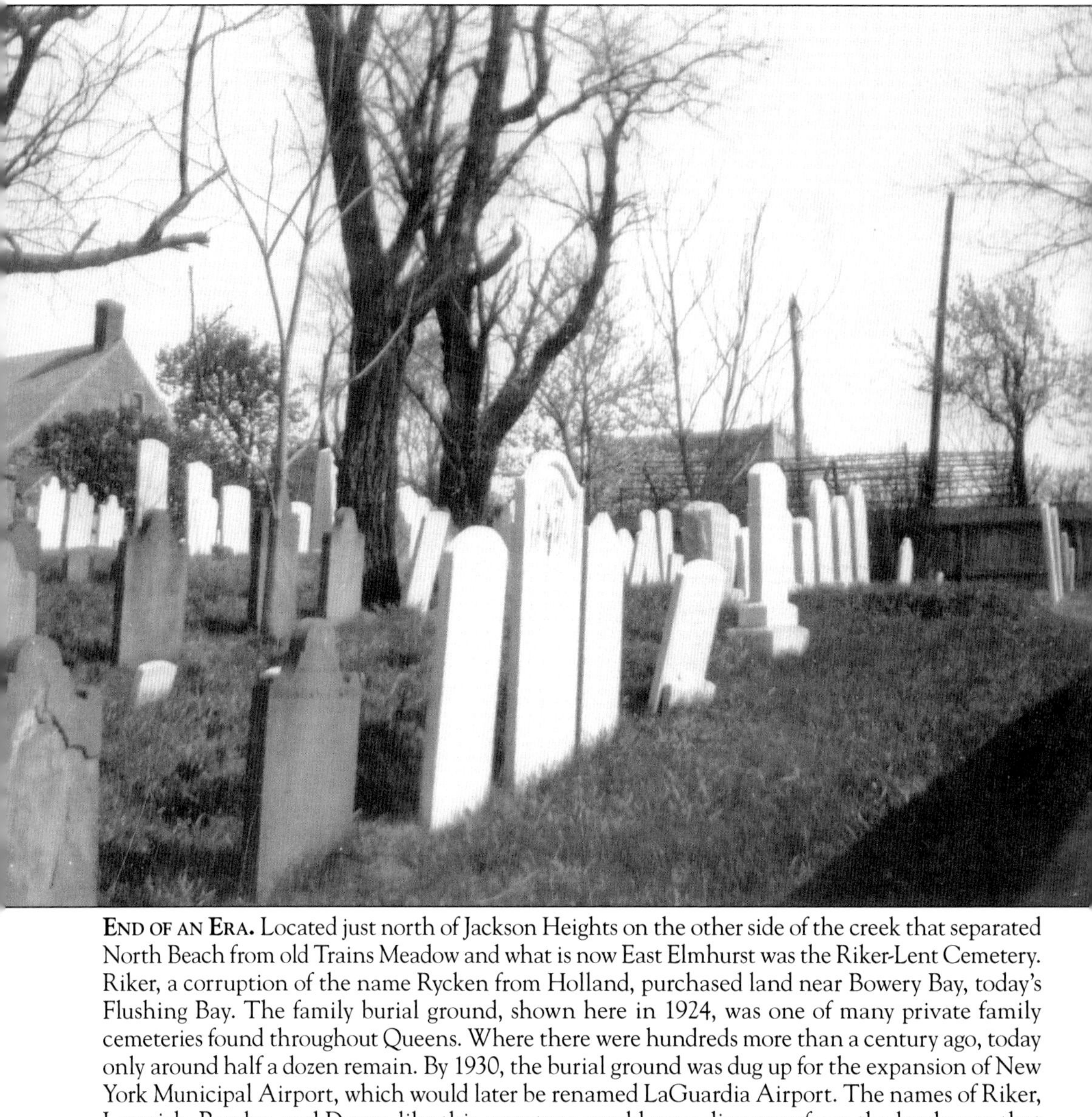

END OF AN ERA. Located just north of Jackson Heights on the other side of the creek that separated North Beach from old Trains Meadow and what is now East Elmhurst was the Riker-Lent Cemetery. Riker, a corruption of the name Rycken from Holland, purchased land near Bowery Bay, today's Flushing Bay. The family burial ground, shown here in 1924, was one of many private family cemeteries found throughout Queens. Where there were hundreds more than a century ago, today only around half a dozen remain. By 1930, the burial ground was dug up for the expansion of New York Municipal Airport, which would later be renamed LaGuardia Airport. The names of Riker, Leverich, Barclay, and Dugro, like this cemetery, would soon disappear from the landscape that they had inhabited for almost 200 years. (Courtesy of the Queens Borough Public Library, Long Island Division, Eugene L. Armbruster Photographs.)

Two

Speculation and Development

On March 30, 1909, the most monumental event of 20th-century Queens took place at the borough's western terminus in Long Island City. For it was on this day that Gustav Lindenthal's 3,700-foot span, the Queensboro Bridge, opened to vehicular, trolley, and pedestrian traffic. With its opening, the fertile and rural landscape of Queens County was now accessible to the millions that crowded Manhattan. From a high vantage point, pedestrians coming to Queens from the city could look out and see farms and prairies stretching for miles in either direction.

Three years earlier, in 1906, the Brooklyn-born Edward A. MacDougall began surveying the land of Trains Meadow, situated between Woodside and Elmhurst, south of Jackson Avenue. He had developed other parts of the borough including Kissena Park, Terminal Heights in Woodside, and Elmhurst Square. On August 12, 1909, MacDougall formed the Queensboro Corporation and entered perhaps the single largest farm buyout in American history. The corporation bought the 128-acre Barclay-Dugro tract, and by the time all was said and done, more than 350 acres of farmland were purchased.

By 1910, almost $500,000 was spent by the Queensboro Corporation grading the old dirt paths, adding miles of sidewalks, sewers, and water and gas mains. Several years later, the first major buildings were erected. This included such masterworks as The Towers, The Chateau, Linden, Laurel Courts, and others—all of which made their eternal marks in modern architectural history.

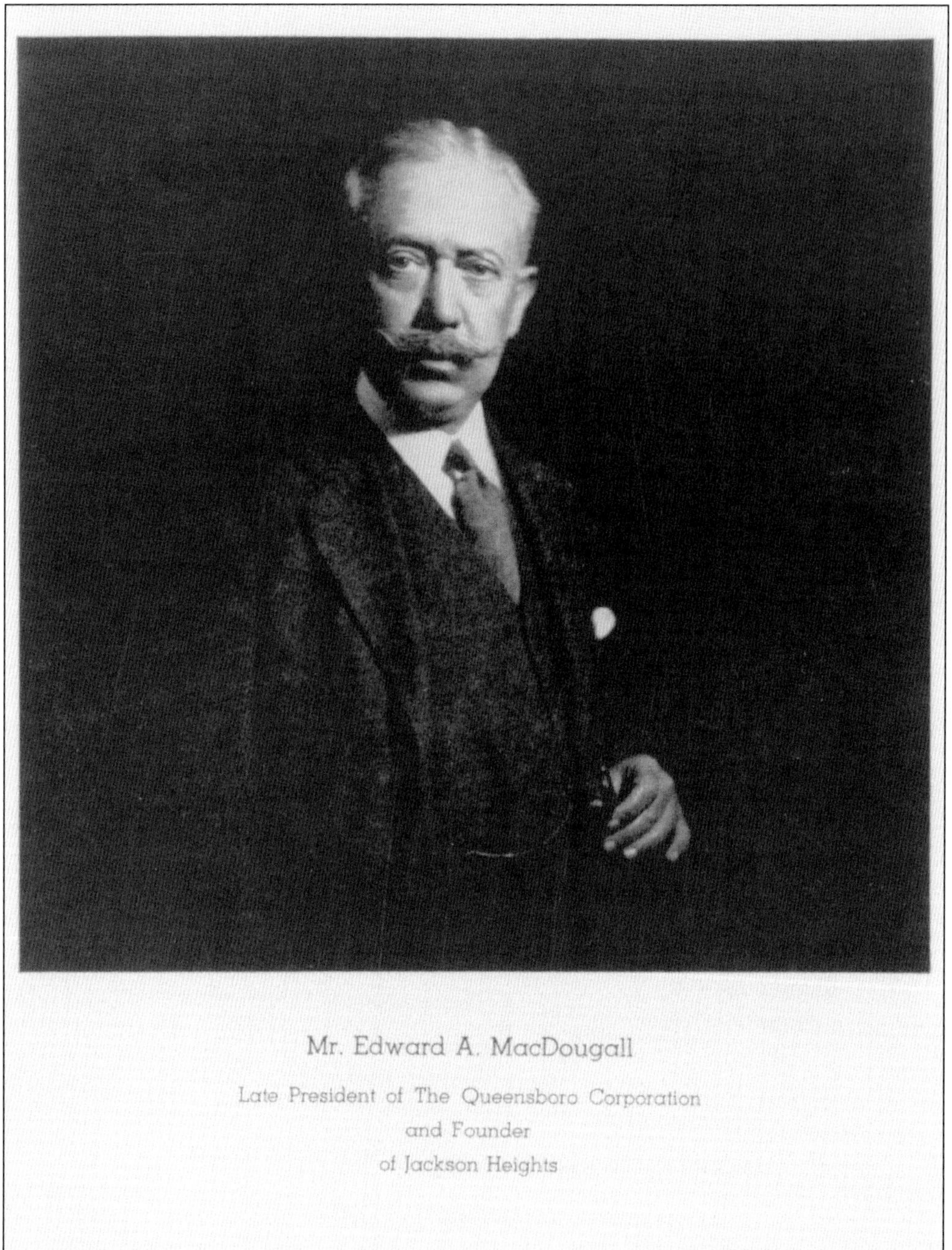

MASTER DEVELOPER. President and founder of the Queensboro Corporation, Edward Archibald MacDougall (1874–1944) was the driving force behind the creation of Jackson Heights. It was MacDougall's vision for Jackson Heights that heralded the coming of the garden apartment concept to Queens and the United States. Born in Brooklyn on July 16, 1874, MacDougall had a career in real estate development that spanned more than four decades. (Courtesy of the Queens Borough Public Library, Long Island Division, Illustrations Collection–Jackson Heights.)

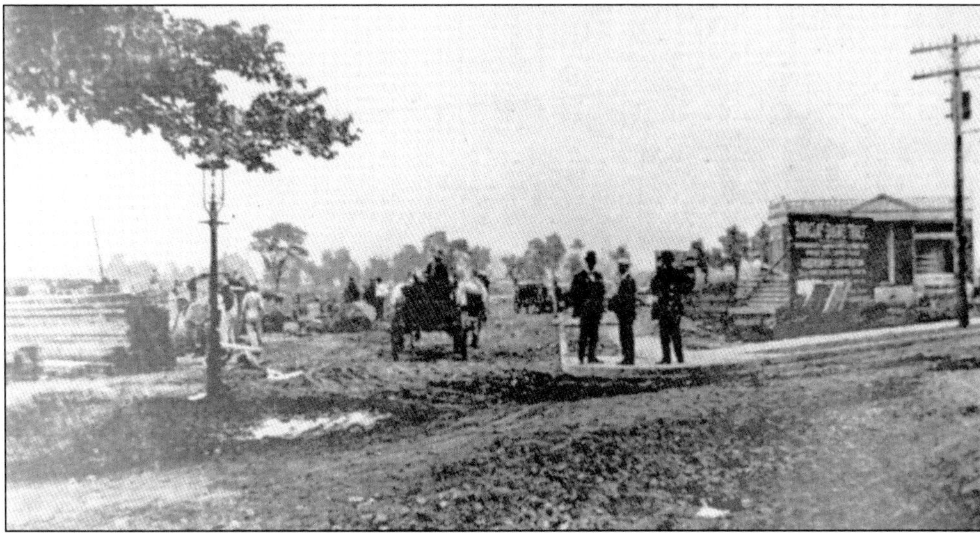

QUEENSBORO CORPORATION. The first location of the Queensboro Corporation was in a temporary building at the corner of Roosevelt Avenue and Eighty-second Street. It was incorporated on August 12, 1909, with William F. Wyckoff its first president. A sign in front of the new headquarters states that this area is the former "Barclay-Dugro Tract," 128 acres that comprised six separate parcels of land. The acquisition of the land amounted to $1.5 million. Between 1910 and 1914, Queensboro would acquire 28 additional farms, equaling about 350 acres. (Courtesy of the Queens Borough Public Library, Long Island Division, Illustrations Collection–Jackson Heights.)

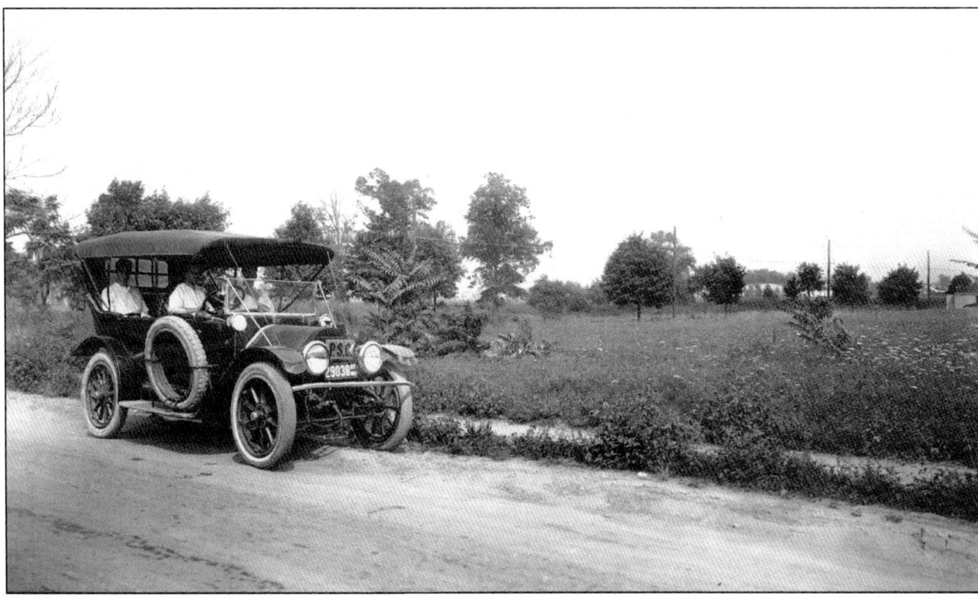

CRUISING ON THE BOULEVARD. Despite its rural appearance, Northern Boulevard served as one of the main arteries for the new Jackson Heights neighborhood, allowing much needed access to and from Manhattan via the Queensboro Bridge. With the opening of the span in March 1909, Queens was finally linked with Manhattan. Here, an early Model T cruises through an undeveloped part of Jackson Heights. The rise of automobile travel signaled a time of profound change for this once bucolic region. (Courtesy of the Queens Borough Public Library, Long Island Division, Borough President of Queens Collection.)

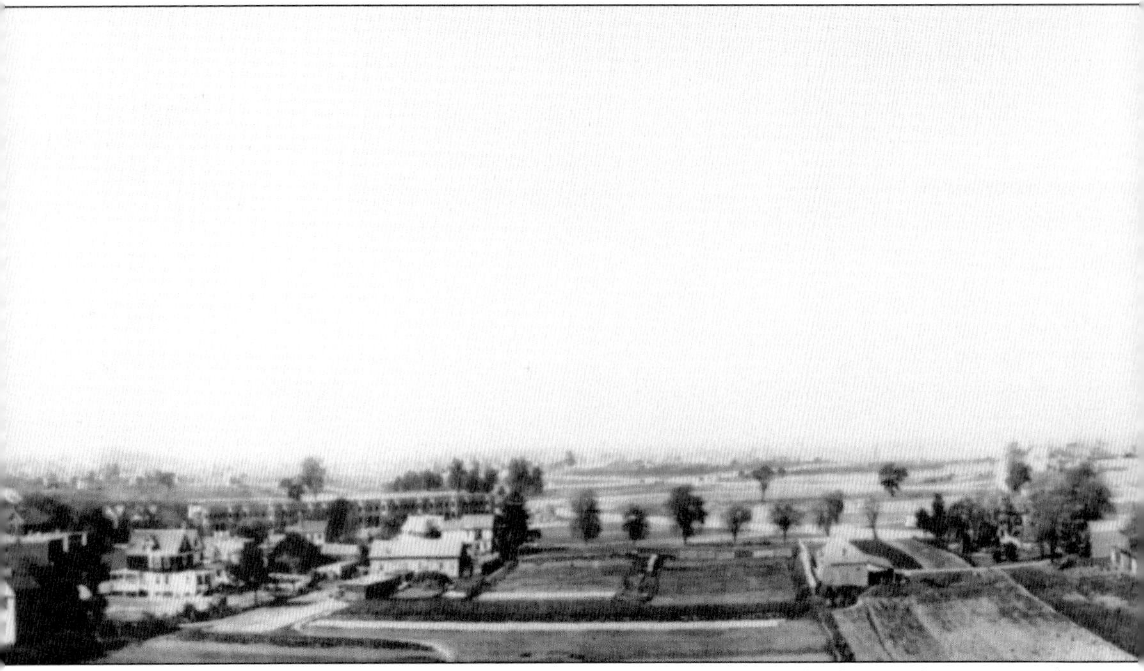

A Fleeting Vista. Reminiscent of a 19th-century oil painting is a final view of Trains Meadow captured in this panoramic photograph from 1910. To the right, the remaining homesteads are

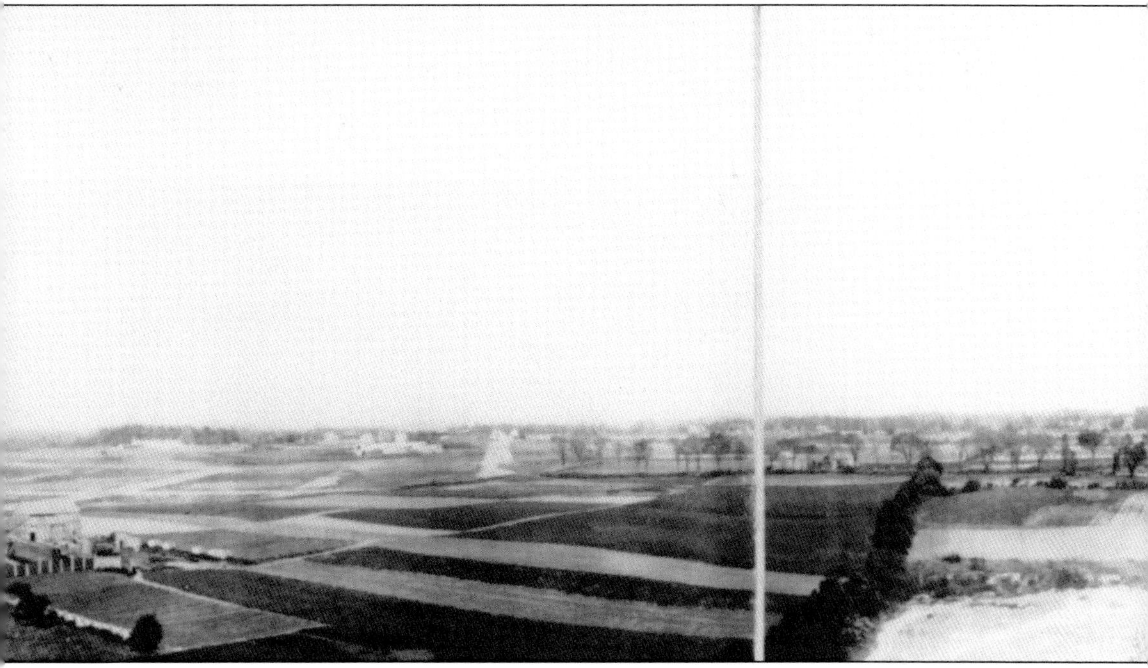

in their final days as early construction has already started to appear on the left. This view looks south from the neighborhood of Elmhurst. (Courtesy of the Queens Historical Society.)

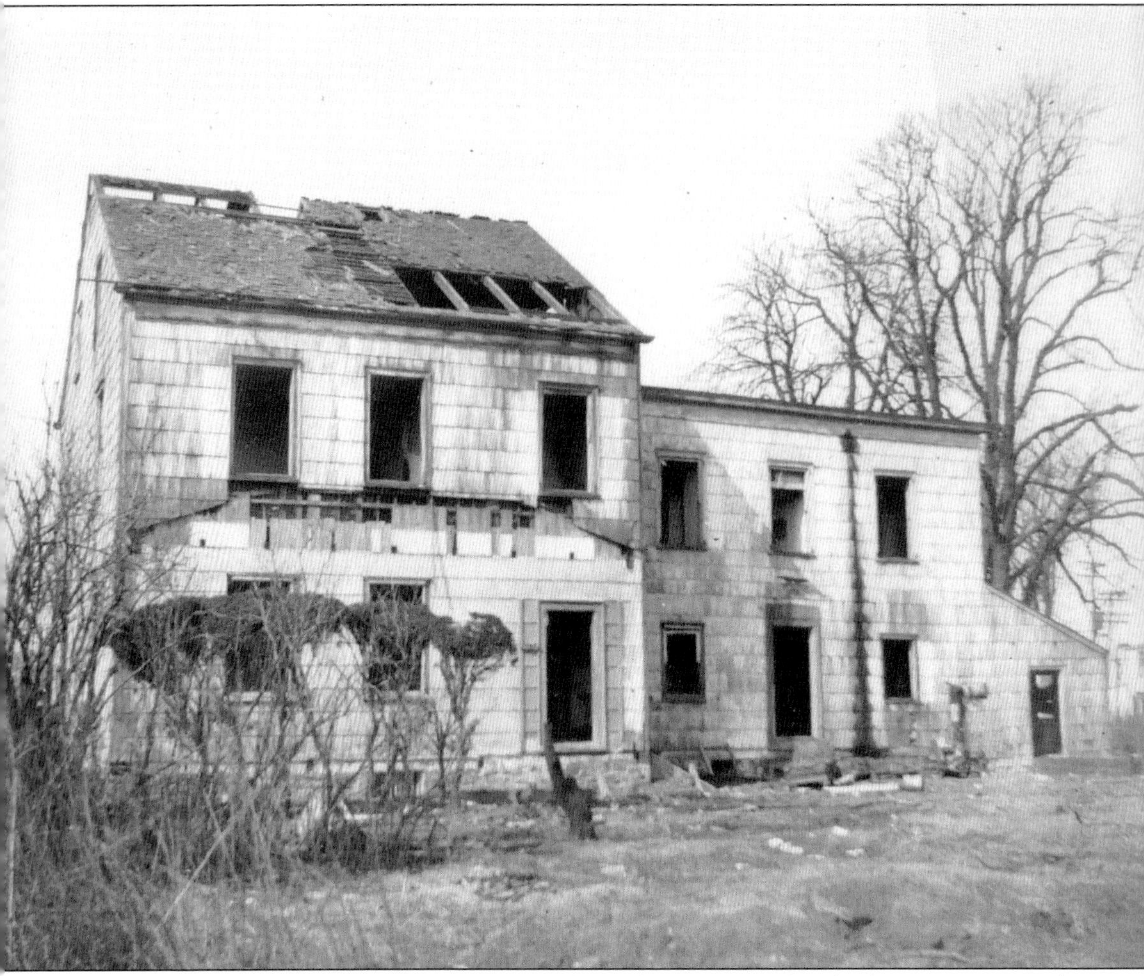

THOMAS FISH HOUSE. The origins of the Fish family in Queens date back to 1659. Located on Thirty-seventh Avenue and Warren Street, this home was originally built in 1800 and occupied by the Fish family until 1820. Successive owners included James Oath, from 1820 until 1852, and J.P. Leverich, from 1852 to 1860, before possession reverted back to the Fish family. Toward the end of the 19th century, a general store was added when the property was reclaimed and renovated by Thomas Fish. Both the home and store succumbed to fire before being demolished. Believed to be related to the old Saxon Fish family of German nobility, Jonathan Fish was the family's first settler in Newtown. (Courtesy of the Queens Borough Public Library, Long Island Division, Eugene L. Armbruster Photographs.)

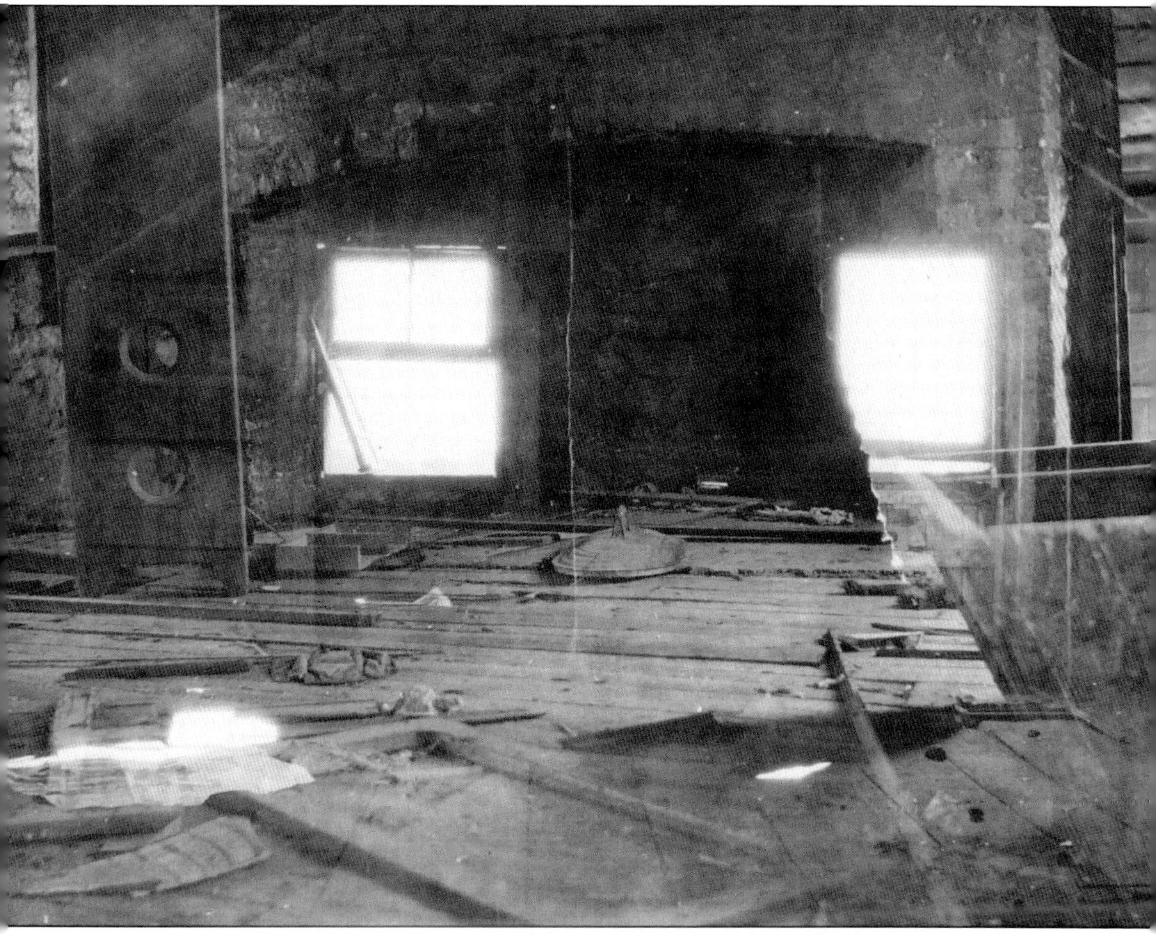

Interior View of Olden Days. The attic of the venerable David Rapalye house is seen here during its demolition. Note the thick wooden slats and large bricks that were typical of such houses. (Courtesy of the Queens Borough Public Library, Long Island Division, Eugene L. Armbruster Photographs.)

A Unique Perspective. For two centuries, the view from this doorway of the David Rapalye house looked upon a vast idyllic landscape of rolling hills and prairie land. Now, as seen in this unusual photograph, the view is of a newly built row house that marked the coming of the Jackson Heights development in the early 20th century. (Courtesy of the Queens Borough Public Library, Long Island Division, Eugene L. Armbruster Photographs.)

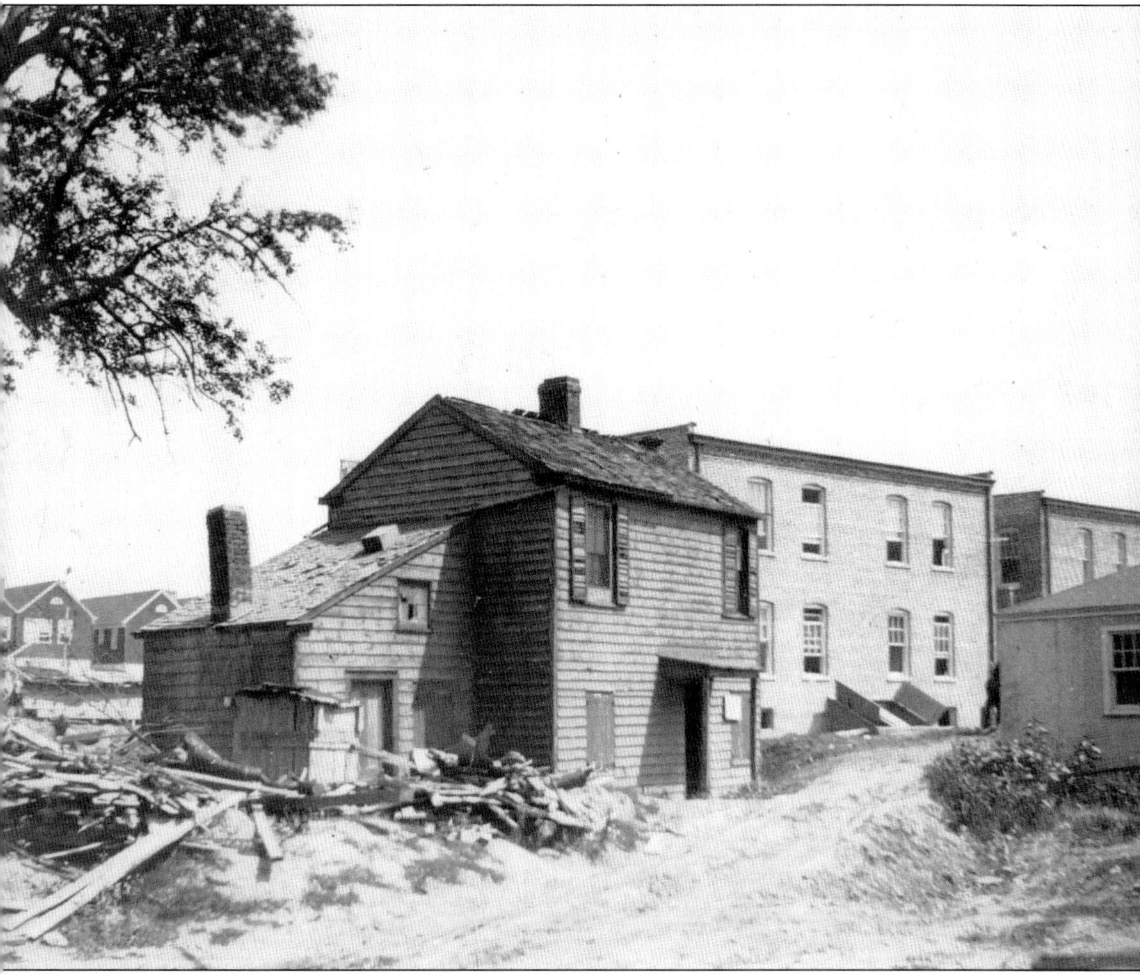

The Last of the Leverich House. This rear view shows the Henry S. Leverich house, located north of Elmhurst Avenue or Shell Road (now Thirty-seventh Avenue and Ninety-third Street). Built in 1841, it was demolished in June 1925, soon after this photograph was taken. Parts of the house were reused for summer homes located at Throgs Neck in the Bronx. Note the outhouse adjacent to the main structure in the foreground and the development of one-family homes taking place in the background. (Courtesy of the Queens Borough Public Library, Long Island Division, Eugene L. Armbruster Photographs.)

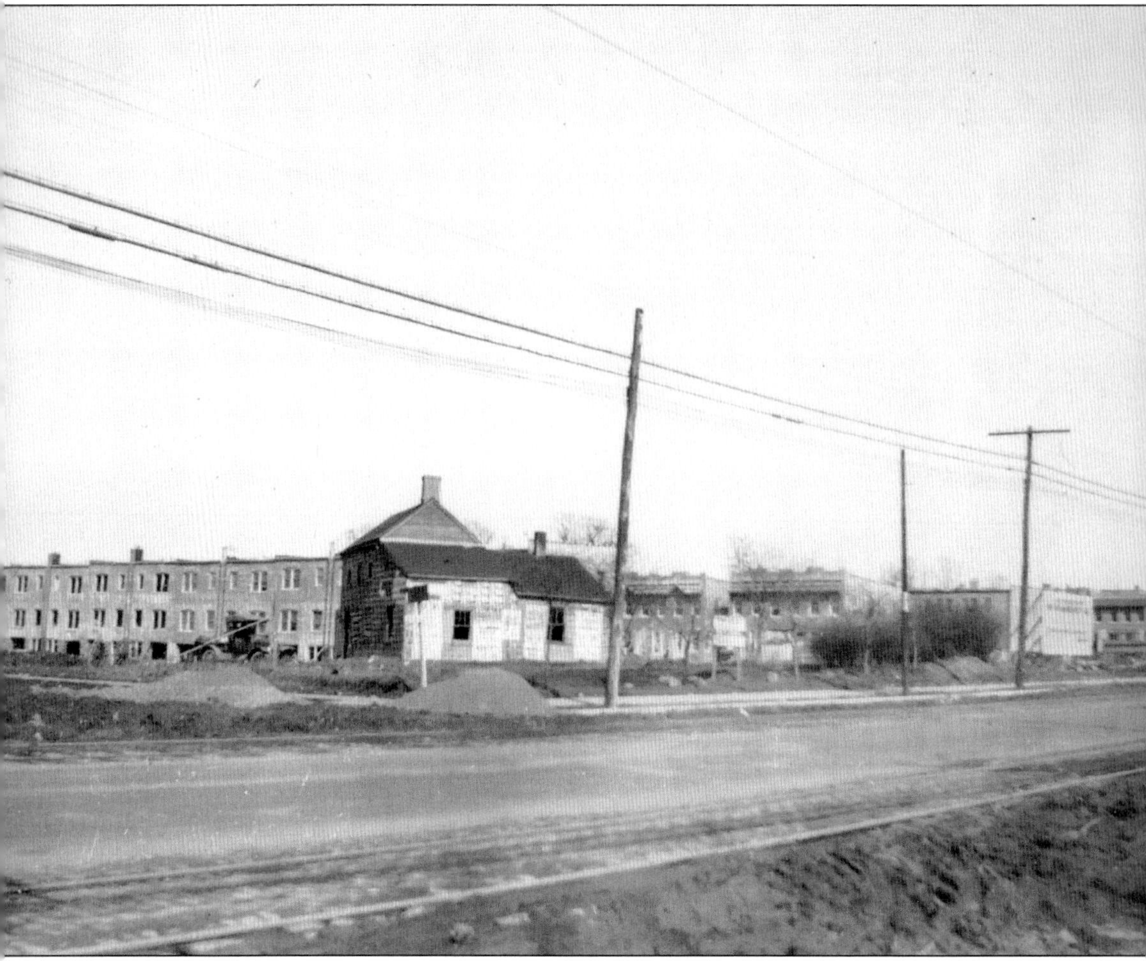

The J.P. Fowler House. One of the final vestiges of old Trains Meadow stands almost defiantly before the first wave of area development. The Fowler property was located on the north side of Northern Boulevard near Seventy-eighth Street. It was finally demolished in 1924. (Courtesy of the Queens Borough Public Library, Long Island Division, Eugene L. Armbruster Photographs.)

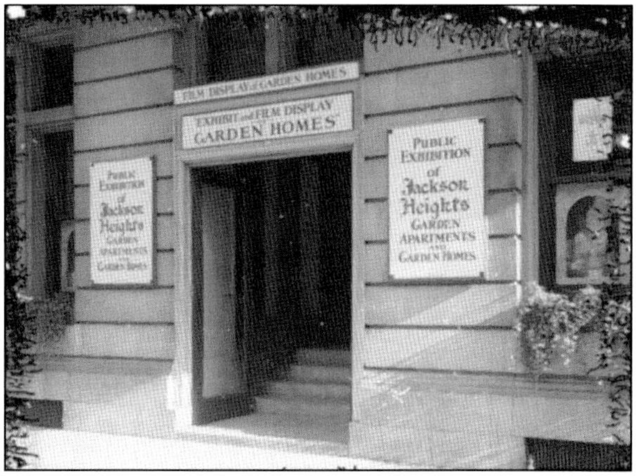

ON DISPLAY. In this never-before-published photograph of Manhattan's Delmonico's Restaurant, a public exhibition arranged by the Queensboro Corporation is promoting the latest innovation in community life: the garden apartments of Jackson Heights. Note that the exhibit featured still photography and motion picture footage to illustrate how garden apartments were healthy alternatives to congested city life. (Courtesy of the Museum of the City of New York.)

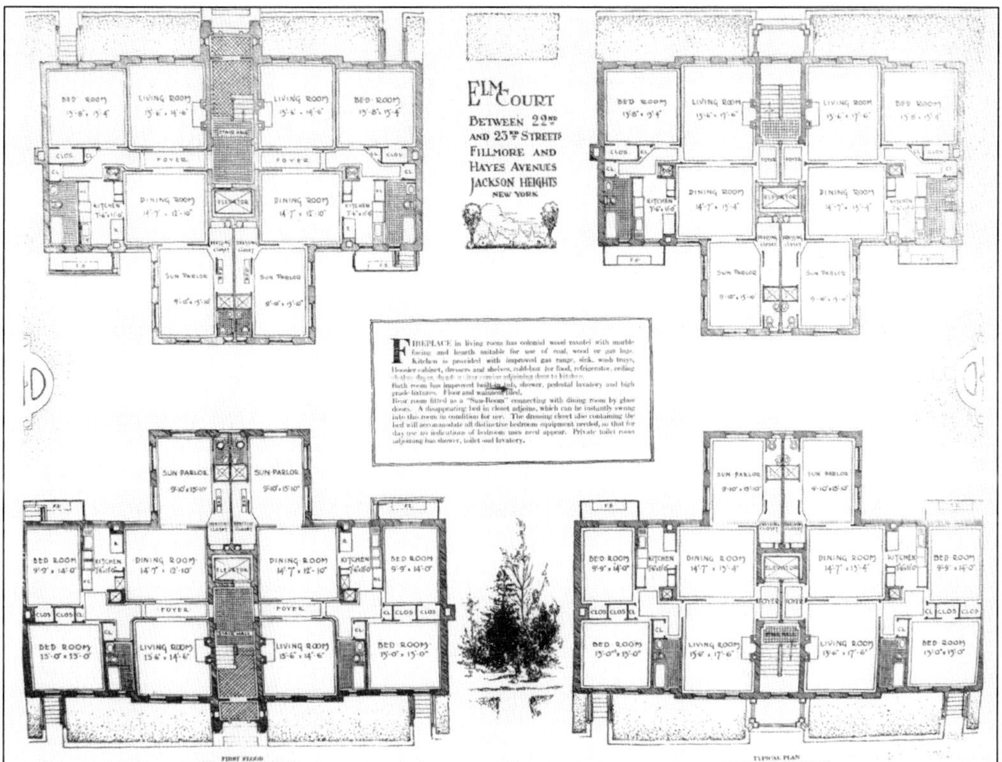

AN ELEGANT FLOOR PLAN. The amenities that would become a hallmark of apartments in Jackson Heights are apparent in this floor plan depicting the layout of Elm Court. Built in 1922 and designed by George H. Wells, the complex is located from 3427–3449 Seventy-ninth Street to 3450 Eightieth Street. Original occupants enjoyed a living room fireplace featuring "a colonial wood mantel with marble facing and a hearth that accommodated either coal, wood or gas logs." In addition, a well-appointed kitchen and bathroom were part of the plan, as were ample-sized bedrooms that ensured comfort and privacy. By the 1970s, fireplaces were deemed a safety hazard and outlawed. Elm Court was originally located between Twenty-second and Twenty-third Streets (now Seventy-ninth and Eightieth Streets) and Hayes and Fillmore Avenues (present-day Thirty-fourth and Thirty-fifth Avenues). (Courtesy of the Queens Borough Public Library, Long Island Division, Illustrations Collection–Jackson Heights.)

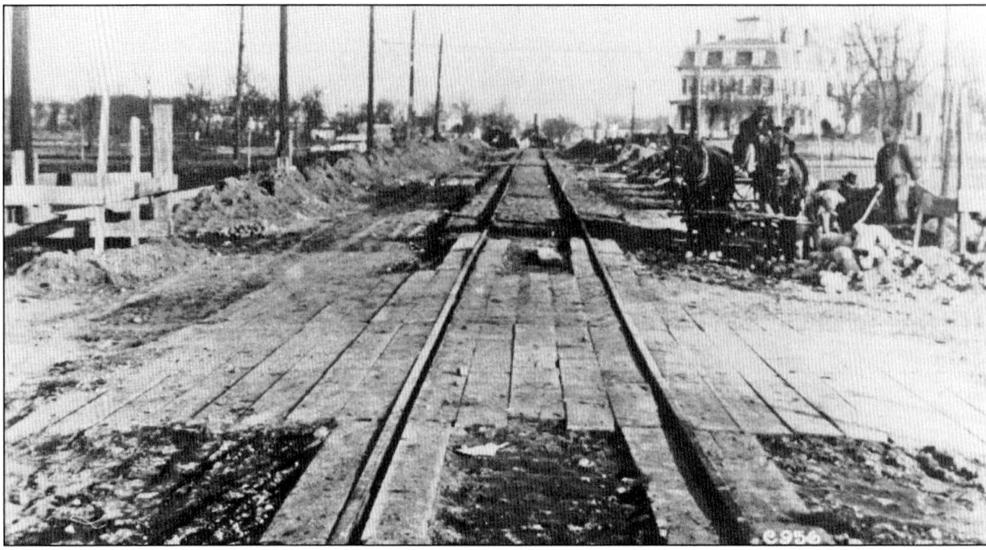

PAVING THE WAY. With the signing of the Dual System contract, Jackson Heights would see the coming of the Interboro Rapid Transit (IRT) by April 1917 with the Corona extension. In this rare photograph, taken in December 1913, the initial phase of construction can be seen here at Roosevelt Avenue and Eighty-second Street. (Courtesy of the Queens Historical Society.)

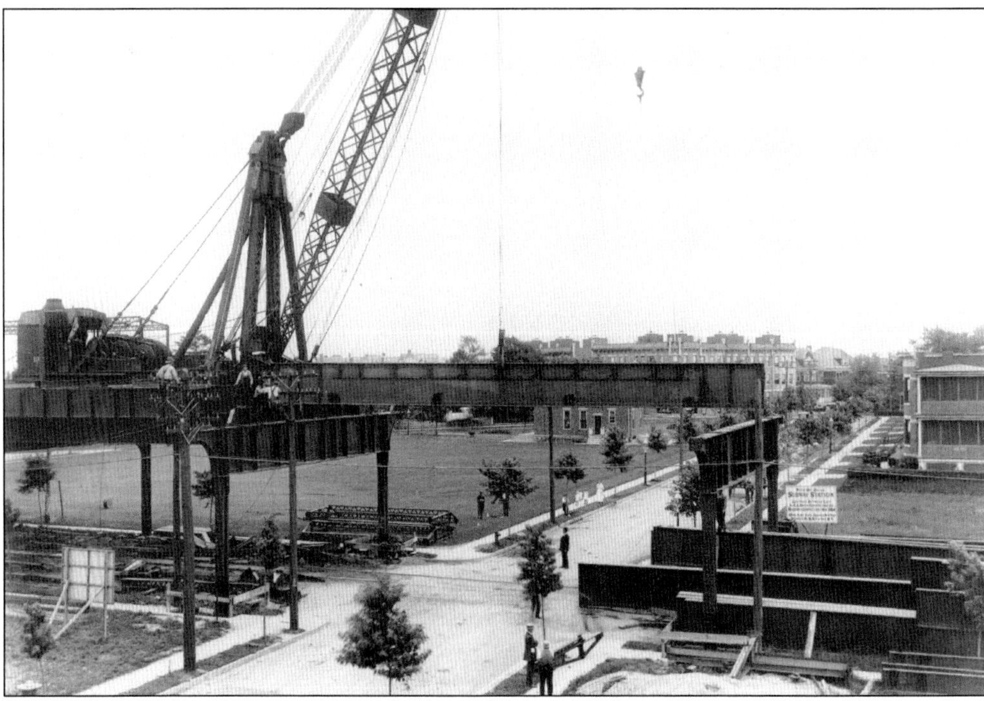

THE SUBWAY IN TOWN. Much to the relief of the local residents in Jackson Heights, the city and two private entities formally agreed to provide subway service to the outer boroughs. By April 1917, the agreement facilitated a Manhattan-bound commute of only 25 minutes, as opposed to an hour and a half beforehand—a most welcomed improvement. This photograph shows the erection of the eleated roadway, or el, that would eventually bring subway service to the area. (Courtesy of the Queens Historical Society.)

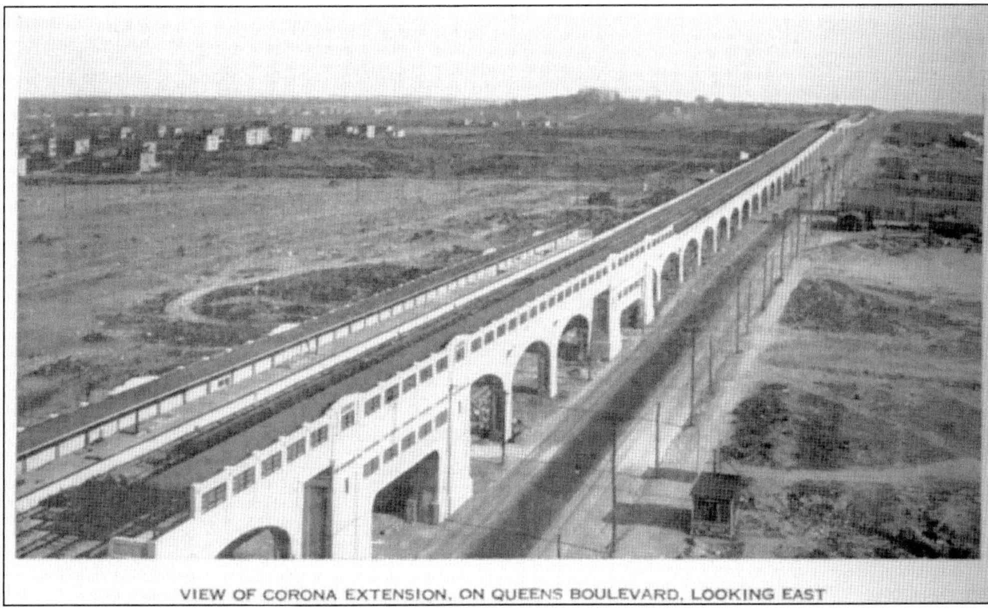

VIEW OF CORONA EXTENSION. This dramatic photograph shows the completed IRT viaduct along Queens Boulevard. Surrounding the el are the open lands that would yield the relocated Sunnyside, formerly known as Blissville. The area of Jackson Heights can be seen in the distance on the high ground.

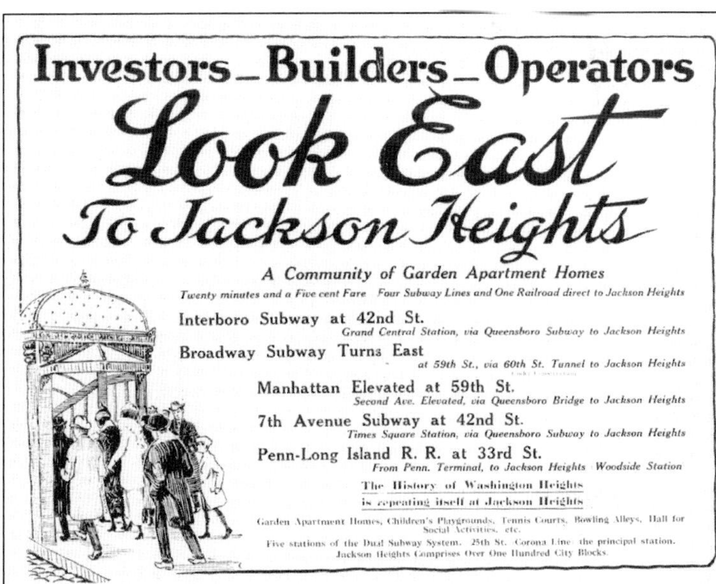

LOOKING EAST. The advantages of subway service became a major selling point in advertisements by the Queensboro Corporation. Touting a commute to the city of 20 to 25 minutes, the corporation apparently felt confident enough to use this to lure potential investors in addition to prospective residents. (Courtesy of the Queens Historical Society.)

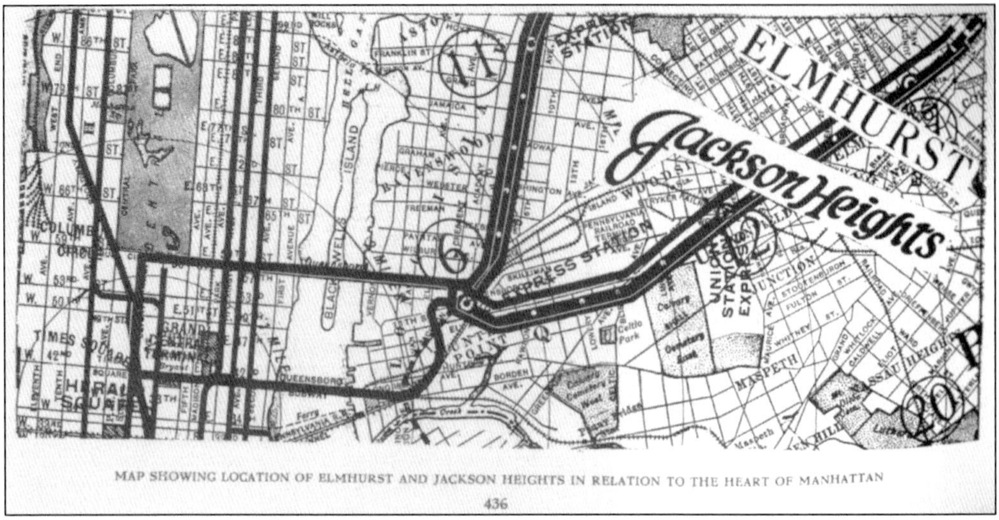

MAPPING THE WAY EAST. This detailed map, published in the December 1920 issue of *Queensborough* magazine, shows the route of the IRT stretching from Manhattan eastward toward Elmhurst and Jackson Heights. Maps like these were used to show prospective buyers how convenient it was to travel to and from the city. (Courtesy of the Queens Chamber of Commerce.)

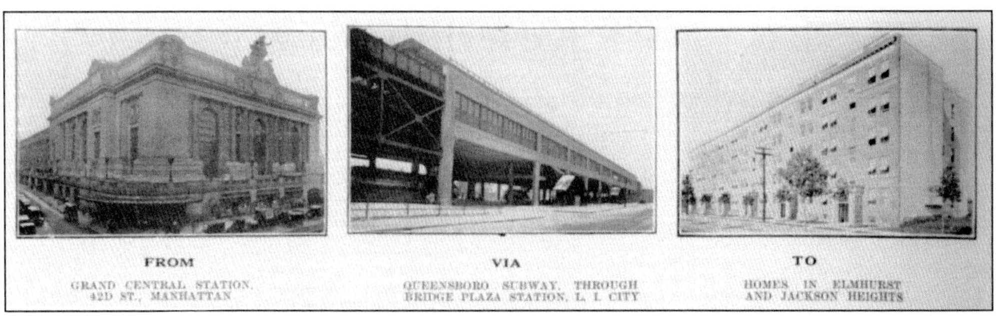

FROM POINT A TO B TO C. *Queensborough* magazine printed three successive images to illustrate the streamlined commute from Jackson Heights to midtown Manhattan as a major selling point. (Courtesy of the Queens Chamber of Commerce.)

THE BENEFITS OF OWNERSHIP. The Queensboro Corporation placed a premium on home ownership. In 1919, a plan was presented in which people were allowed to purchase their own apartments, thus making it one of the first cooperative communities in the nation. This advertisement tries to deter prospective residents from renting by showing the financial advantages of purchasing. An owner could save up to $600 a year for seven years or more. (Courtesy of the Queens Chamber of Commerce.)

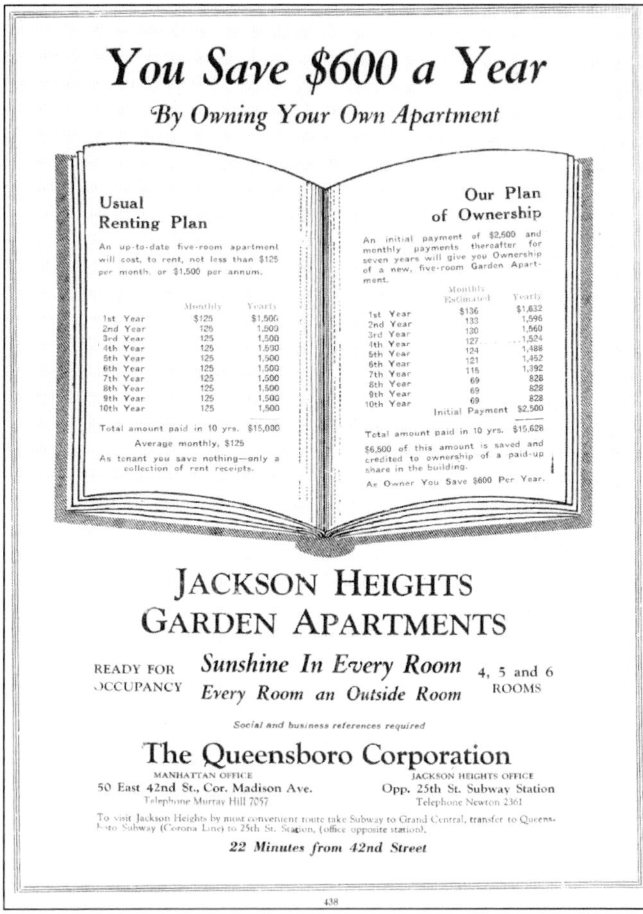

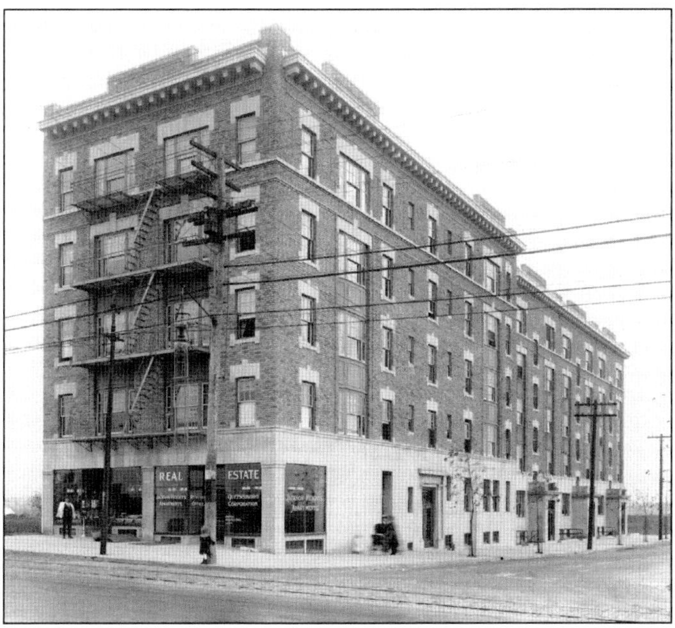

LAUREL COURT. In 1914, Laurel Court was completed as the first apartment building to appear in Jackson Heights. The development consisted of four 5-story buildings in tan brick. Laurel Court, situated on the southeast corner of Eighty-second Street and Northern Boulevard, housed another location of the Queensboro Corporation's sales office. (Courtesy of the Queens Borough Public Library, Long Island Division, Borough President of Queens Collection.)

Another project to which the Cham-

A Group of Winners in the Building Competition

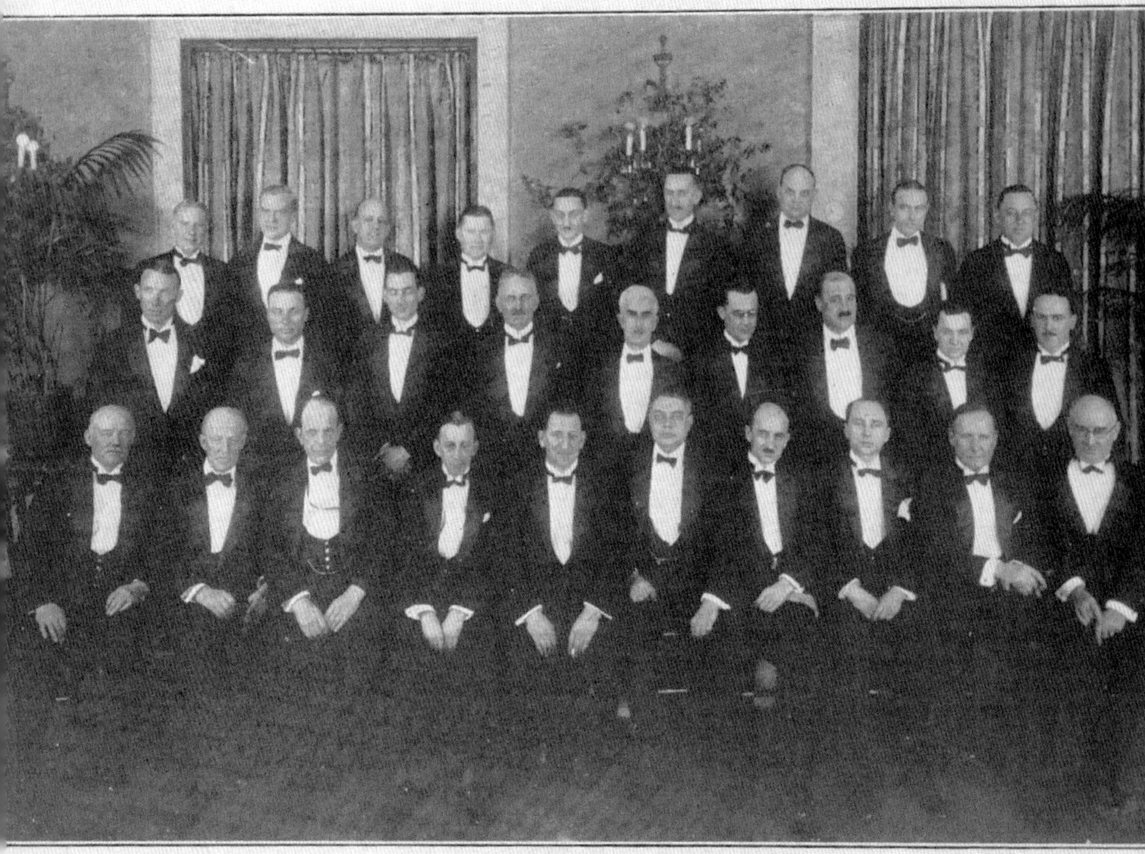

FRONT ROW—Fred T. Youngs, Jacob & Youngs; Charles H. Roberts, Roberts, Nash & Co.; Clarence M. Lowes, Pr Flushing National Bank; P. A. Rowley, Treas. of the Chamber and Vice-Pres., Bank of the Manhattan Co.; Judge Fr F. Adel, President of the Chamber; J. D. Dusenberry, Pres., United Fireproofing Co.; William J. Hollister; A. E. Da LeRoy Latham, Pres., Latham Litho & Printing Co.; H. A. Bernhardt.
SECOND ROW—William Hueg, Dick, Meyer Corp.; George C. Meyer, Cord Meyer Development Co.; Alexander Alex der, Cord Meyer Development Co.; William J. Hamilton; William W. Knowles, Architect; R. I. Ballinger, Pres., The linger Co.; Walter Kidde, Pres., Walter Kidde Co.; Hunter McDonnell, Architect; William Collins, Walter Kidde Co.
THIRD ROW—Robert Tappan, Architect; H. Q. Kennedy, J. G. White Engineering Co.; Andrew J. Thomas, Architect; W Moore, Sec., Treo Co.; Charles Hayes, Treas., Treo Co.; John G. Ahlers, Barney-Ahlers Co.; Steward Wagner, Fellhei & Wagner, Architects; Roger H. Bullard, Architect; Richard P. Weber.

Queens Needs More Rapid Transit—The Chamber Is Helping to Get It

PIONEERS OF DEVELOPMENT. Published in *Queensborough* magazine in February 1927, this group photograph shows the winners of the Queens Chamber of Commerce's building competition. Significantly, two architects integral to the development of Jackson Heights are present—Robert Tappan (third row, first from left) and Andrew J. Thomas (third row, third from left). Tappan is credited with designing the English Garden homes and the Garden Country Day School, while Thomas designed The Towers, considered to be the premier complex in Jackson Heights; Linden Court; Dunnolly Gardens; and the Queensboro Corporation's final location in 1947. It was Thomas who brilliantly executed MacDougall's plan for garden apartments, especially in The Chateau. (Courtesy of the Queens Chamber of Commerce.)

A MORAL MESSAGE. Significantly, this *Queensborough* magazine cartoon appeared in 1922, one year after the country experienced the Red Scare. Its underlying message is clear: home ownership (read: private property), a source of pride and contentment, is the key to avert radicalism. (Courtesy of the Queens Chamber of Commerce.)

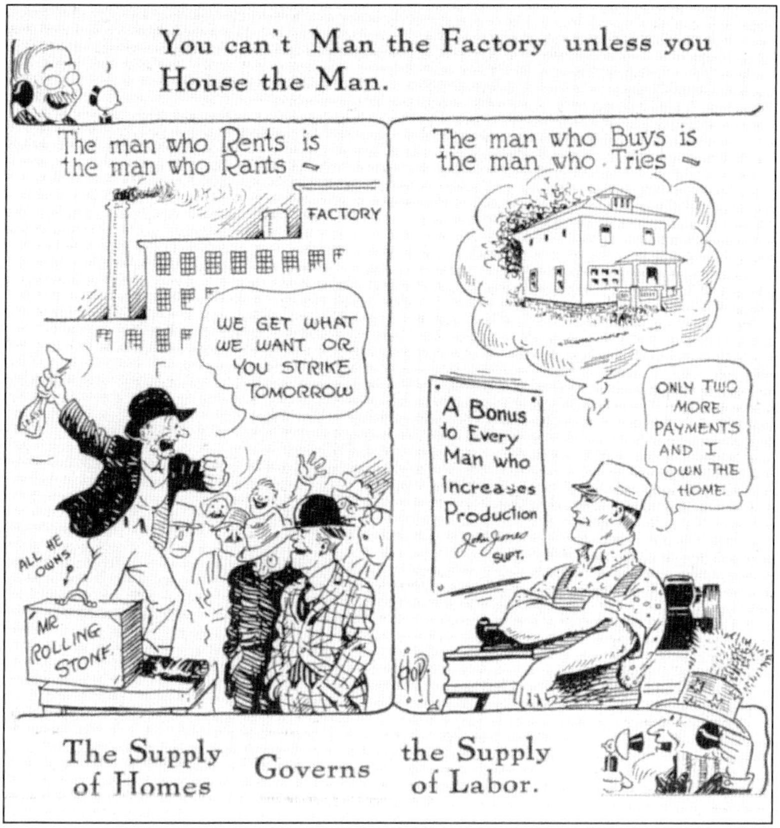

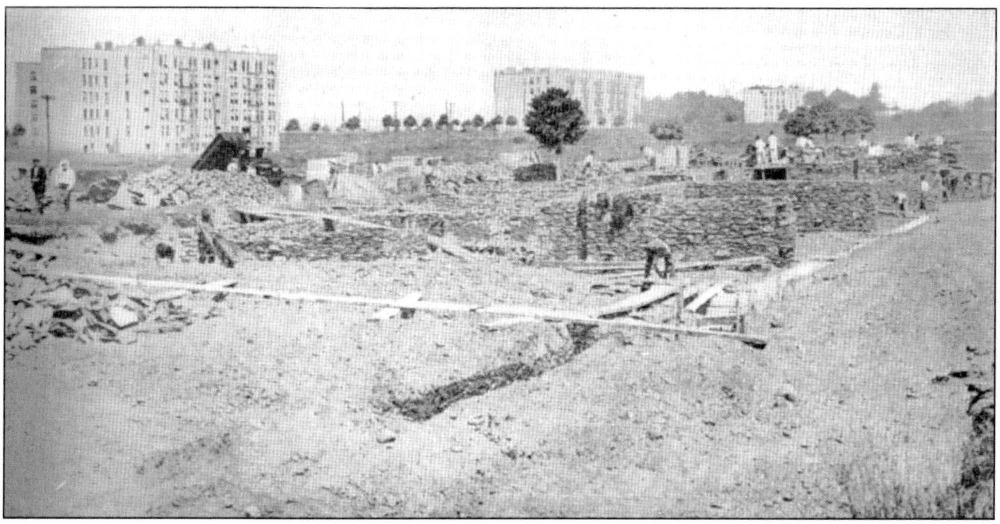

EARLY CONSTRUCTION. Rising out of the meadows, the new garden apartments are seen in a rare early construction photograph. Laborers are laying the foundation for Linden Court between Twenty-seventh and Twenty-eighth Streets (now Eighty-fourth and Eighty-fifth Streets) from Roosevelt Avenue to Polk Avenue (now Thirty-seventh Avenue). (Courtesy of the Queens Chamber of Commerce.)

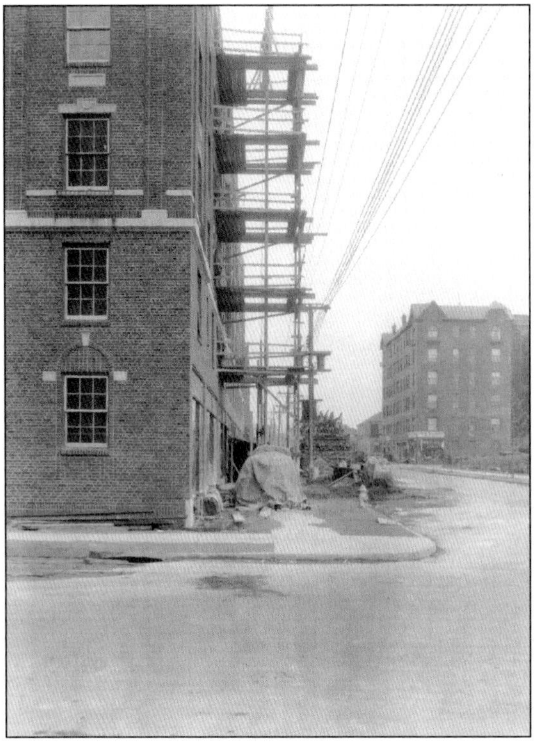

Nearing Completion. Another complex nears completion. In the background is La Mesa Verde Apartments complex, built in 1926. (Courtesy of the Queens Borough Public Library, Long Island Division, Borough President of Queens Collection.)

A Neighborhood Taking Shape. Built in 1915, the Colonial was the third apartment complex to be erected. The buildings seen at left are located along Eighty-second Street between Thirty-fourth and Thirty-fifth Avenues (then known as Hayes and Fillmore Avenues, respectively). This view, facing south toward Roosevelt Avenue, shows the tennis court and open lots waiting to be filled. In the center background are Plymouth Courts (built 1916), Willow Court (1916) on the far left, and the Greystone Apartments (1917–1918) to the right. (Courtesy of the Queens Borough Public Library, Long Island Division, Borough President of Queens Collection.)

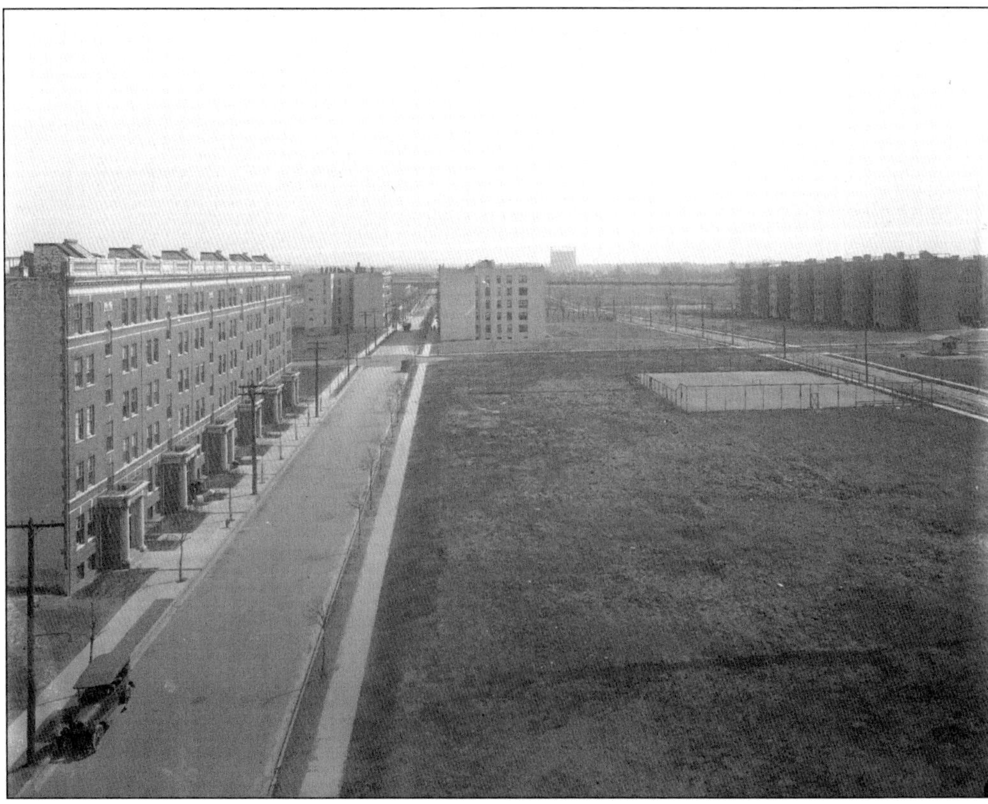

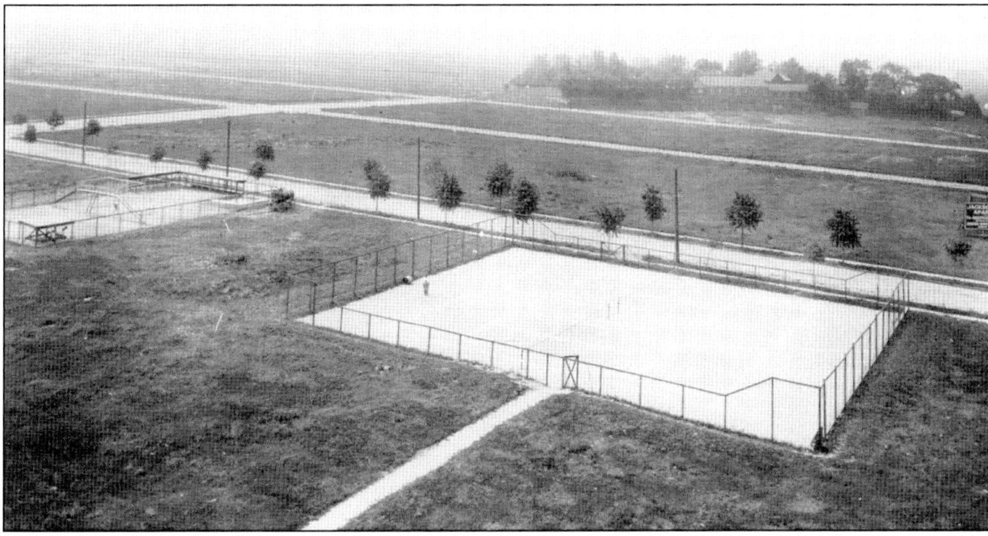

Tennis, c. 1921. To enhance the sense of luxury for its residents, tennis courts in Jackson Heights were built in 1915 on the north side of Thirty-fifth Avenue between Eighty-first and Eighty-second Streets. By 1917, there were almost a dozen such courts built. A year later, in 1918, a Jackson Heights tennis team was established to compete against other area tennis clubs. During the winter months, the courts were flooded and used as ice-skating rinks. The country-like atmosphere in this photograph is accentuated by the open space that was characteristic of the borough of Queens in its early years. (Courtesy of the Queens Borough Public Library, Long Island Division, Borough President of Queens Collection.)

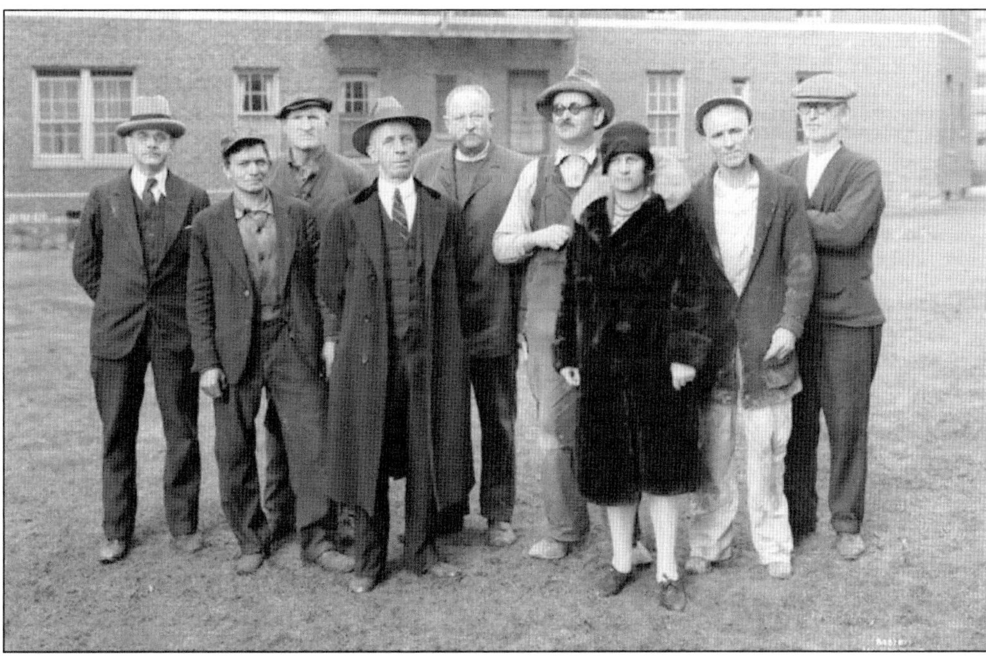

A Humble Lot. Seen here are the employees of the Queensboro Corporation who handled the day-to-day demands of the new garden community. The behind-the-scenes work of these people, who were concerned with daily maintenance issues, groundskeeping, carpentry, and so on, continually kept the neighborhood attractive. (Courtesy of the New-York Historical Society.)

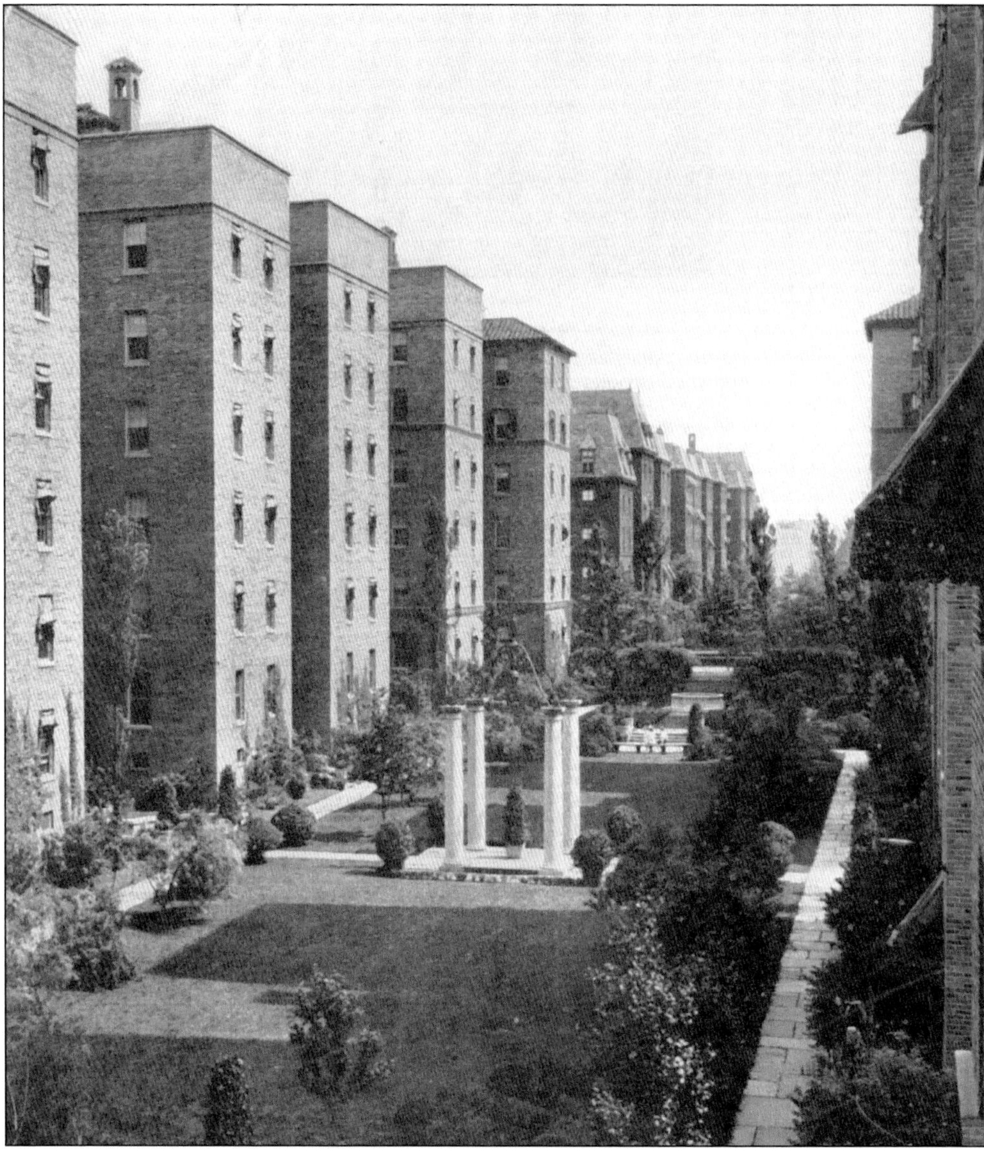

A GARDEN VISTA. This 1924 view, taken from an apartment window, shows the outdoor splendor of the Tower Garden Apartments, the most opulent structure by the Queensborough Corporation. Edward Archibald MacDougall moved here with his family from their home in Flushing. The MacDougalls lived on the top floor, a 14-room duplex situated on the corner of Eightieth Street and Thirty-fourth Avenue. Penthouse apartments, located on the seventh floor, served as dwellings for servants. The Towers were built by the J.G. White Engineering Corporation. (Courtesy of the Queens Chamber of Commerce.)

INSPECTION DAY. In the spring of 1925, more than 300 delegates attending the International Town, City, and Regional Planning Conference in Manhattan were taken on a trip through Queens on Friday, April 24. Delegates represented Great Britain, France, Germany, New Zealand, Norway, Belgium, Greece, and the Far East. The motorcade passed through several new and revolutionary developments situated in the neighborhoods of Sunnyside, Forest Hills, Kew Gardens, and Jackson Heights, where all gathered at the Queensboro Corporation for a luncheon. (Courtesy of the Queens Chamber of Commerce.)

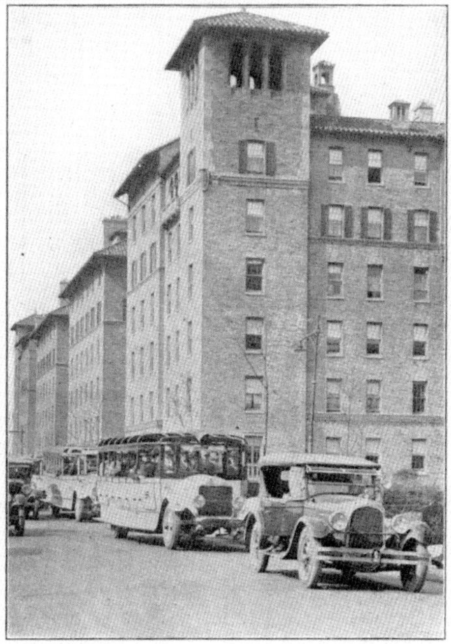

The Inspection Party seated in automobiles in front of The Towers at Jackson Heights

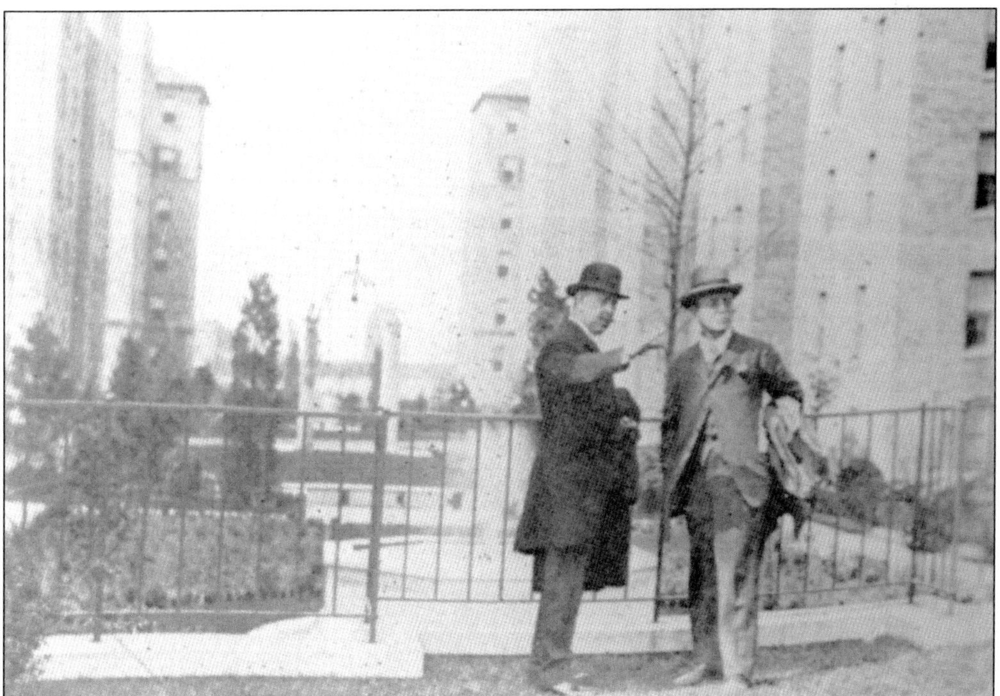

SHOWING OFF HIS CREATION. Edward A. MacDougall (left) is proudly showing off many of the neighborhood's state-of-the-art features to Raymond Unwin, chief architect to the British Ministry of Health. Upon viewing what MacDougall presented to him, Unwin was quoted as saying, "It is particularly a pleasure to me to see the cooperation that is taking place in such communities as is typified by Jackson Heights." (Courtesy of the Queens Chamber of Commerce.)

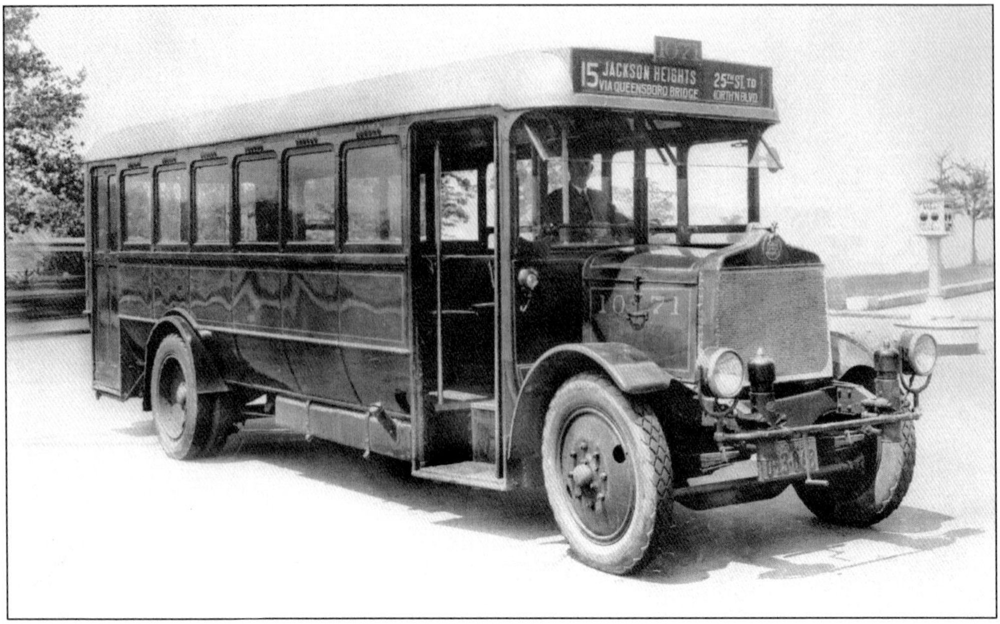

A New Mode of Transportation. Beginning in 1925, residents were able to commute via the Fifth Avenue Coach Company to Manhattan with express service from the Waldorf-Astoria Hotel at Thirty-fourth Street and Fifth Avenue (later the location of the Empire State Building). The fare, originally 35¢, was later reduced to 25¢.

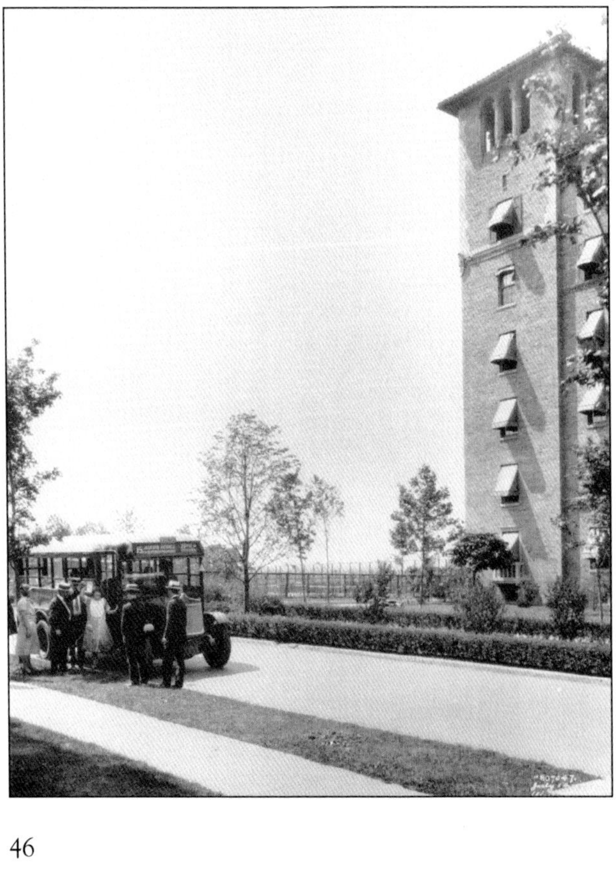

The First Pickup. This photograph, taken July 14, 1925, shows residents boarding on (or disembarking from) the inaugural run of the Fifth Avenue Coach Company service to Jackson Heights. The bus route traveled from Twenty-fifth Street and Fifth Avenue in Manhattan to Eighty-second Street and Northern Boulevard. Note the vast space found behind The Towers, the period straw hats the men are wearing, and the flapper outfits of the women.

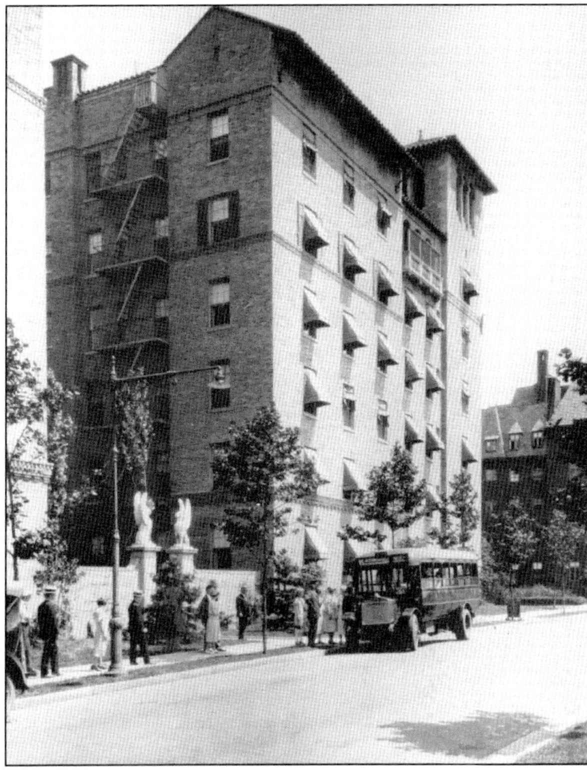

Another Fare. Here is another view of The Towers with the Fifth Avenue Coach, showing people boarding in front. The Towers covered an area from Eightieth to Eighty-first Streets between Thirty-fourth Avenue and Northern Boulevard. The structures featured marble hallways, oak parquet floors, solid plaster construction, sunrooms, and fireplaces. Notice the griffins that stand guard by the entryway to the garden. (Courtesy of the Queens Historical Society.)

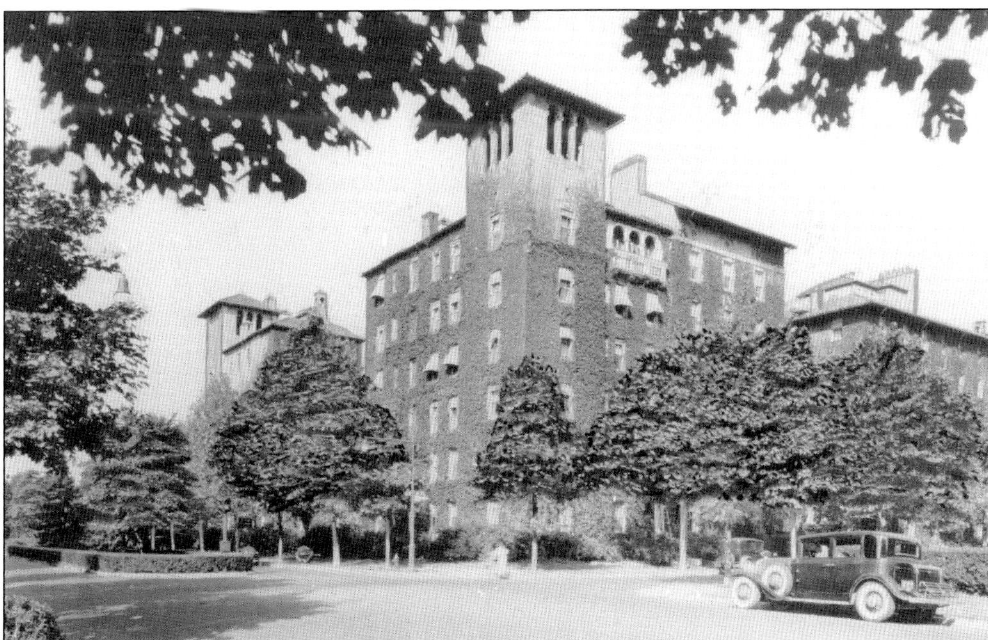

Revolutionary Construction. The Towers cost more than $2.5 million when they were built in 1924 (nearly $34 million in 2012 dollars). Prices for individual apartments ranged between $18,000 and $25,000. Despite their architectural splendor, The Towers did not bring in the amount of money the Queensboro Corporation expected. (Courtesy of the Queens Historical Society.)

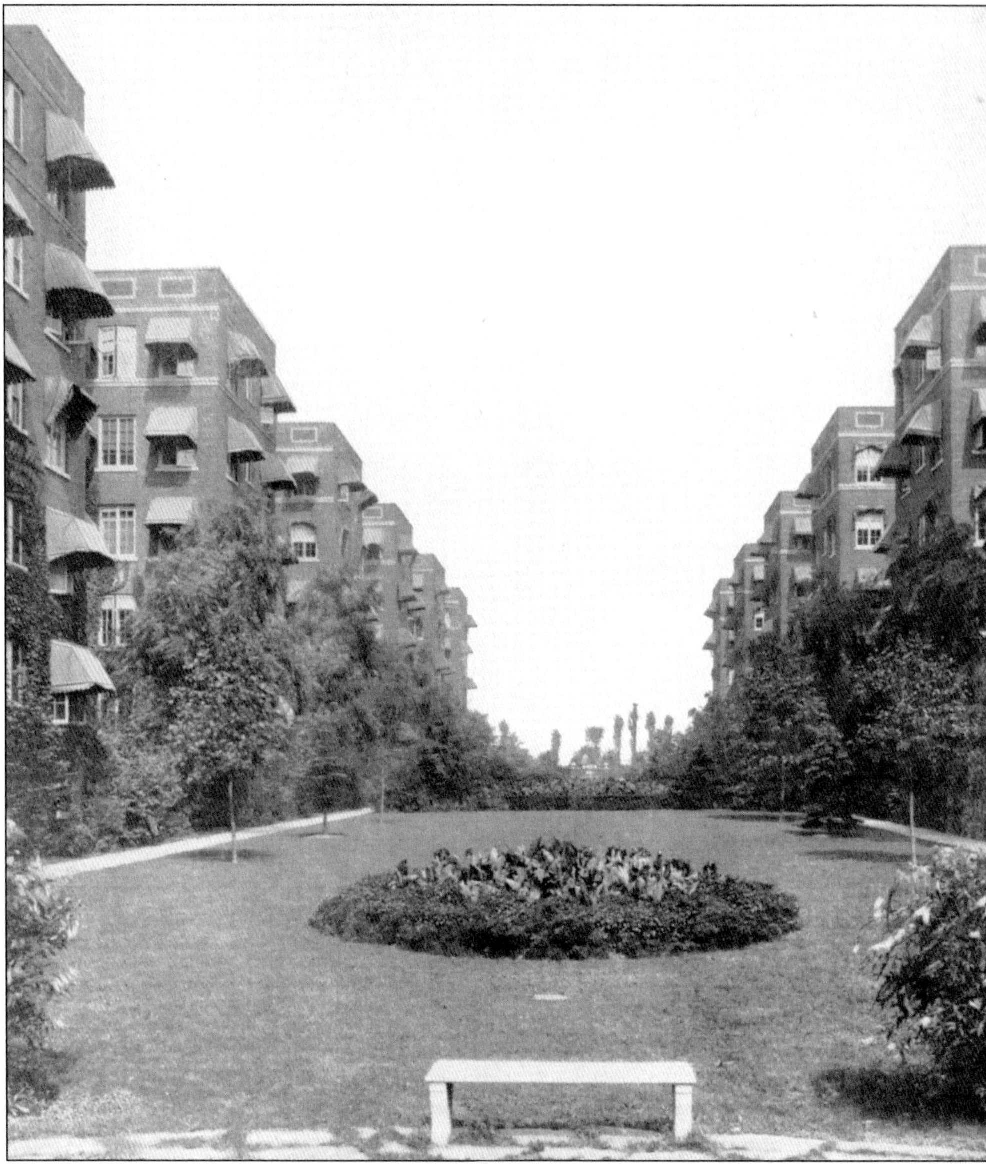

SPACIOUS AND BEAUTIFUL. Hawthorne Courts was constructed in 1922 as part of the second generation of Jackson Heights complexes and was modeled after the dormitories at Harvard. Again, one sees the garden apartment concept in full bloom. Hawthorne Court was part of the success experienced by MacDougall and the Queensboro Corporation, and by the early 1920s, the majority of the buildings were almost totally occupied because of a real estate tax exemption passed by the city board of estimate. This bill stated that any building four stories or more built between April 1920 and April 1922 would be exempt from real estate taxes until 1932. (Courtesy of the Queens Borough Public Library, Long Island Division, Illustrations Collection–Jackson Heights.)

ANOTHER PERSPECTIVE. A car drives past The Towers in this photograph taken on a sunny April day in 1930. (Courtesy of the Queens Chamber of Commerce.)

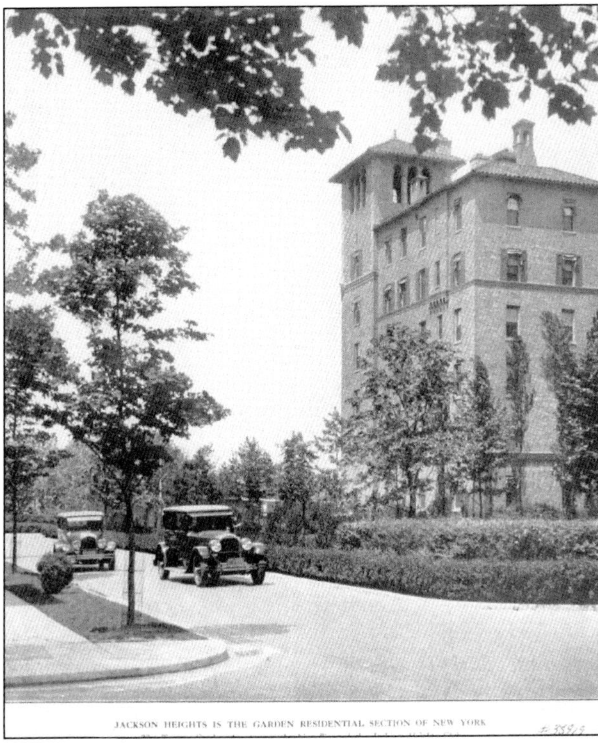

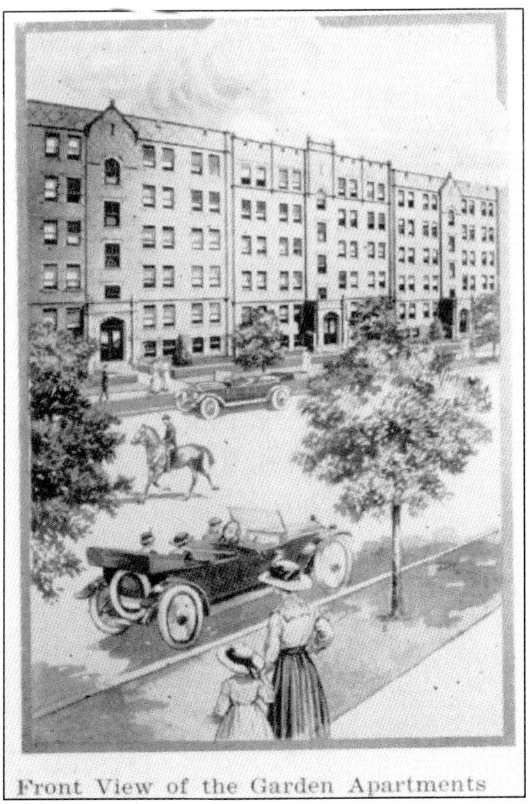

ADVERTISING GENTILITY. Fancifully depicted is the garden apartment ideal at Jackson Heights. Note the combination of open-air automobiles and a man on horseback in this promotional rendering. (Courtesy of the Queens Borough Public Library, Long Island Division, Illustrations Collection–Jackson Heights.)

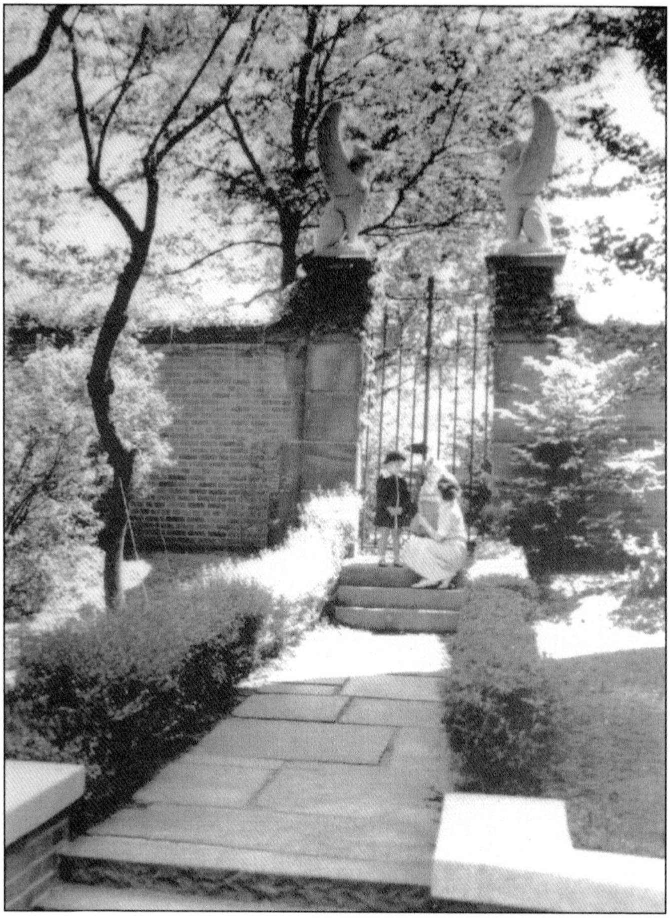

A Tender Moment. A mother and her two children are situated before a gate guarded by griffins inside the garden of The Towers complex. (Courtesy of the Queens Historical Society.)

Georgian Hall. Located on the north side of Thirty-seventh Avenue, between Eighty-third and Eighty-fourth Streets, Georgian Hall was constructed in 1930. It was built as the second building under the Jackson Heights Realty Investment Plan and featured retail stores on its main level. The realty plan was implemented just after the crash of the stock market in 1929. (Courtesy of the Queens Historical Society.)

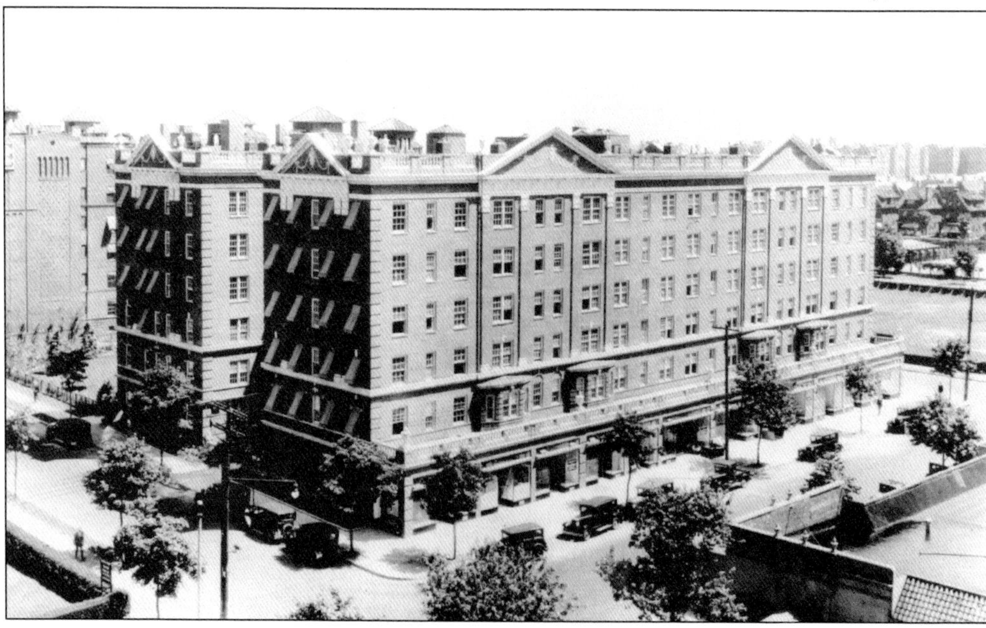

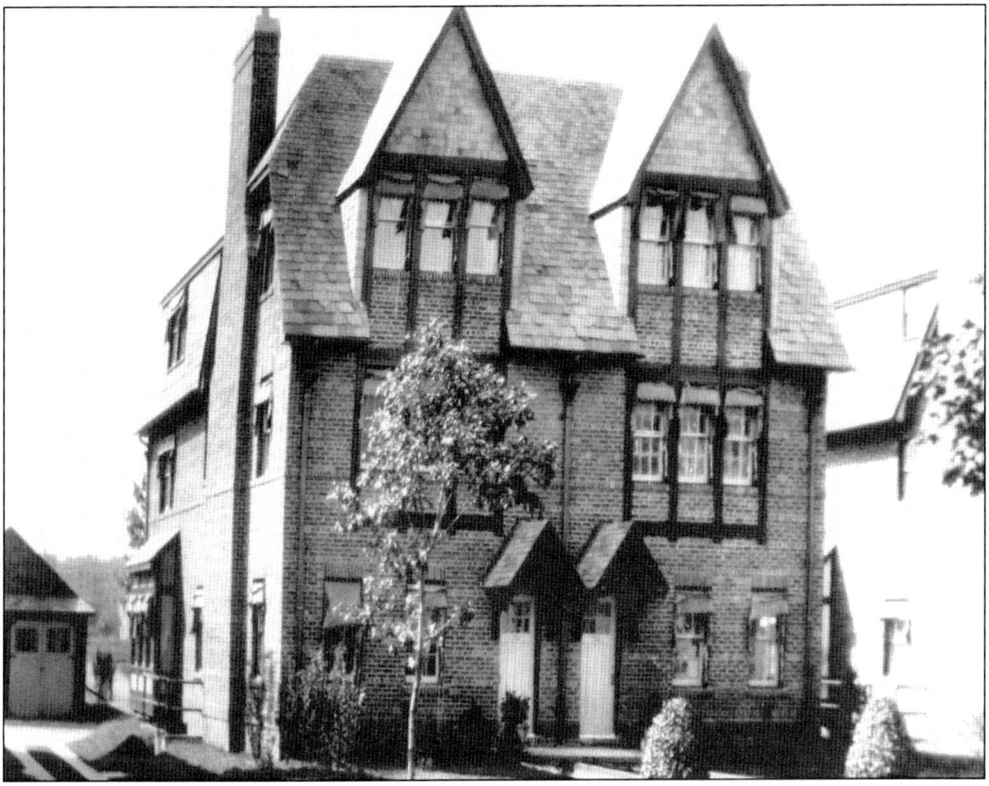

THE LUXURY OF PRIVATE HOMES. Along with apartment complexes, the Queensboro Corporation also erected private homes fashioned in the English Garden style. Located on Eighty-seventh Street between Thirty-fifth and Thirty-seventh Avenues, the English Garden homes featured oak parquet floors in both living and dining rooms, generous front and rear gardens, brick facades, rear garages, fireplaces, and roofs of slate or tile. Designed by Robert Tappan and Pierce L. Kieswetter, the English Garden homes sold for $20,000 to almost $40,000, a princely sum when one considers that the average Queens home then sold for under $1,500. These structures were also known as convertible garden homes, which meant the third story had a two-bedroom apartment accessible by a separate internal staircase. The apartment could be rented out to supplement existing household income. (Courtesy of the Queens Historical Society.)

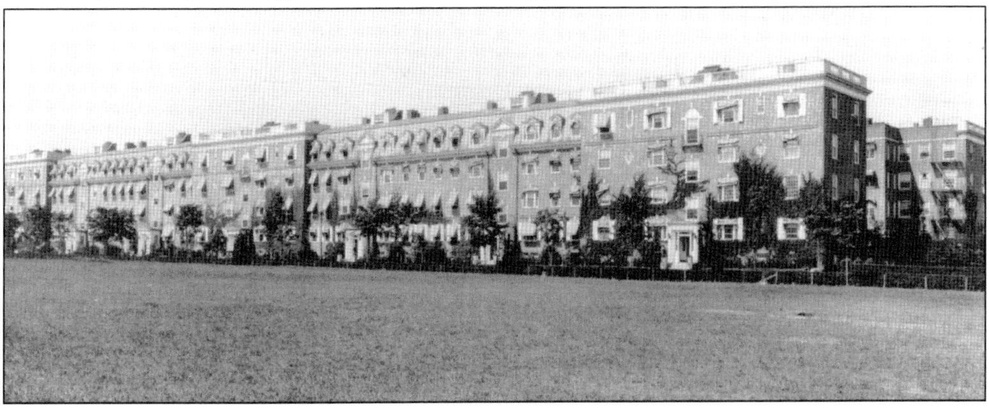

CAMBRIDGE COURT. Built in 1923, Cambridge Court was conceived as an eight-block-long super structure. (Courtesy of the Queens Historical Society.)

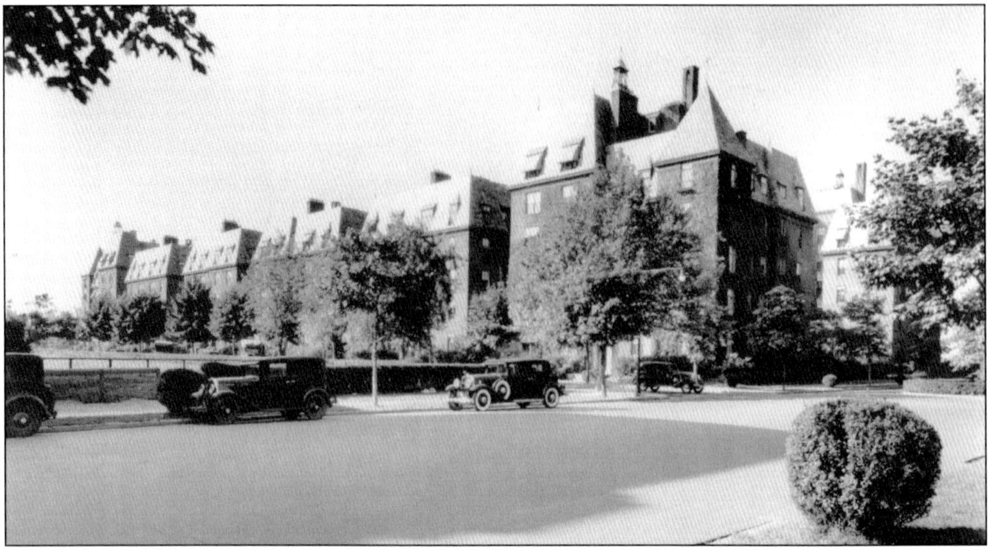

A Touch of Class. One of the most iconic structures in Jackson Heights is The Chateau, located by Eightieth and Eighty-first Streets between Thirty-fourth and Thirty-fifth Avenues. Designed by Andrew J. Thomas, The Chateau Apartments would be the 12th such complex built. The opulent-looking cars indicate the kind of clientele the Queensboro Corporation aimed to attract. (Courtesy of the Queens Historical Society.)

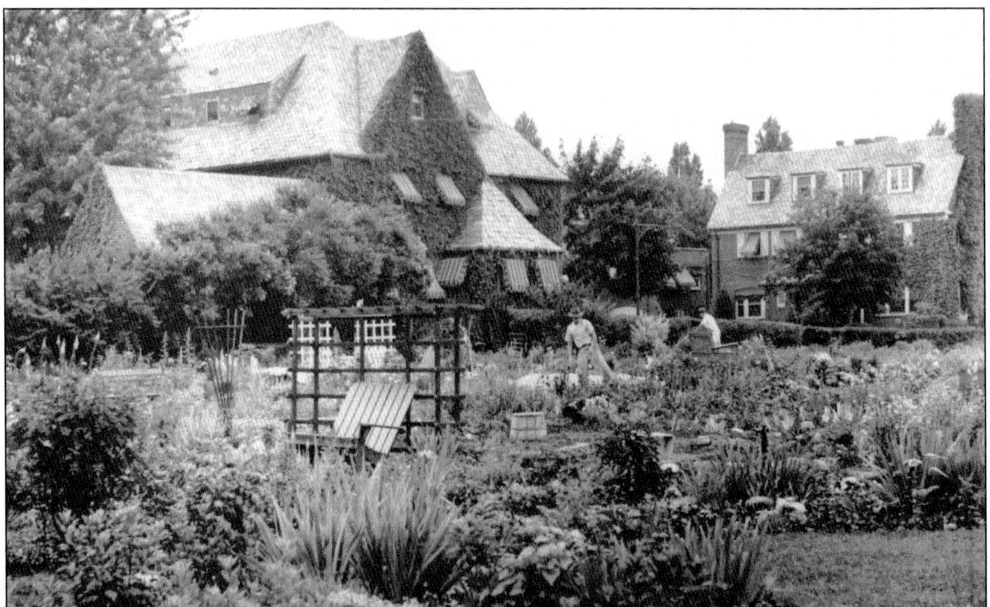

The Garden Ideal. Appearing as though they came straight from England, the back lots of many Jackson Heights dwellings came the closest of any American development to epitomizing the garden apartment ideal espoused in the late 19th century by English social reformer Ebenezer Howard. Howard's principles outlined the creation of garden-based cities as healthy alternatives to the congested atmosphere found in metropolitan centers. Here, two men are tending to a community garden situated behind the English Garden homes. (Courtesy of the Queens Historical Society.)

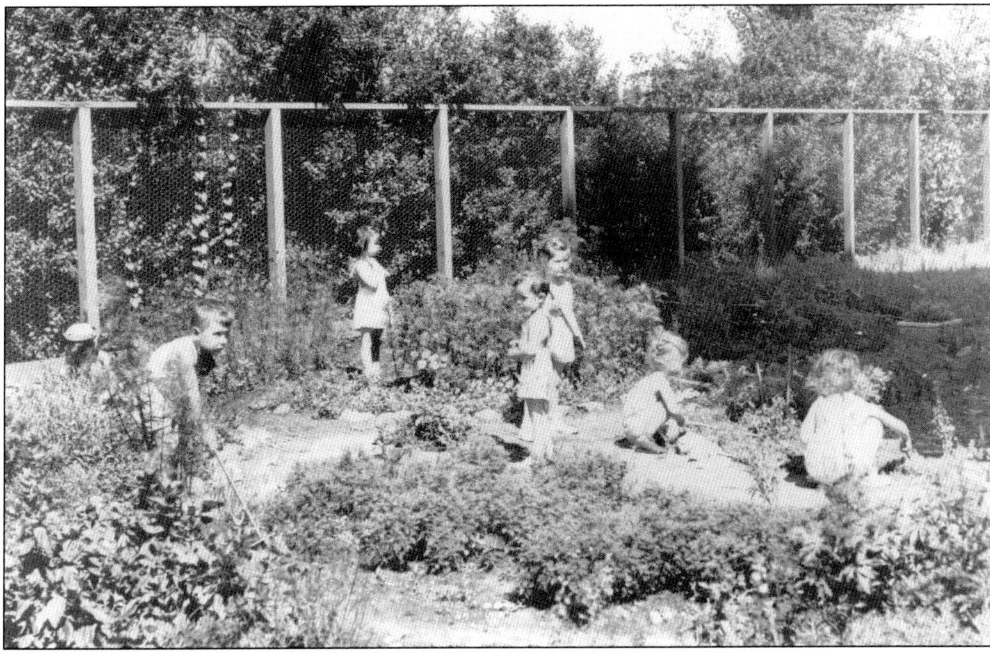

TENDING THE GARDEN. Even the children of Jackson Heights were encouraged to participate in garden activities, like the one shown here at the clubhouse. This kept in line with Queensboro's plan that a positive environment nurtured positive child development. (Courtesy of the Queens Historical Society.)

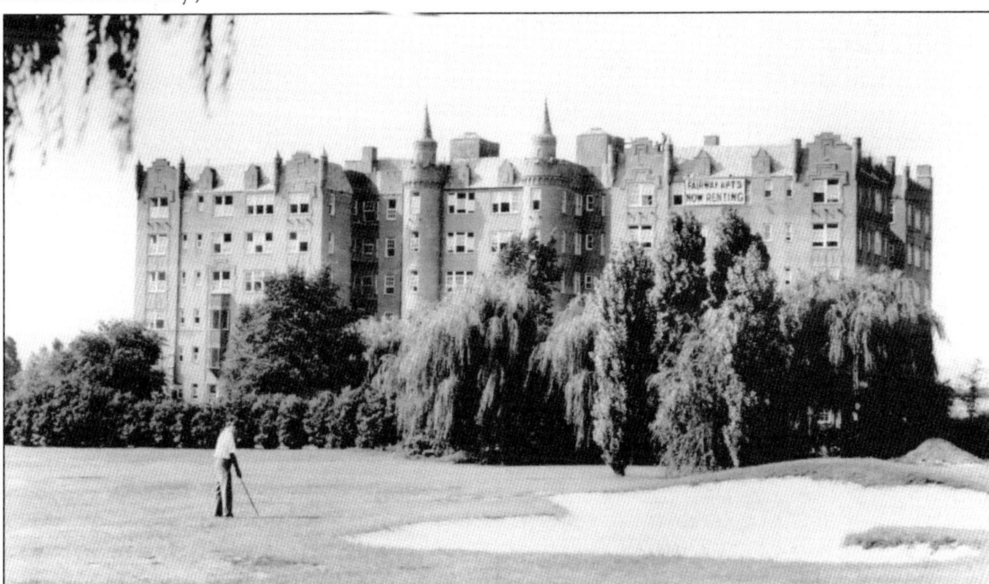

FAIRWAY APARTMENTS. Built in 1937, the Fairway Apartments were named for its proximity to the community golf course. Architect Joshua Tabatchnik chose the Tudor Revival style to reflect the romantic revival designs that predominated in the neighborhood. Tabatchnik designed the structure to resemble a Tudor castle, featuring an arched batten-style wooden entry door with flanking semicircular towers up to the roofline of turrets, battlements, and ramparts. (Courtesy of the Queens Historical Society.)

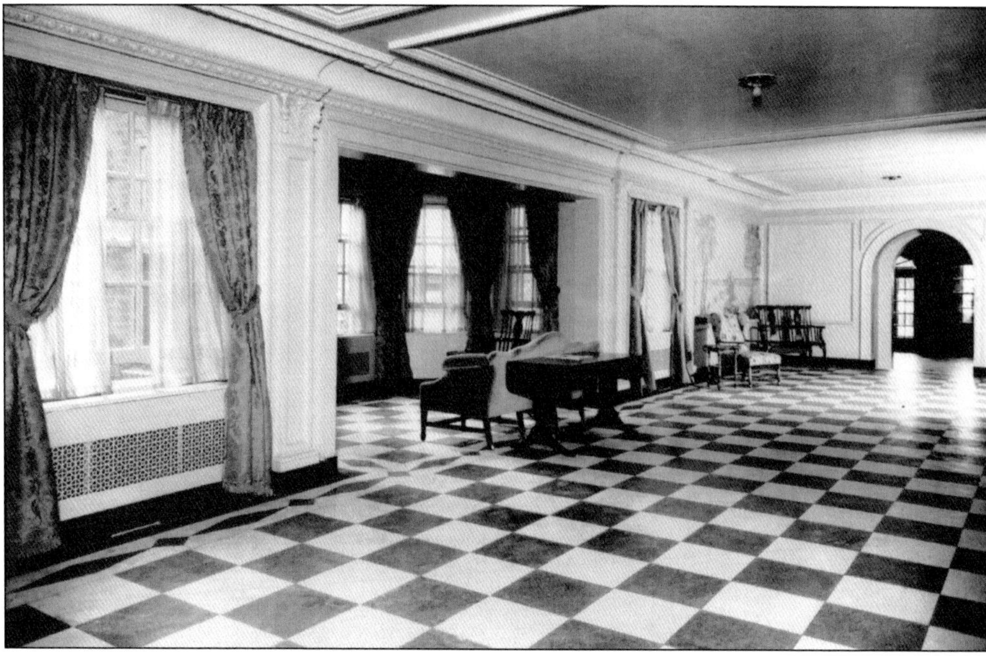

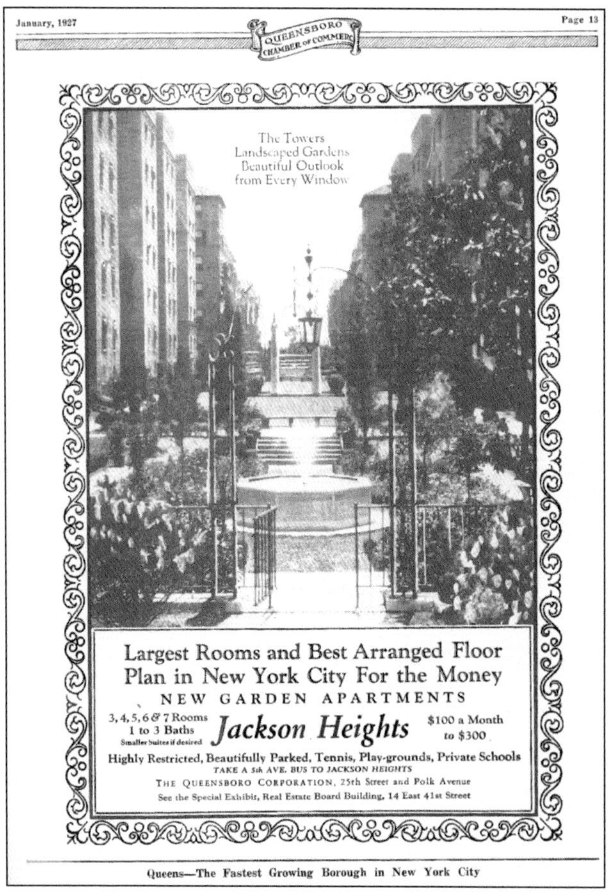

January, 1927 — Page 13

Queensboro Chamber of Commerce

The Towers
Landscaped Gardens
Beautiful Outlook
from Every Window

Largest Rooms and Best Arranged Floor Plan in New York City For the Money

NEW GARDEN APARTMENTS

3, 4, 5, 6 & 7 Rooms
1 to 3 Baths
Smaller Suites if desired

Jackson Heights

$100 a Month to $300

Highly Restricted, Beautifully Parked, Tennis, Play-grounds, Private Schools

TAKE A 5th AVE. BUS TO JACKSON HEIGHTS

THE QUEENSBORO CORPORATION, 25th Street and Polk Avenue

See the Special Exhibit, Real Estate Board Building, 14 East 41st Street

Queens—The Fastest Growing Borough in New York City

Georgian Hall Lobby. The lobby of Georgian Hall featured exquisite attention to detail as evidence by parquet floors, drapes, lounge furniture, and wall and ceiling moldings with Corinthian column inlays. (Courtesy of the Queens Historical Society.)

Period Advertisement. The Queensboro Corporation and the Queens Chamber of Commerce promoted the luxury of Jackson Heights, as seen in this advertisement from the January 1927 issue of *Queensborough* magazine. (Courtesy of the Queens Chamber of Commerce.)

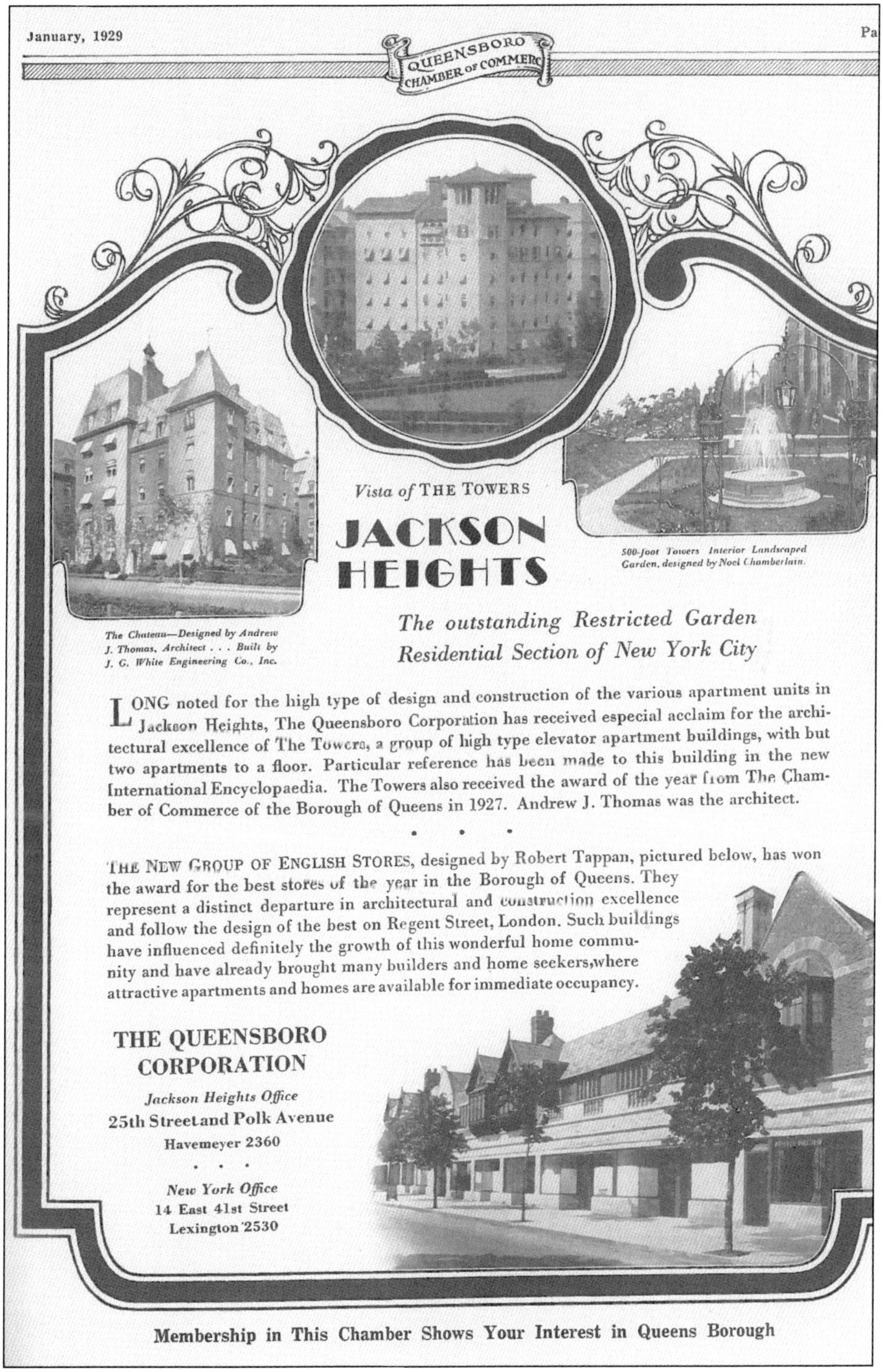

January, 1929

QUEENSBORO CHAMBER OF COMMERCE

Pa

The Chateau—Designed by Andrew J. Thomas, Architect . . . Built by J. G. White Engineering Co., Inc.

Vista of THE TOWERS

JACKSON HEIGHTS

500-foot Towers Interior Landscaped Garden, designed by Noel Chamberlain.

The outstanding Restricted Garden Residential Section of New York City

LONG noted for the high type of design and construction of the various apartment units in Jackson Heights, The Queensboro Corporation has received especial acclaim for the architectural excellence of The Towers, a group of high type elevator apartment buildings, with but two apartments to a floor. Particular reference has been made to this building in the new International Encyclopaedia. The Towers also received the award of the year from The Chamber of Commerce of the Borough of Queens in 1927. Andrew J. Thomas was the architect.

• • •

THE NEW GROUP OF ENGLISH STORES, designed by Robert Tappan, pictured below, has won the award for the best stores of the year in the Borough of Queens. They represent a distinct departure in architectural and construction excellence and follow the design of the best on Regent Street, London. Such buildings have influenced definitely the growth of this wonderful home community and have already brought many builders and home seekers, where attractive apartments and homes are available for immediate occupancy.

THE QUEENSBORO CORPORATION

Jackson Heights Office
25th Street and Polk Avenue
Havemeyer 2360

• • •

New York Office
14 East 41st Street
Lexington 2530

Membership in This Chamber Shows Your Interest in Queens Borough

OUTSTANDING RESTRICTED GARDEN COMMUNITY. In this advertisement from January 1929, the notable Towers and Chateau complexes, designed by Andrew J. Thomas, and new group of English stores, designed by Robert Tappan, are spotlighted. (Courtesy of the Queens Chamber of Commerce.)

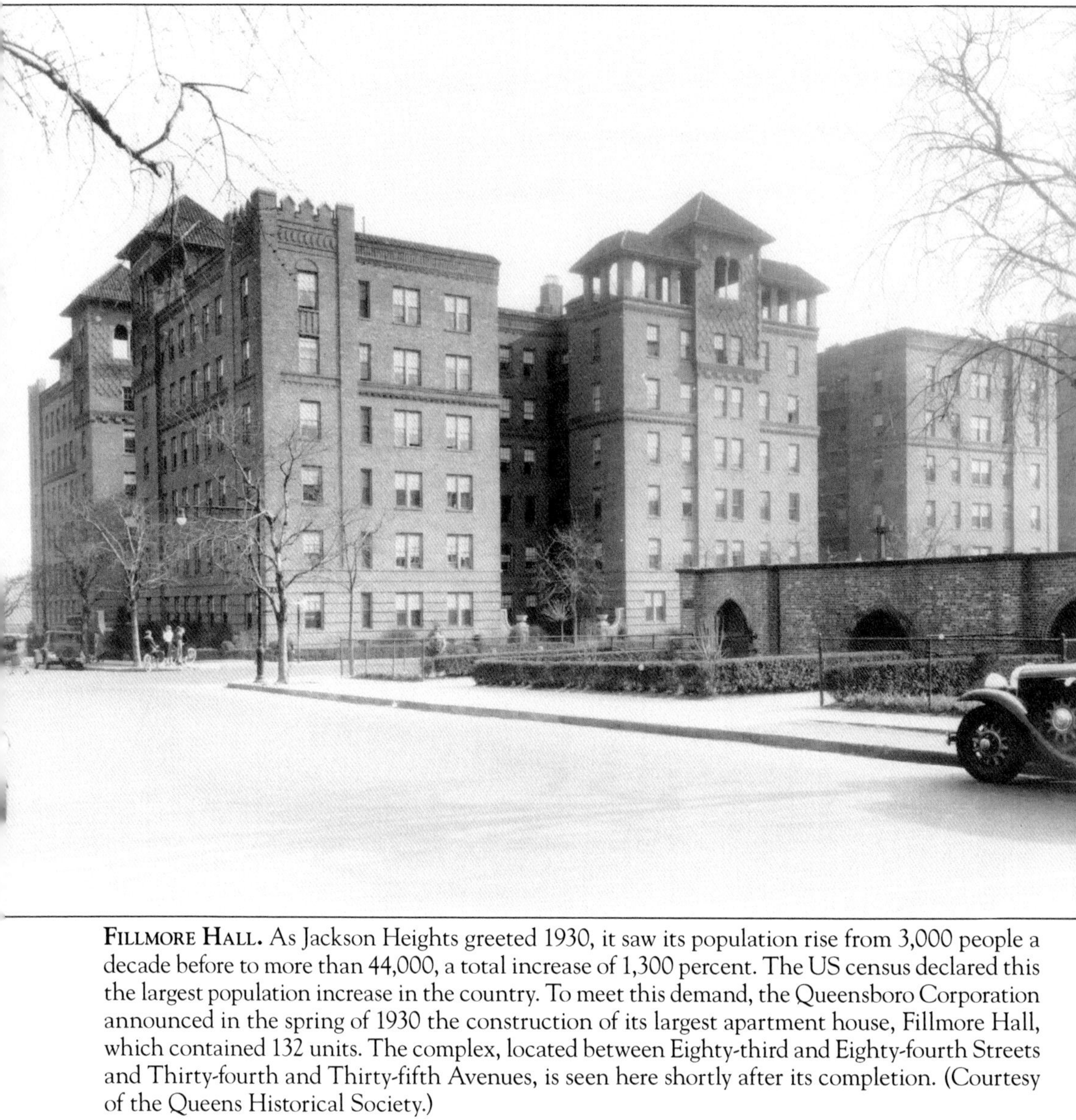

FILLMORE HALL. As Jackson Heights greeted 1930, it saw its population rise from 3,000 people a decade before to more than 44,000, a total increase of 1,300 percent. The US census declared this the largest population increase in the country. To meet this demand, the Queensboro Corporation announced in the spring of 1930 the construction of its largest apartment house, Fillmore Hall, which contained 132 units. The complex, located between Eighty-third and Eighty-fourth Streets and Thirty-fourth and Thirty-fifth Avenues, is seen here shortly after its completion. (Courtesy of the Queens Historical Society.)

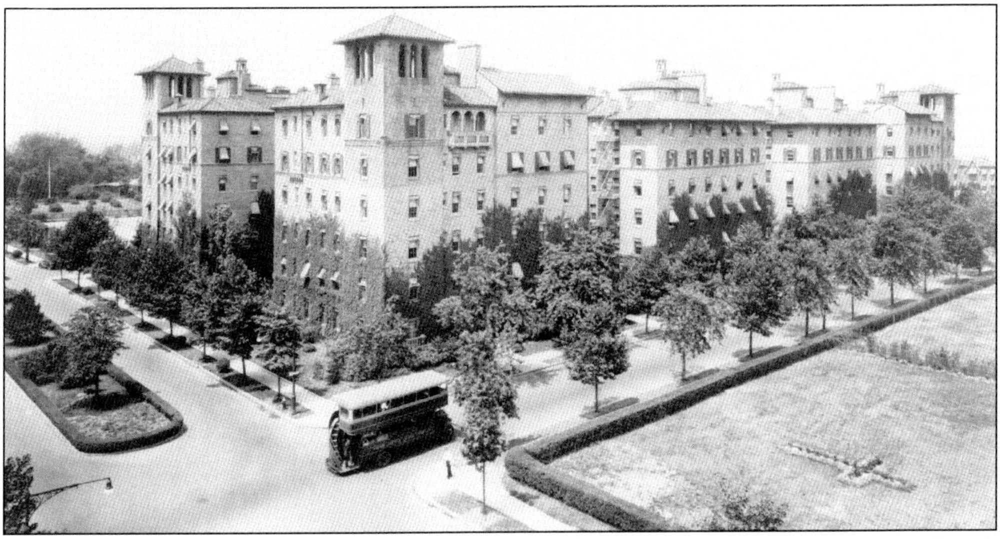

A View from Church. The Towers are seen here in all their glory at the corner of Thirty-fourth Avenue and Eighty-first Street. This dramatic photograph was taken from St. Mark's Episcopal Church. Note the property bearing the sign of the cross on the right. St. Mark's, like many structures in Jackson Heights, was designed by Robert Tappan and opened on Christmas Eve 1927. (Courtesy of the Queens Historical Society.)

The value of restrictions

One phase of the standards set by the Queensboro Corporation is that of restrictions. Jackson Heights is a restricted community. This means that you as a member of the community will always enjoy congenial, intelligent neighbors. The people you find at Jackson Heights are only those people you want to associate with. In addition, the Queensboro Corporation passes on every house to be built. There is no possibility as there is in other places, of property depreciating through the building of cheap or ugly houses. These restrictions are an insurance policy that protects your investment values.

"The Value Of Restrictions." In this message to prospective residents printed in a Queensboro Corporation brochure, the use of coded, and not so coded, language making Jackson Heights a restricted community is evident: "The people you find at Jackson Heights are only those people you want to associate with." There is also the promise that no "cheap or ugly" houses will be built. Accordingly, it assures the reader (a prospective resident) that "these restrictions are an insurance policy that protects your investment values." Practices such as these were aimed at excluding Catholics, Jews, and African Americans from living in the neighborhood. (Courtesy of the Queens Historical Society.)

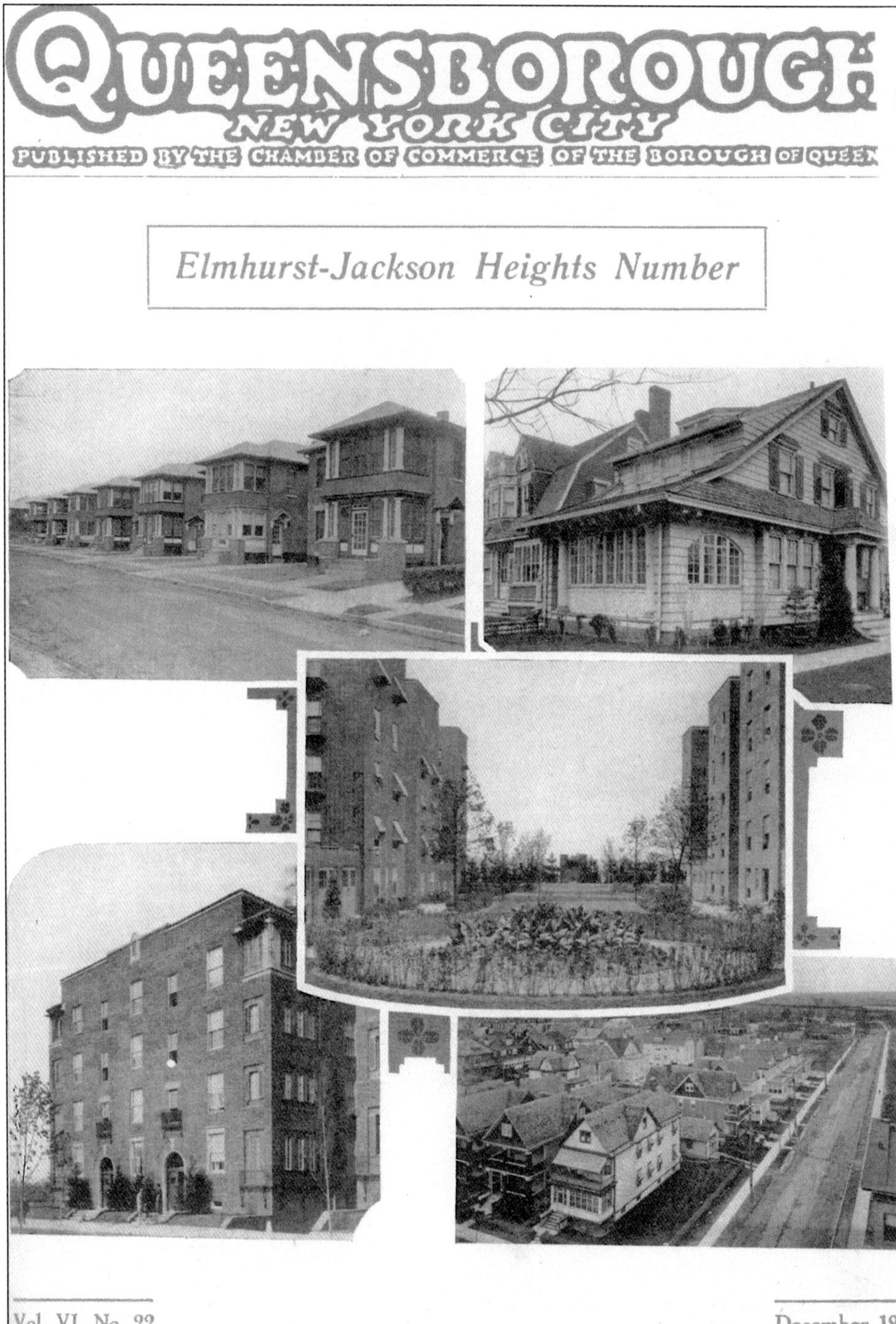

MAKING THE COVER. As the 1920s came to a close, development was in full swing. Elmhurst and Jackson Heights were featured on the cover of *Queensborough* magazine in December 1928 in an attempt to draw more people to Queens by showing newly built homes and expanded communities. Notice how prominently Jackson Heights is featured in the center. (Courtesy of the Queens Chamber of Commerce.)

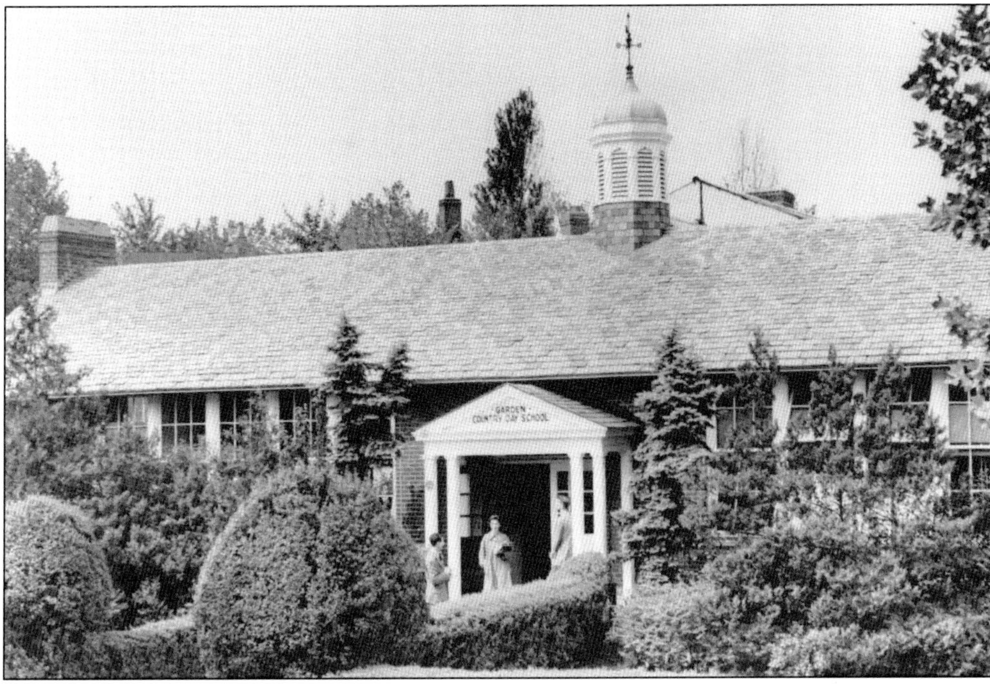

Garden Day School. A Jackson Heights icon, the Garden Country Day School, was created in 1923 by a group of parents who wanted an alternative to a public school education. The school took its name from the garden apartments surrounding it. The first classes, including students in kindergarten through the third grade, met in the Laburnum Court Apartments under the guidance of Dorothy Glenn, Charles Townshend, and Josephine Wech. Two years later, in 1925, grades four to six were added, and John Bosworth Laing became the director. In 1927, Otis Flower assumed the position of headmaster. With the help of the Queensboro Corporation, the Garden Country Day School moved to its current location at 33-16 Seventy-ninth Street. (Courtesy of the Queens Historical Society)

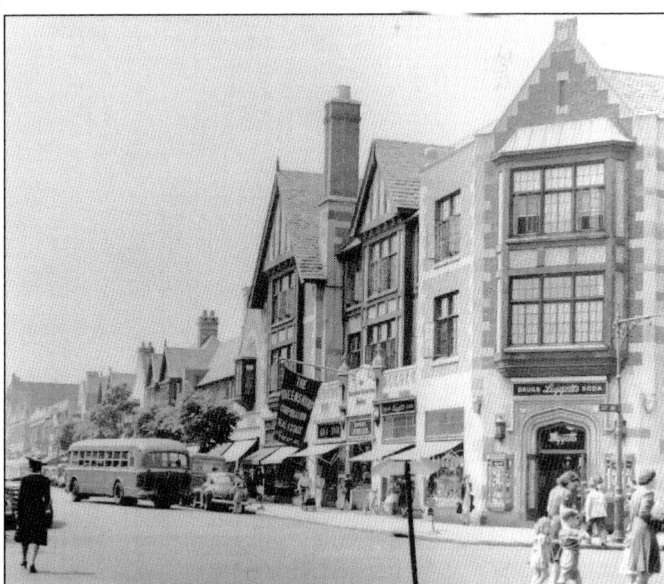

A Thriving Community. Moving toward mid-20th century, Jackson Heights was a bustling community that included a thriving commercial area. The offices of the Queensboro Corporation headquarters are seen in the corner (note its waving banner) of this 1942 image. Designed by Morrell Smith, this three-story Neo-Tudor structure cost $500,000 to build. It opened in May 1929 and housed the corporation's 250 employees. (Courtesy of the Queens Historical Society.)

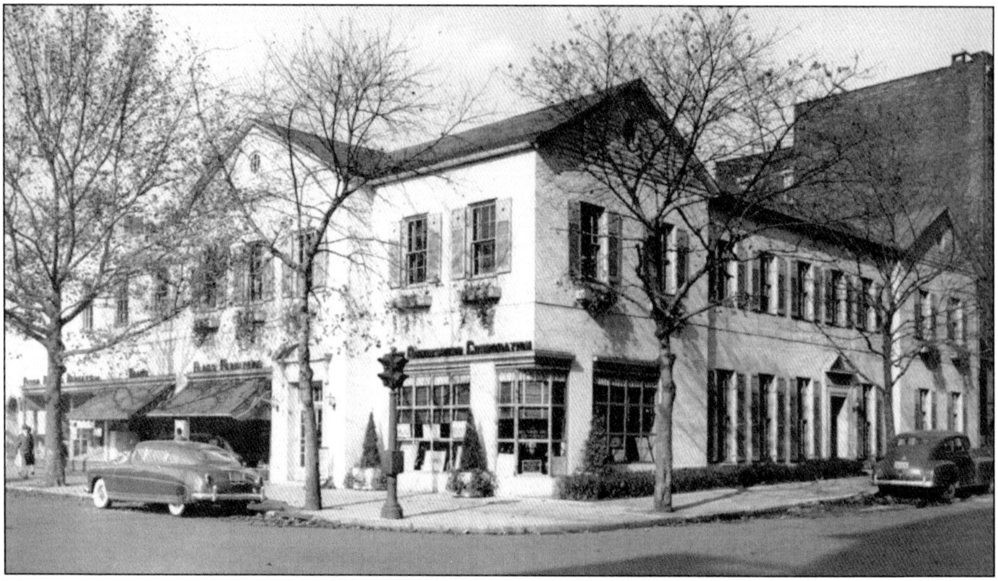

The Last Location. After World War II, the Queensboro Corporation moved into its new and final offices at the corner of Seventy-ninth Street and Thirty-seventh Avenue. Andrew J. Thomas designed the structure in the Neo-Georgian tradition. Opening on November 17, 1947, the location would be Thomas's final project for the Queensboro Corporation after a relationship that lasted almost three decades. (Courtesy of the Queens Historical Society.)

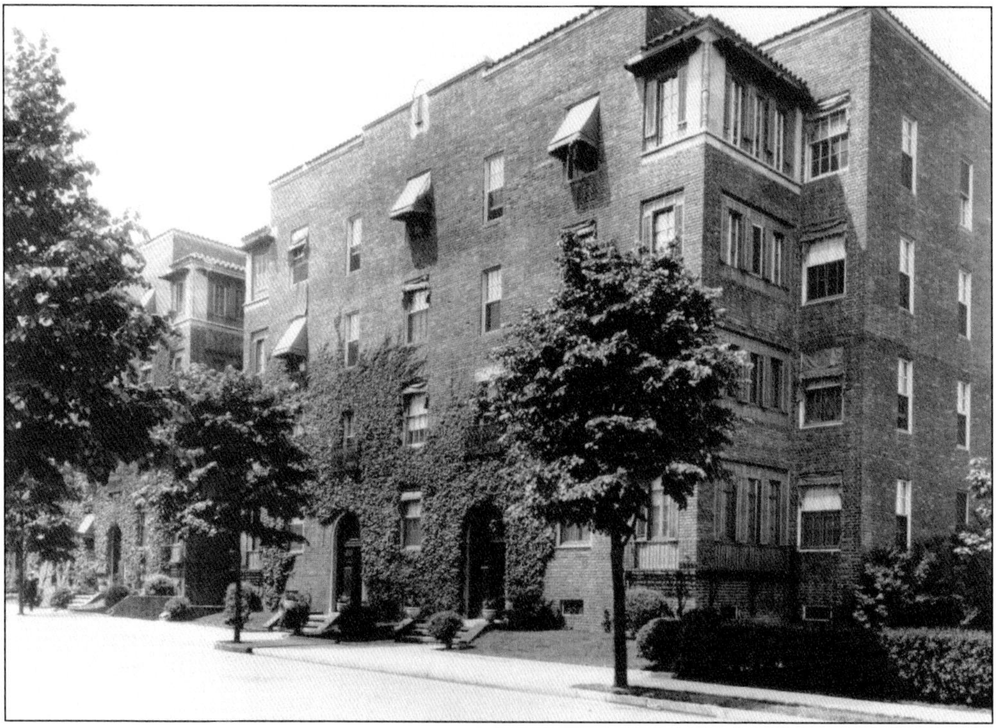

Linden Court. Designed by Andrew J. Thomas, Linden Court is located between Eighty-fourth and Eighty-fifth Streets and Thirty-seventh and Roosevelt Avenues. It opened in 1921. (Courtesy of the Queens Historical Society.)

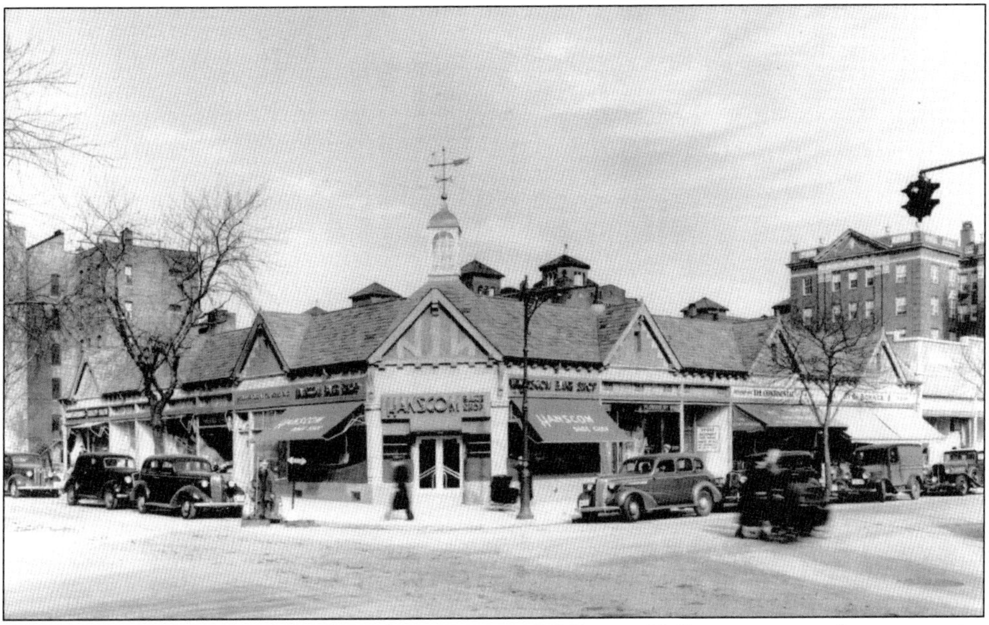

Local Businesses. In the shadow of Georgian and Fillmore Halls is a group of stores on the corner of Thirty-seventh Avenue and Eighty-second Street (around 1940). At the center of the photograph is Hanscom Bakery. Note the weather vane above. Originally, this very intersection was slated to be the location of the Jackson Heights Hotel. The project never came to fruition. (Courtesy of the Queens Historical Society.)

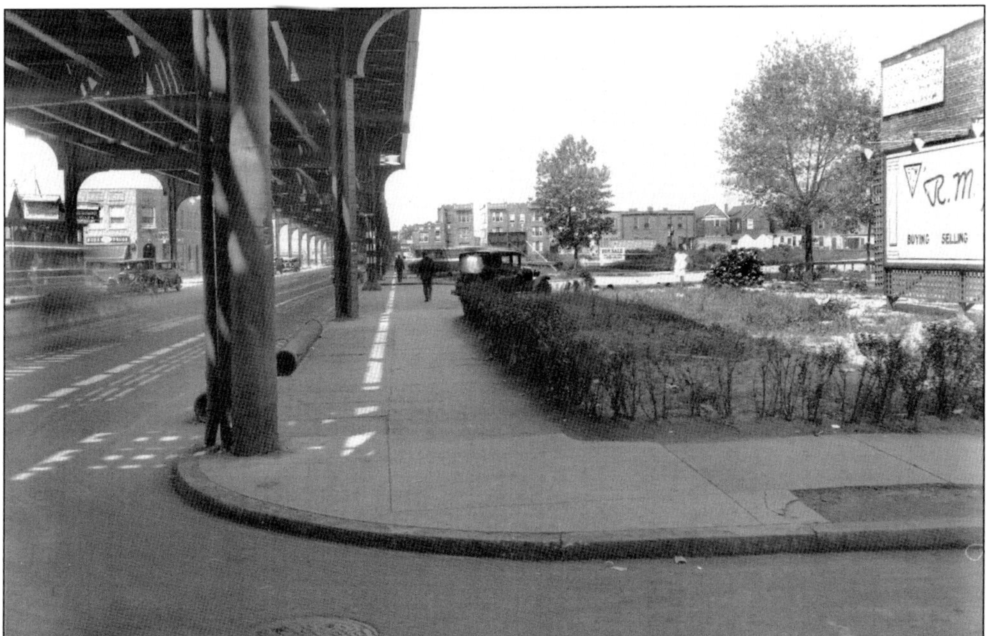

Limited Space. This empty lot on the right represented a valuable buying opportunity, for this section along Roosevelt Avenue was probably one of the last undeveloped sections of what was by now a bustling urban center. This 1940s scene includes For Sale signs for the last amount of available space. (Courtesy of the Queens Historical Society.)

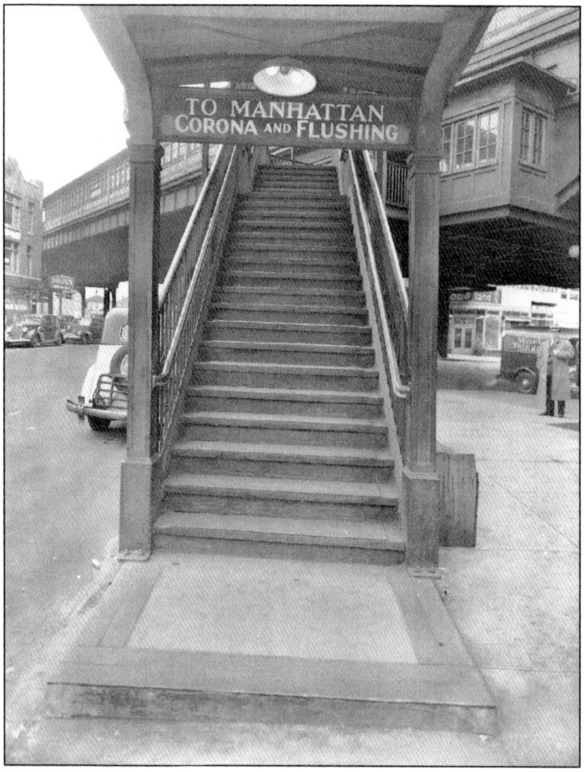

TO MANHATTAN. At the time of the Great Depression, mass transit was seen as a more economical option to travel to Manhattan or eastern Queens.

PRESERVING A NEIGHBORHOOD'S IDENTITY. In September 1947, the New York City Housing Authority announced its proposal to build public housing (or projects) in Jackson Heights. The Queensboro Corporation and the neighborhood fought Robert Moses, the city planner who endorsed the plan. By January 1948, the plan was abandoned, and instead additional modern cooperatives were built, thus preserving the neighborhood's character.

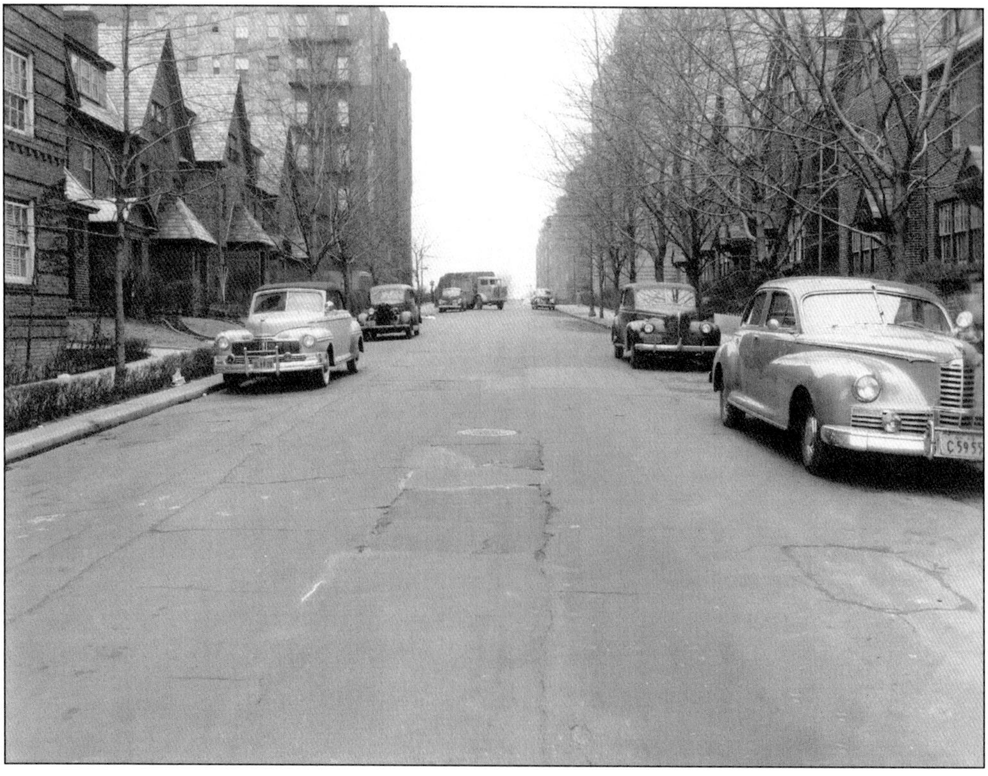

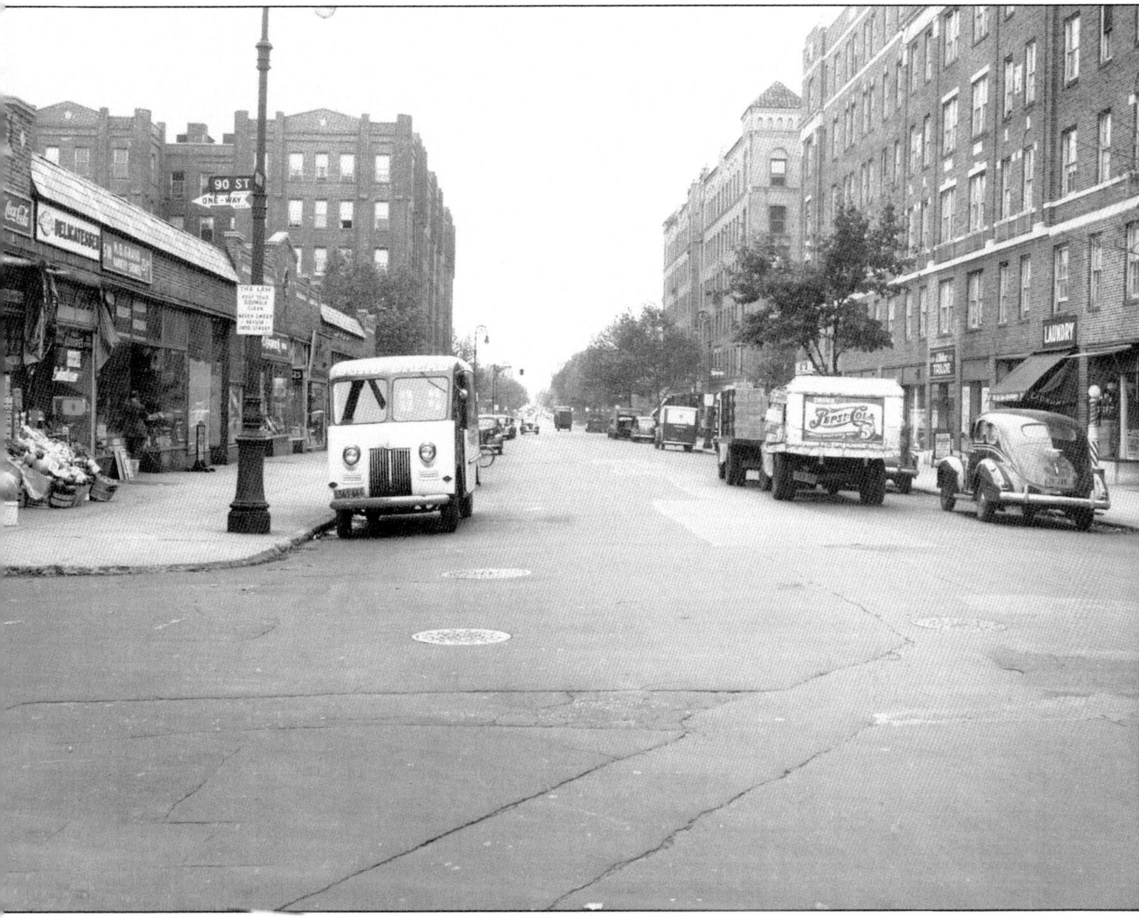

JACKSON HEIGHTS, C. 1950. A morning scene along Thirty-seventh Avenue shows delivery trucks bringing goods to local stores. Note the Pepsi-Cola delivery truck on the right. To the left are Stahl-Meyer Delicatessen, N.B. Grand Five-and-Dime Variety Store, and a C. Bohack grocery. The sign on the ornate lamppost at the corner of Ninetieth Street serves to remind the owners of these small businesses to keep their portions of the sidewalk clean. (Courtesy of the Queens Borough Public Library, Long Island Division, President of Queens Borough Collection.)

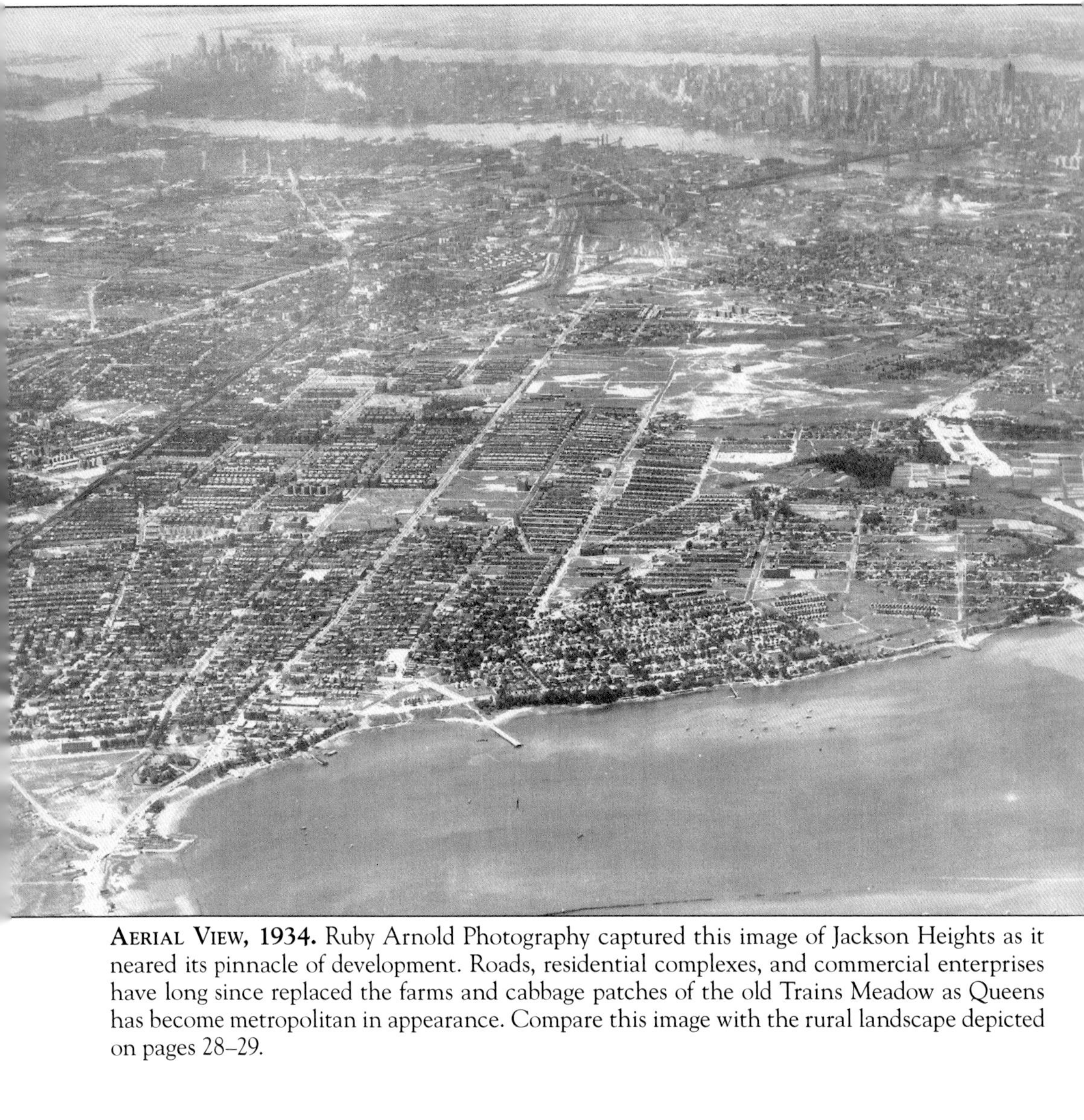

Aerial View, 1934. Ruby Arnold Photography captured this image of Jackson Heights as it neared its pinnacle of development. Roads, residential complexes, and commercial enterprises have long since replaced the farms and cabbage patches of the old Trains Meadow as Queens has become metropolitan in appearance. Compare this image with the rural landscape depicted on pages 28–29.

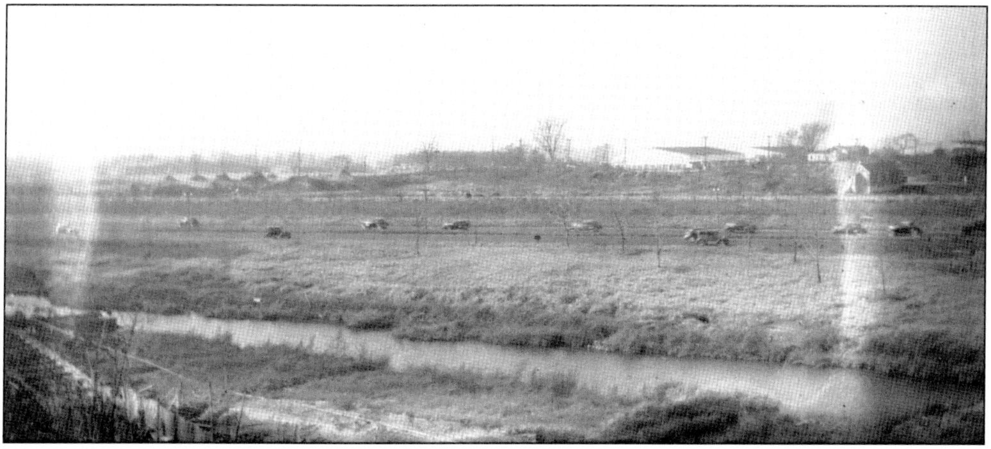

North Beach Airport and Grand Central Parkway. As the 1920s came to a close, New York City continued to expand its infrastructure. Transportation needs exceeded that of housing. The Grand Central Parkway was built in 1931. At one of the northern tips of Queens, just opposite Jackson Heights, stood the North Beach Amusement Park, which would become the Glenn Curtiss Field. (Courtesy of the Queens Borough Public Library, Long Island Division, Ralph Solecki Photographs.)

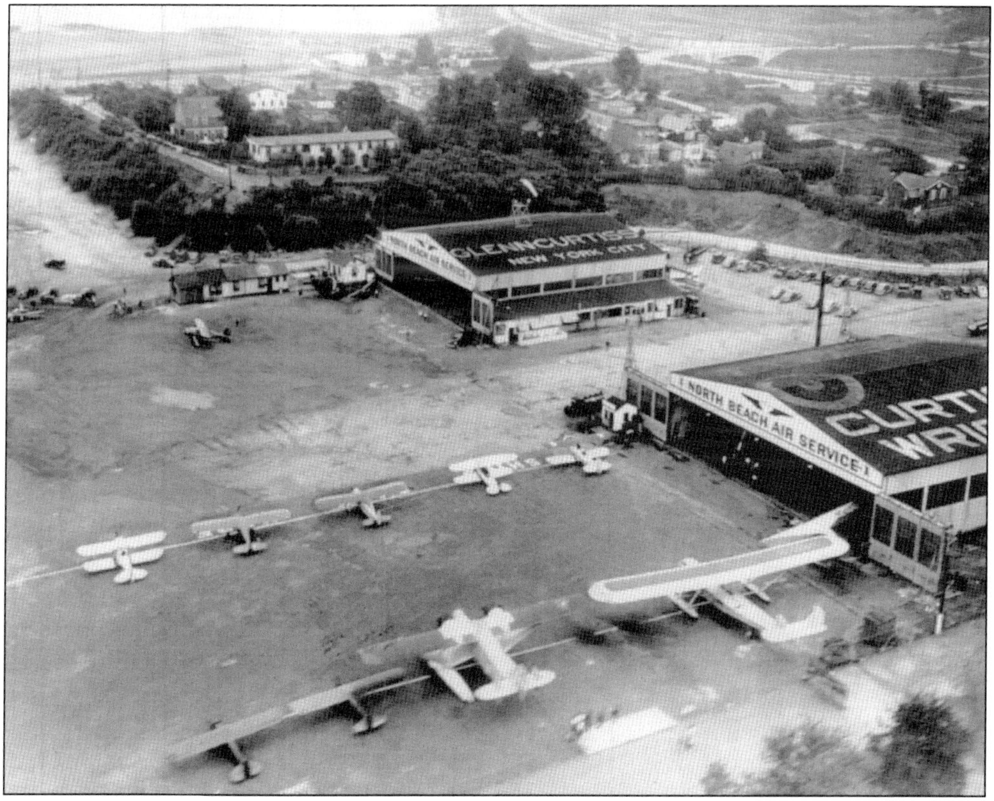

Glenn Curtiss. This aerial view of Glenn Curtiss Field was taken right after its renaming to North Beach Airport. The airport boasted multiple runways, three hangars, a blimp dock, and a seaplane ramp. It was renamed in 1939 to New York Municipal Airport–LaGuardia Field and again in 1953 to LaGuardia Airport in honor of New York City mayor Fiorello LaGuardia.

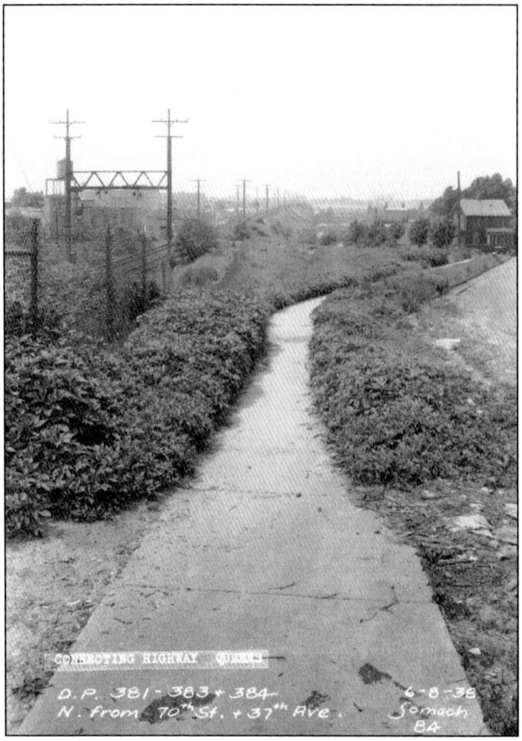

Brooklyn-Queens Expressway (BQE). The BQE, as it is sometimes called, came into being in 1936 to provide direct access to Brooklyn from Queens. This June 8, 1938, photograph shows the proposed path that would be led through Elmhurst and Jackson Heights. This view looks north from Seventieth Street and Thirty-seventh Avenue. (Courtesy of the Queens Borough Public Library, Long Island Division, Borough President of Queens Collection.)

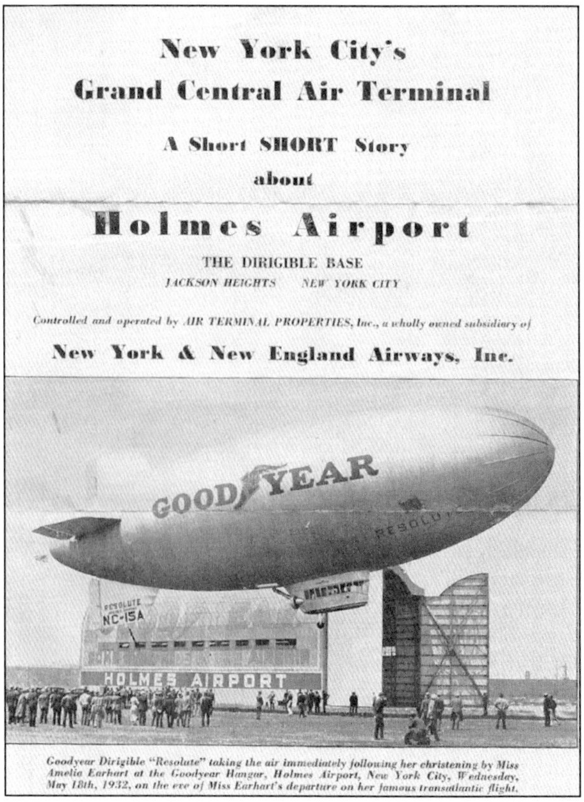

Holmes Airport. Real estate developer E.H. Holmes built this small airport on 220 acres of undeveloped land in Jackson Heights. In February 1929, Clarence Chamberlin, aviatrix Viola Gentry, and Dorothy Stone broke ground for the new airport. It featured two hangars, an office, and two gravel runways, measuring 2,800 and 3,000 feet. Holmes Airport opened on March 16, 1929, attracting 100,000 on its second day of operation. Later in 1929, the first scheduled flights from New York City began operations from the airport when Eastern Air Express started a two-day run to Miami. Goodyear erected a 220-foot blimp hangar at the airport in 1931 and conducted sightseeing flights. In 1936, the blimps were used for the first aerial traffic reports in recorded history. Today, the acres once occupied by the airport are filled with residential homes and the Bulova Watch Building.

Three

The Bulova Watch Company

Bulova's many achievements, some of which were groundbreaking, are well known. For a time, its product quality and marketing strategy stood unparalleled. Bulova was not only the first company to run radio commercials— landing the phrase "Bulova Time" in the vernacular—but also the first to air one on television, right before the start of a Brooklyn Dodgers game. Yet, its philanthropy still warrants appreciation. At the close of World War II, Bulova availed itself to help disabled veterans make the transition to civilian life, "a small measure," chairman Ardé Bulova acknowledged, "of the gratitude . . . [owed] to these men for their service to our country in this greatest of all wars." Bulova realized that being on the right side of history only started with victory on the battlefield.

Its commitment was further realized in selecting retired five-star general Omar Bradley as head of the company in 1953. Bradley's brand of leadership made him well suited to the task, but what stood out was his overriding concern for disabled ex-servicemen. As administrator for Veterans Affairs, he declined to speak before enormous V-J Day crowds but not at a graduation ceremony at the Bulova Watchmaking School (which, unfortunately, no longer exists). Before 20 graduates of the rehab program he helped institute there in 1945, he conveyed the following:

> You're here in this graduating class, ready and able to move out into the world as self-reliant, independent, productive citizens. You have the ability and determination to make your business careers count for something. . . . [Your] graduation marks a new step forward in joint government and Industry cooperation to insure that there will be no repetition of the wasteful and costly practice of ignoring the talents and abilities of disabled veterans. . . . You wouldn't let your body quit. You worked on it, and you licked it. You taught it new skills. You will live for yourselves, for your community, and for your nation.

Bradley's pride in his men was as unwavering as ever, but his foresight carried the day. And, like its famed timepieces, Bulova marked time in excellent style.

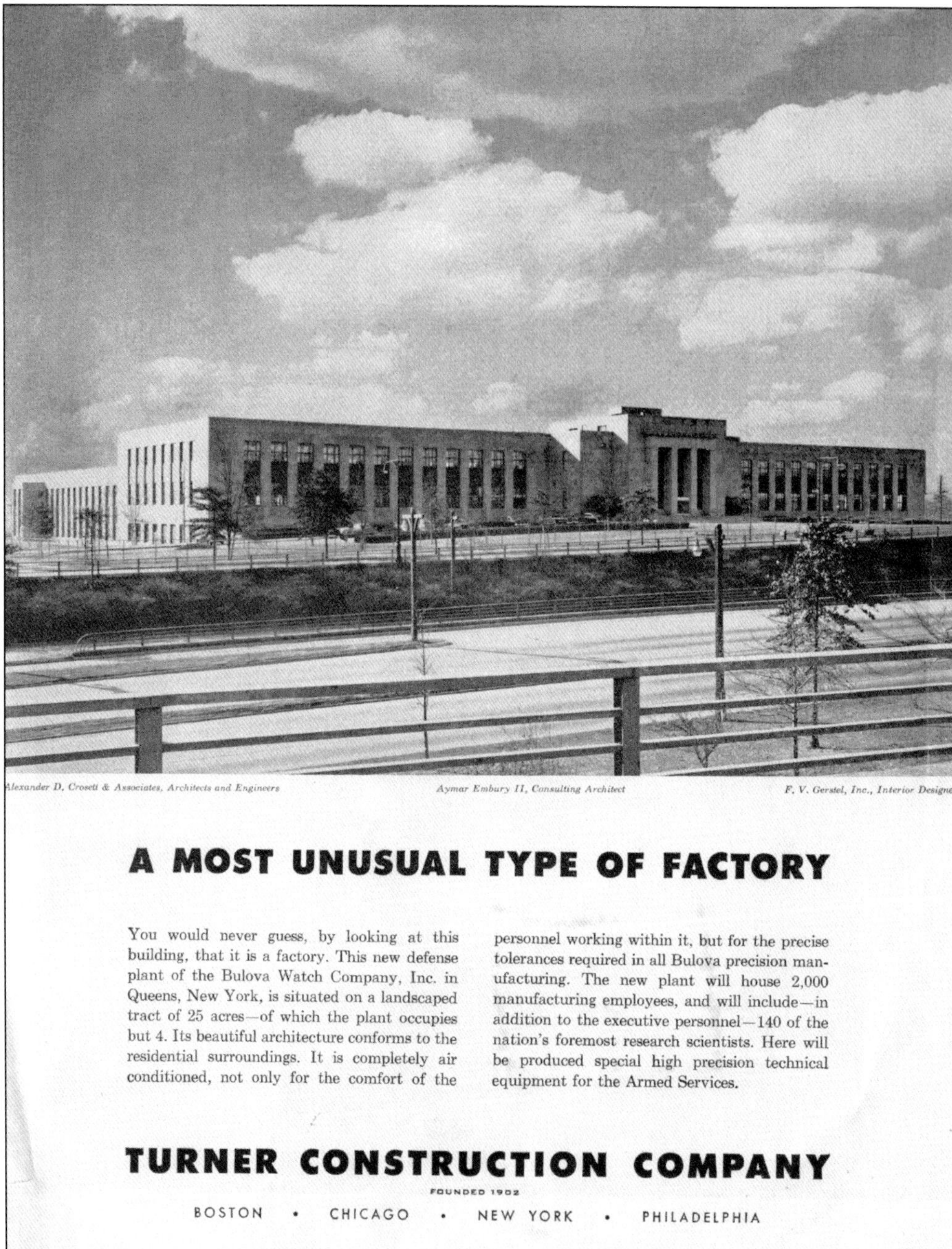

A MOST UNUSUAL TYPE OF FACTORY. The Bulova Watch Company built the most advanced assembly complex in its history on the 25-acre tract that was once Holmes Airport. Located just south of the Grand Central Parkway where it splits into the Brooklyn-Queens Expressway, the facility was designed by Alexander D. Crosett and Associates. F.V. Gerstel designed the interior, and Aymar Embury II served as a consulting architect. Built as a defense plant, it housed 2,000 manufacturing employees and 140 of the nation's foremost research scientists. Workers helped design and produce special high-precision technical equipment for the armed services. The plant, located on the easternmost border of Jackson Heights, opened in 1953.

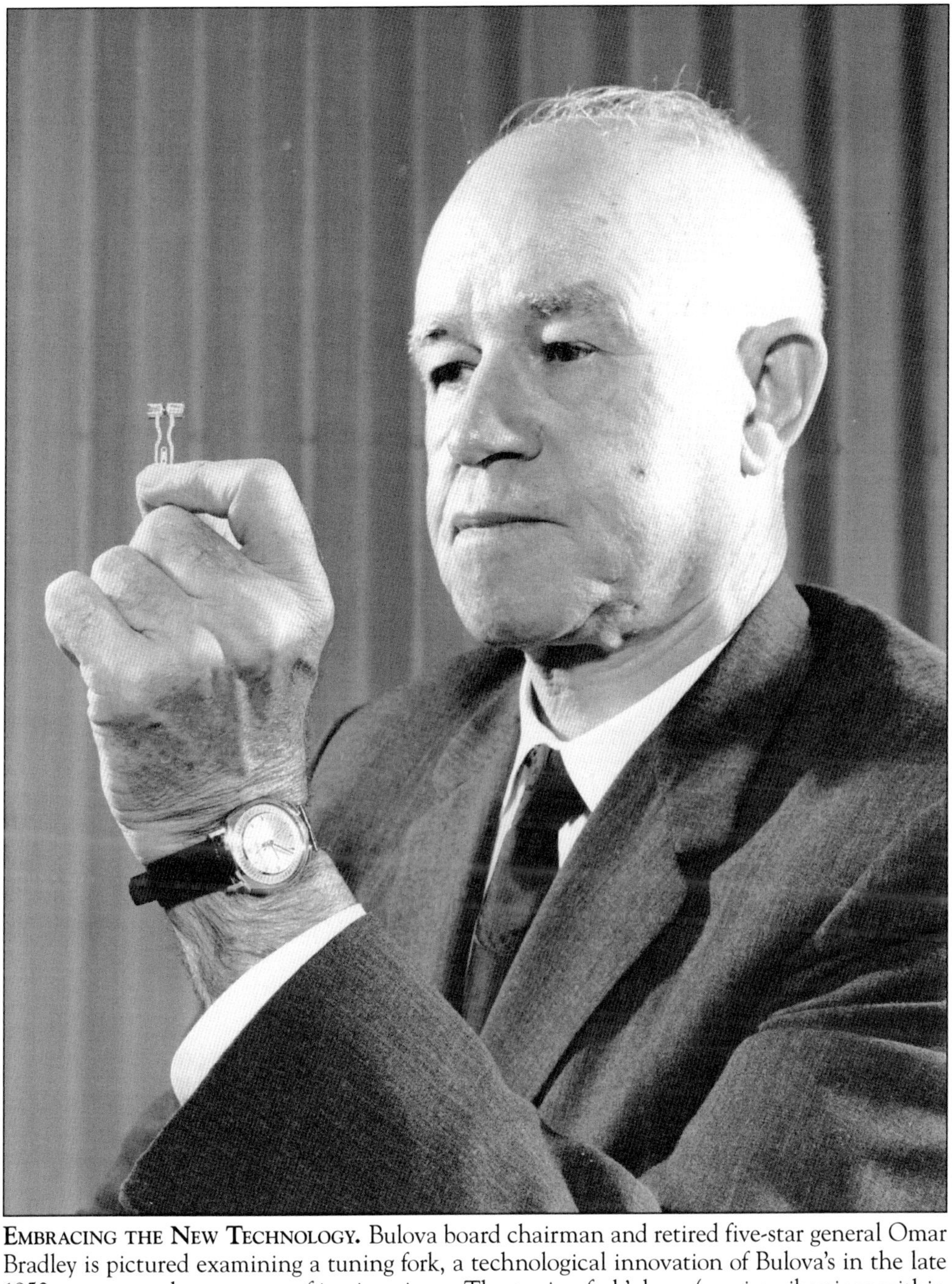

EMBRACING THE NEW TECHNOLOGY. Bulova board chairman and retired five-star general Omar Bradley is pictured examining a tuning fork, a technological innovation of Bulova's in the late 1950s to ensure the accuracy of its timepieces. The tuning fork's hum (precise vibrations within a transistorized electronic circuit) was seen as cutting edge, meant to supersede the traditional ticking sound of current watches. Notice that Bradley is wearing a new Accutron, the watch with the new tuning fork technology, which debuted a month before this photograph was taken in November 1960.

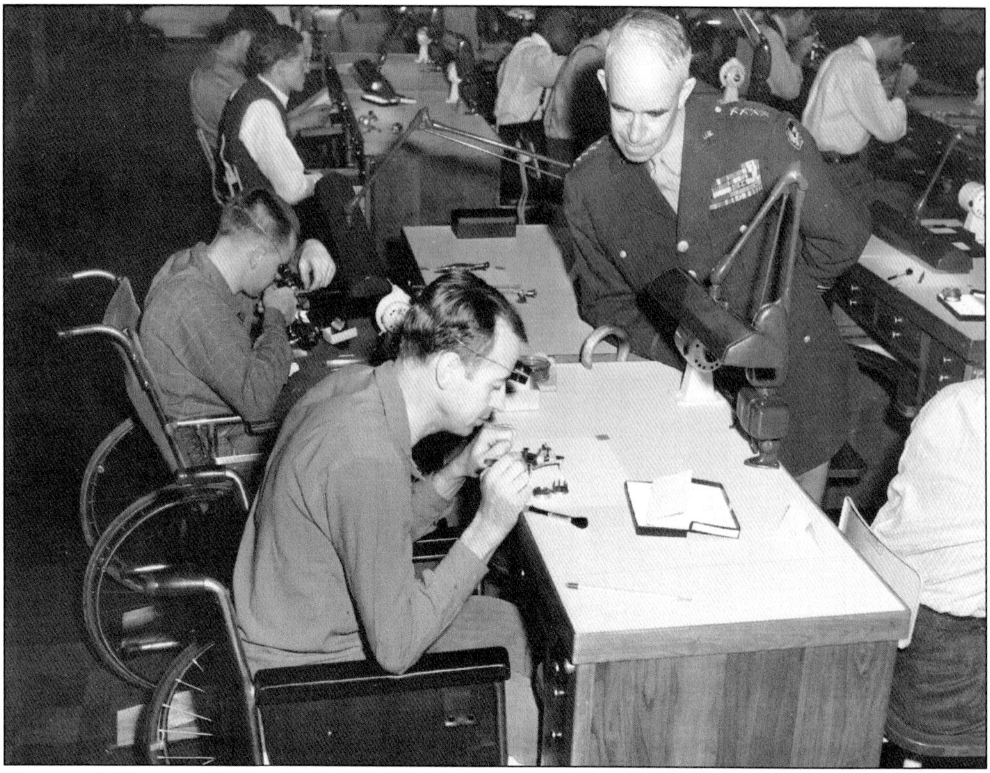

Bradley's Bulova Tour. As head of the Veterans Affairs after World War II, General Bradley took a keen interest in the welfare of disabled veterans. Here, he appears visibly impressed as he looks upon a group of unidentified heroes at the Bulova Watchmaking School. The students are applying their acquired knowledge of watch repair and manufacture. At the time, the Bulova School had a capacity of 125 students and operated at no cost to the government or the vets themselves; it was the first school of its kind to set up a training program with veterans in mind. Bradley took what he gathered here to express a desire to see the same policy emulated in other industries.

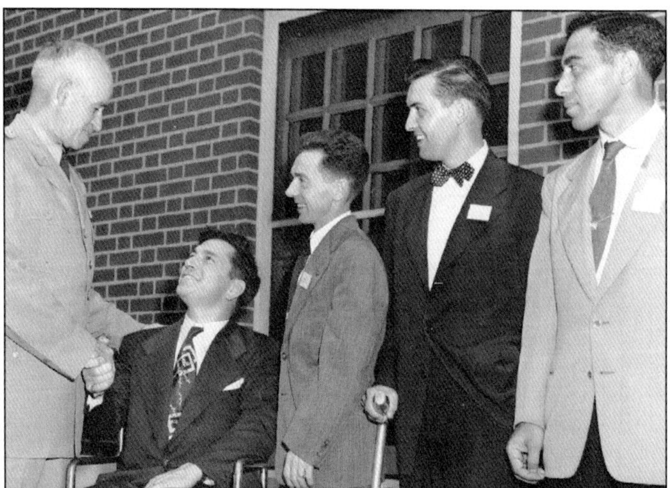

Omar's Men. This is the fifth anniversary of the first graduating class of the Bulova Watchmaking School in August 1951. Here, Bradley (left) takes a moment to chat with four of those graduates who had become expert watch repairmen. They are, from left to right, Edgar Winstead, Harry Cowper, Paul Tylowski, and John Mercoglan. Also present at the event was Vice Pres. Alben Barkley, who spoke to the 3,000 people in attendance.

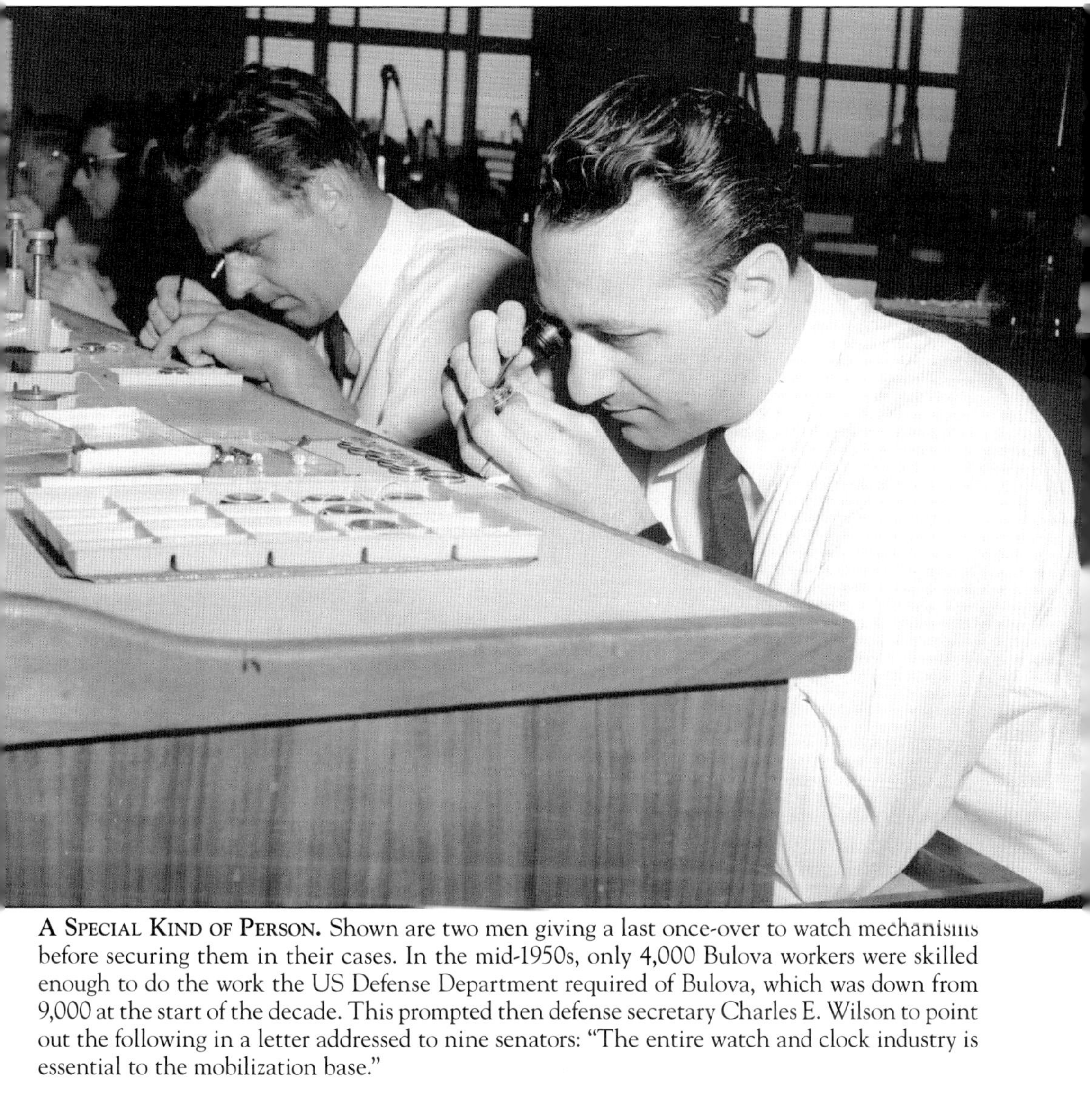

A SPECIAL KIND OF PERSON. Shown are two men giving a last once-over to watch mechanisms before securing them in their cases. In the mid-1950s, only 4,000 Bulova workers were skilled enough to do the work the US Defense Department required of Bulova, which was down from 9,000 at the start of the decade. This prompted then defense secretary Charles E. Wilson to point out the following in a letter addressed to nine senators: "The entire watch and clock industry is essential to the mobilization base."

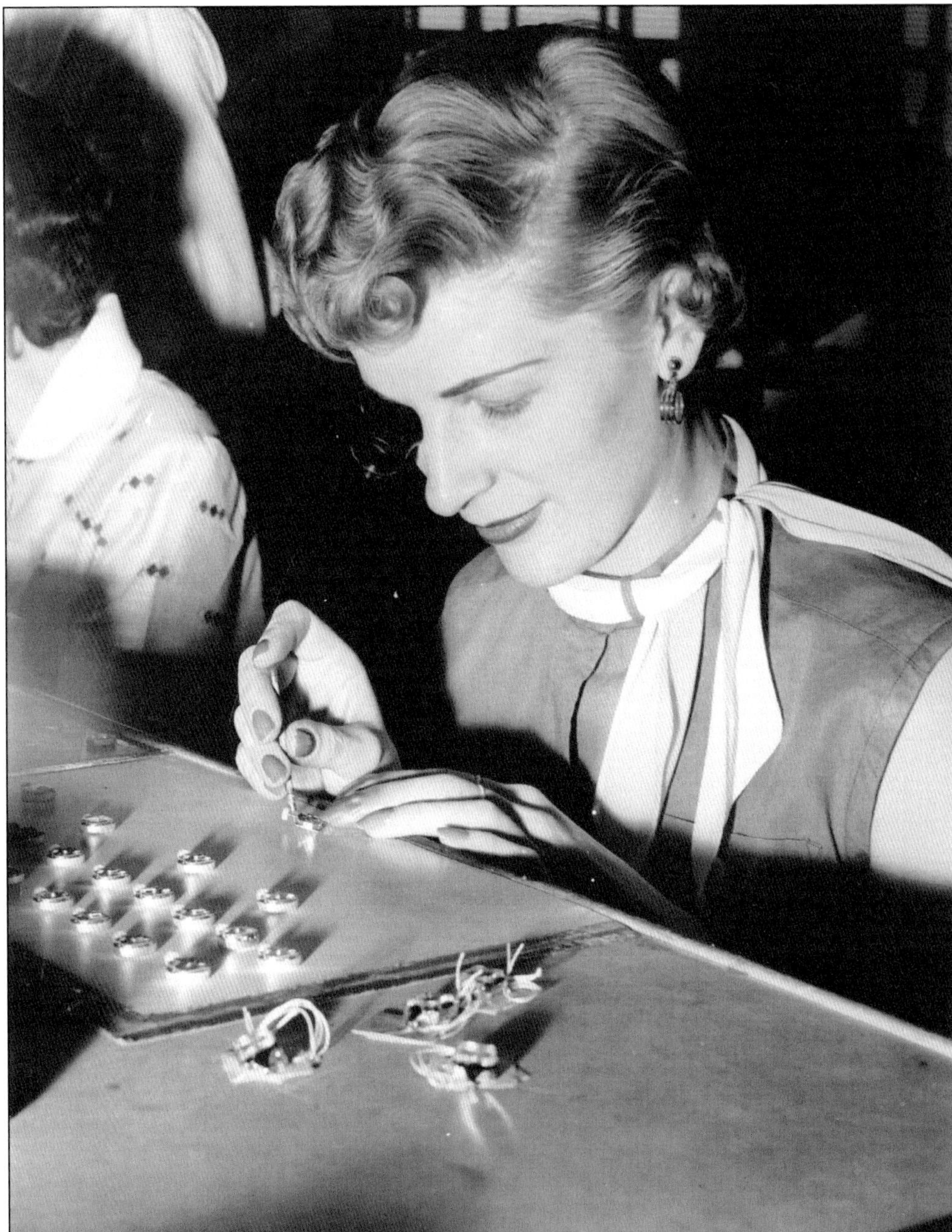

A Day's Work. Make no mistake; women, too, were a valued part of the Bulova workforce. Just imagine the keen eye and steady hand needed to assemble a watch as small as a dime and to do so repeatedly as one's daily work required.

DIAMONDS, DIAMONDS, AND MORE DIAMONDS. When this photograph was first published in 1960, the diamonds before Jerome Light's scrutiny were valued at about $120,000 (more than $900,000 today). A diamond buyer for Bulova, Light planned to use these jewels in an upcoming Christmas line of diamond wristwatches. The tray shown held enough diamonds for use in nearly 60,000 men's and women's watches.

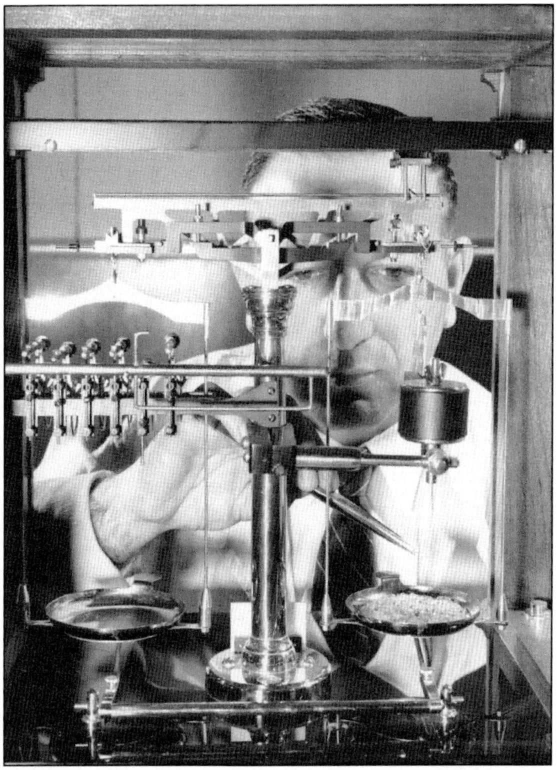

INSPECTING A TIME FUSE. Since American watchmakers were also responsible for classified military technology, Bulova deemed it essential to augment their skills. This nameless employee, with badge No. 01412, was photographed carefully checking a tool of war, and yet beside her is a machine also used to make parts for watches. This photograph was taken in 1955.

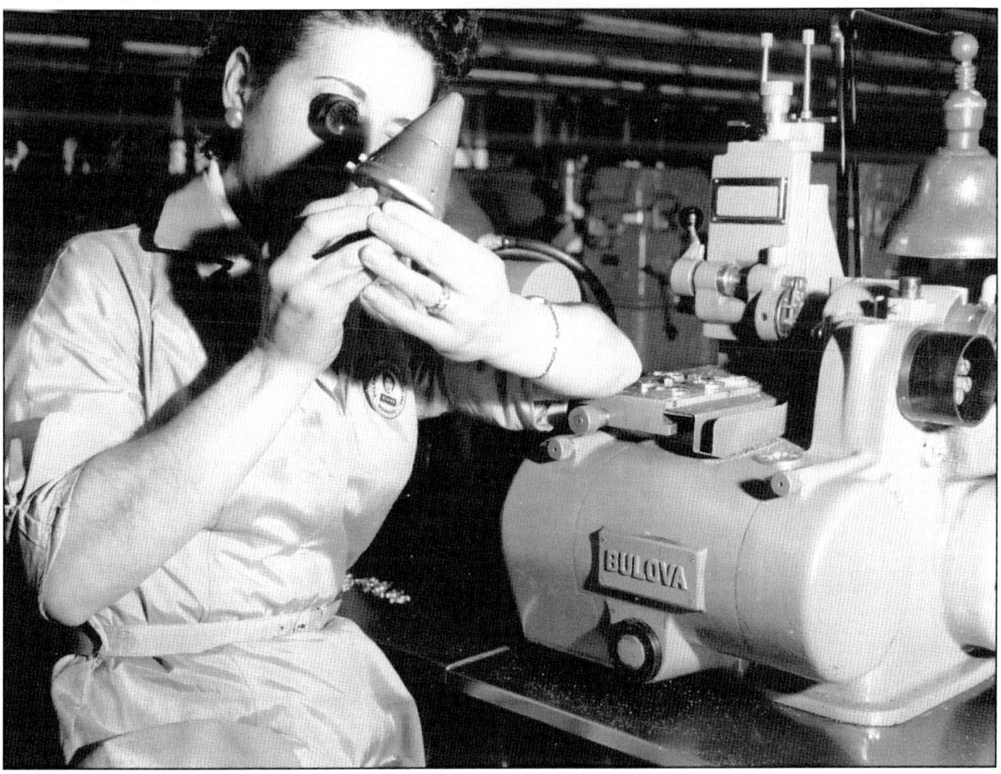

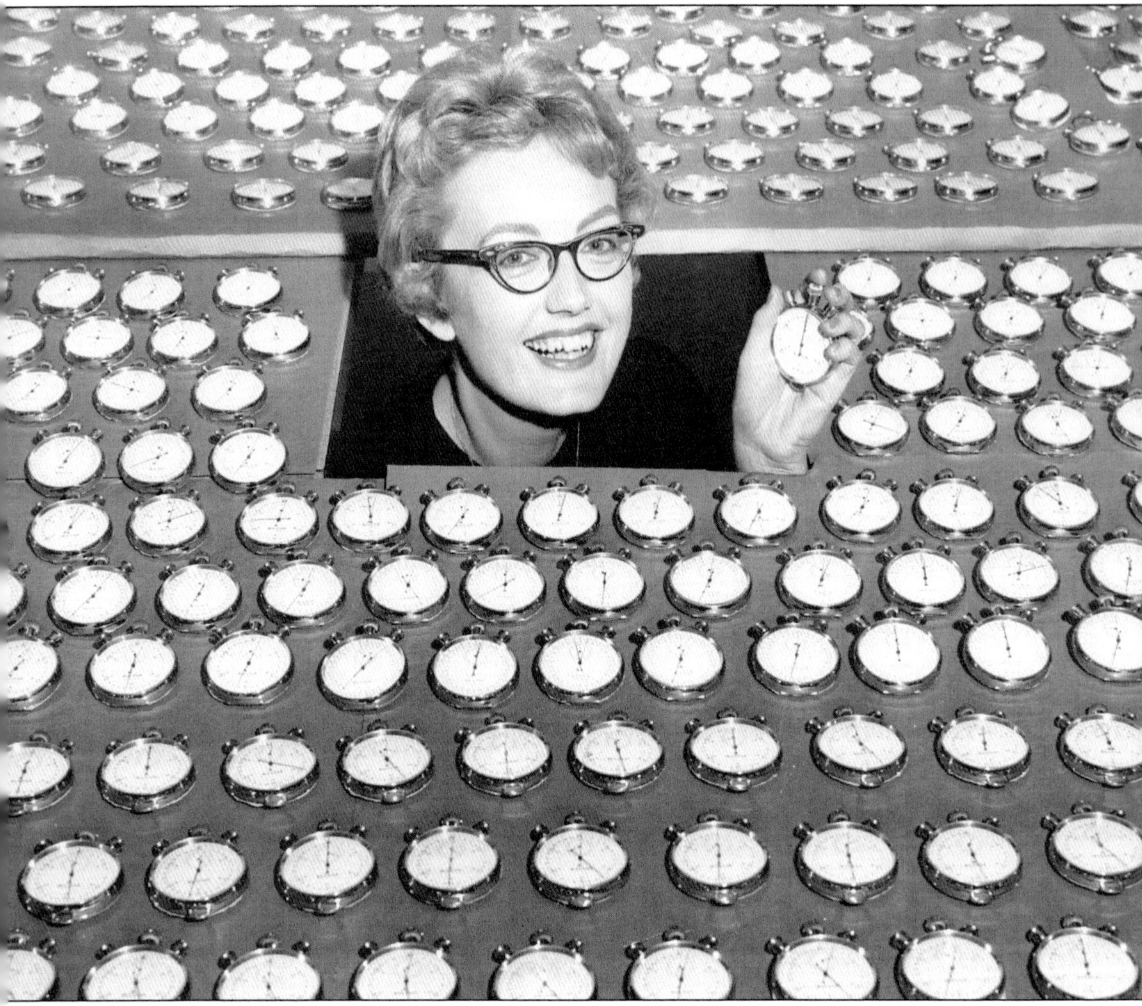

An Appealing Face of Time. Standing out amid a sea of Bulova stopwatches is a beaming Ruth Joels, whose job was to ensure their accuracy before shipment. This photograph was taken in 1962.

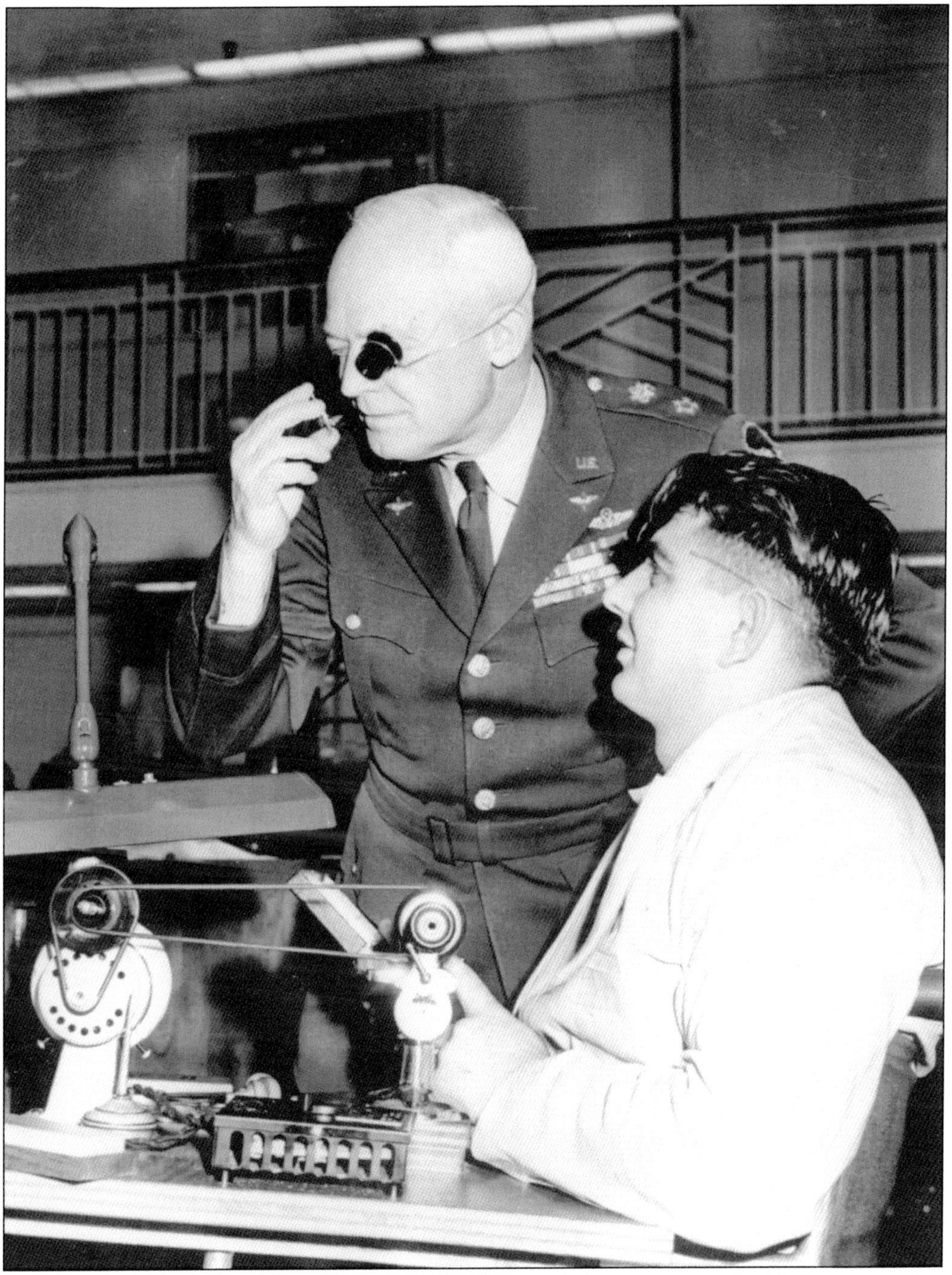

A "Hap" Inspection. Omar Bradley was widely known for his interest in disabled veterans after the war, but Air Force general Henry "Hap" Arnold was not lacking in this respect either. Here, in a photograph dated 1946, the general uses a loupe to inspect the precision work of Bulova Watchmaking School trainee Walter Suchanoff. After just three weeks into combat, Suchanoff was wounded in France and was left paralyzed from the waist down. General Arnold died in 1950.

BOROUGH'S OUTSTANDING AWARD - 1953

Special Bronze Plaque

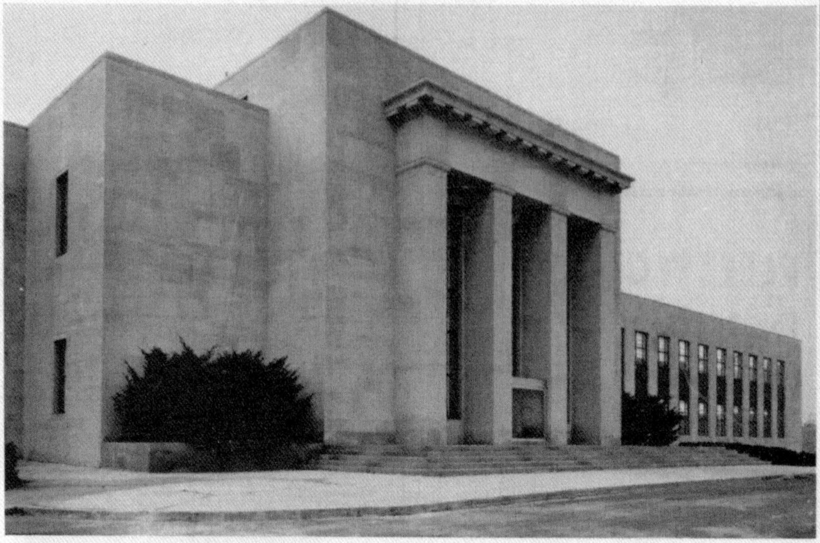

BULOVA WATCH COMPANY, INC.

Bulova Park, 77th Street & Astoria Boulevard, Jackson Heights

Location of Building: BULOVA WATCH COMPANY, INC.
77th Street & Astoria Boulevard, Jackson Heights

ARCHITECT
ALEXANDER D. CROSETT & ASSOCIATES
27 William Street
New York City

BUILDER
TURNER CONSTRUCTION COMPANY
420 Lexington Avenue
New York City

INSPIRED BY THE design of the Federal Reserve Bank in Washington, D. C., the Bulova Watch Company building in Jackson Heights is unique in modern industrial planning. The classic two-story structure 450′ wide by 350′ deep houses the company's administrative headquarters, research and development laboratories, and manufacturing area. Total space, including 160,000 square feet for manufacturing, is 400,000 square feet.

Overall height, in keeping with civil aeronautic regulations, does not exceed 50 feet. It boasts spacious, imaginative and forward-looking design throughout. Entirely finished in rustic buff Indiana limestone, it is completely air-conditioned by an elaborate unit providing dust-free, humidity-controlled atmosphere. Designed and columned to provide 25′ by 50′ bays of uncluttered working space, the building's lobby is of Italian ondagata marble. The floor is white travertine marble.

Covering only 3.7 acres or 15 percent of its 24-acre site, the plant is an outstanding example of cooperation between private business and public agencies. It was approved by the City Planning Commission and the Board of Estimate. Construction involved a zoning change to permit light manufacturing.

DECEMBER, 1953 39

AN AWARD FOR EXCELLENCE. In December 1953, just after its opening, the Bulova Watch Company factory was awarded the Borough's Outstanding Award for Architecture by the Queens Chamber of Commerce. The building's design was inspired by the Federal Reserve Bank in Washington, DC, and the structure was built by Turner Construction Company. It not only housed the research and development and factory floor but also served as Bulova's administrative headquarters. With a facade of rustic, buff Indiana limestone, the building was air-conditioned throughout, which eliminated dust and humidity. The lobby was decorated with Italian Ondagata with a floor made of white travertine marble. Ironically, the structure, which still stands at Seventy-seventh Street and Astoria Boulevard, now houses the Queens Chamber of Commerce as well as various city agencies. (Courtesy of the Queens Chamber of Commerce.)

Four

PERSONALITIES

Hollywood celebrities associated with Jackson Heights include some revered names in cinematic history. Word has it that Douglas Fairbanks and Mary Pickford resided in The Towers, though Jackson Heights historian Daniel Karatzas debunks this through the recollection of Gladys Gilbert, a former Queensboro Corporation employee who was certain that Edward MacDougall failed to lure the famed couple. No matter the case, other luminaries include Charlie Chaplin, Montgomery Clift, and Victor Moore. Rita Hayworth attended Public School No. 69. Academy Award–winners Susan Sarandon and Mercedes Ruehl grew up locally, as did actor and activist Lucy Liu. Alfred Hitchcock captured Jackson Heights to great effect in *The Wrong Man*, a classic film noir based on the wrongful arrest of Christopher Emmanuel "Manny" Balestrero. Night scenes of the neighborhood underscore the movie's film noir quality.

Television actors include Kevin Dobson (*Kojak*); Richard Kline (*Three's Company*); Emmy Award–winner Thom Christopher (*One Life to Live*); and Young Tommy Rettig, who played Jeff Miller in the first Lassie series. Comedians are well represented, and John Leguizamo's talents also merited the Rita Moreno Award for Excellence from the Hispanic Organization of Latin Actors (HOLA). Then there is the incomparable Don Rickles, whose comedic insults and invectives are legendary.

Musicians include pianist Clive Lythgoe, cornet player Bobby Hackett, and Kiss's Gene Simmons. Legendary guitarist Les Paul, along with Mary Ford, recorded "How High the Moon" in his studio apartment. Other performers include Helen Kane, who voice and physiognomy inspired the creation of Betty Boop. After achieving prominence in 2001, Pakistani-born Nadia Ali went on to produce *Embers*, *The Queens of Clubs Trilogy*, and presently, *Phoenix*. Not to be overlooked is transgender beauty queen Lady Catiria, a presence at the nightclub La Escuelita before her death in 1990.

In other fields, there are Xerox machine inventor Chester Carlson, photographer Albert Eisenstaedt, and Marvel Comics editor-in-chief Joseph Quezada. Former Pennsylvania governor Bob Casey hails from the area, along with career diplomat Edward Djerejian, former assistant defense secretary Robert Ross, *Newsweek*'s Eleanor Clift (née Roeloffs), and baseball announcer Dave Fleming. Lastly, Alfred Mosher Butts, known for a game perfected at the Community Methodist Church in 1938, was also a resident here.

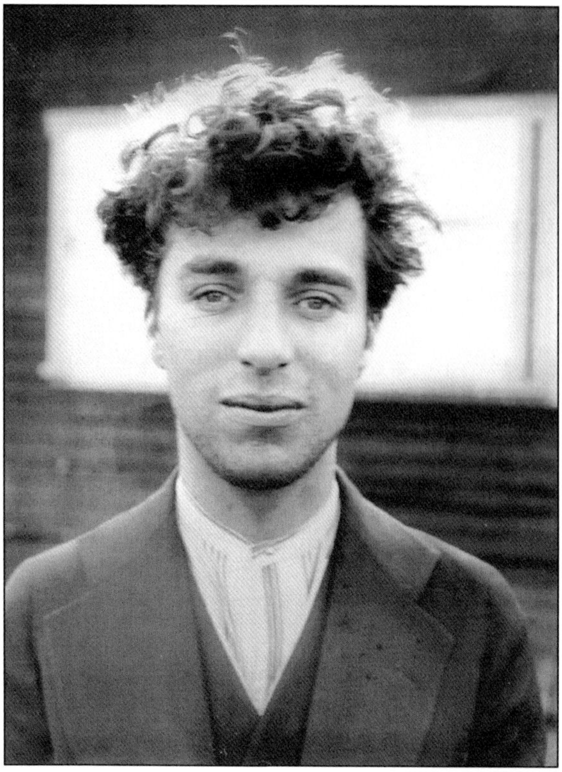

CHARLIE CHAPLIN (1889–1977). Sir Charles Spencer "Charlie" Chaplin was a legendary comic actor, film director, and composer and an icon of the silent era of film. Universally recognized as the Tramp, one of his most endearing roles, Chaplin (seen here without makeup) took up residence in The Towers. (Courtesy of Culver Pictures Archives.)

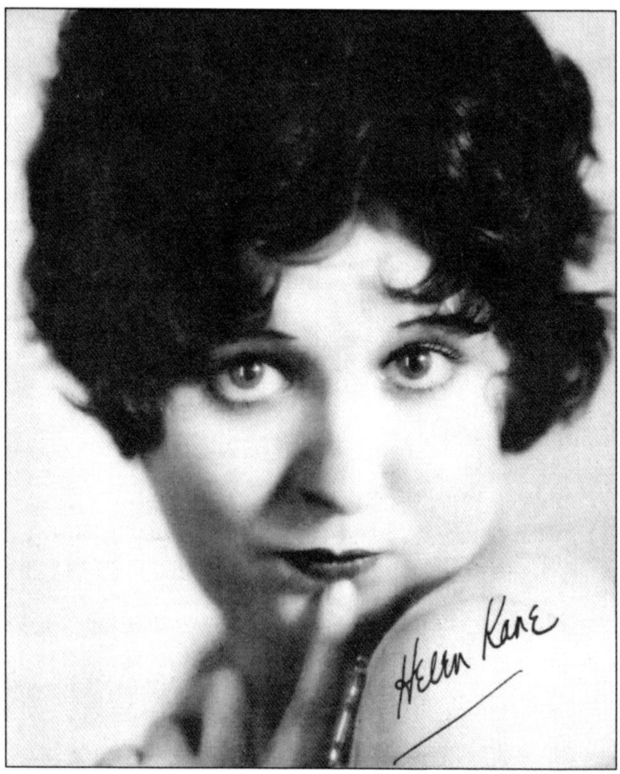

HELEN KANE (1904–1966). The popular singer's appearance and unmistakable baby-like rendition of the song "I Wanna Be Loved By You" served as the inspiration for the popular cartoon character Betty Boop. Amid all its cuteness, Kane's voice has a distinct New York accent; she was born in the Bronx.

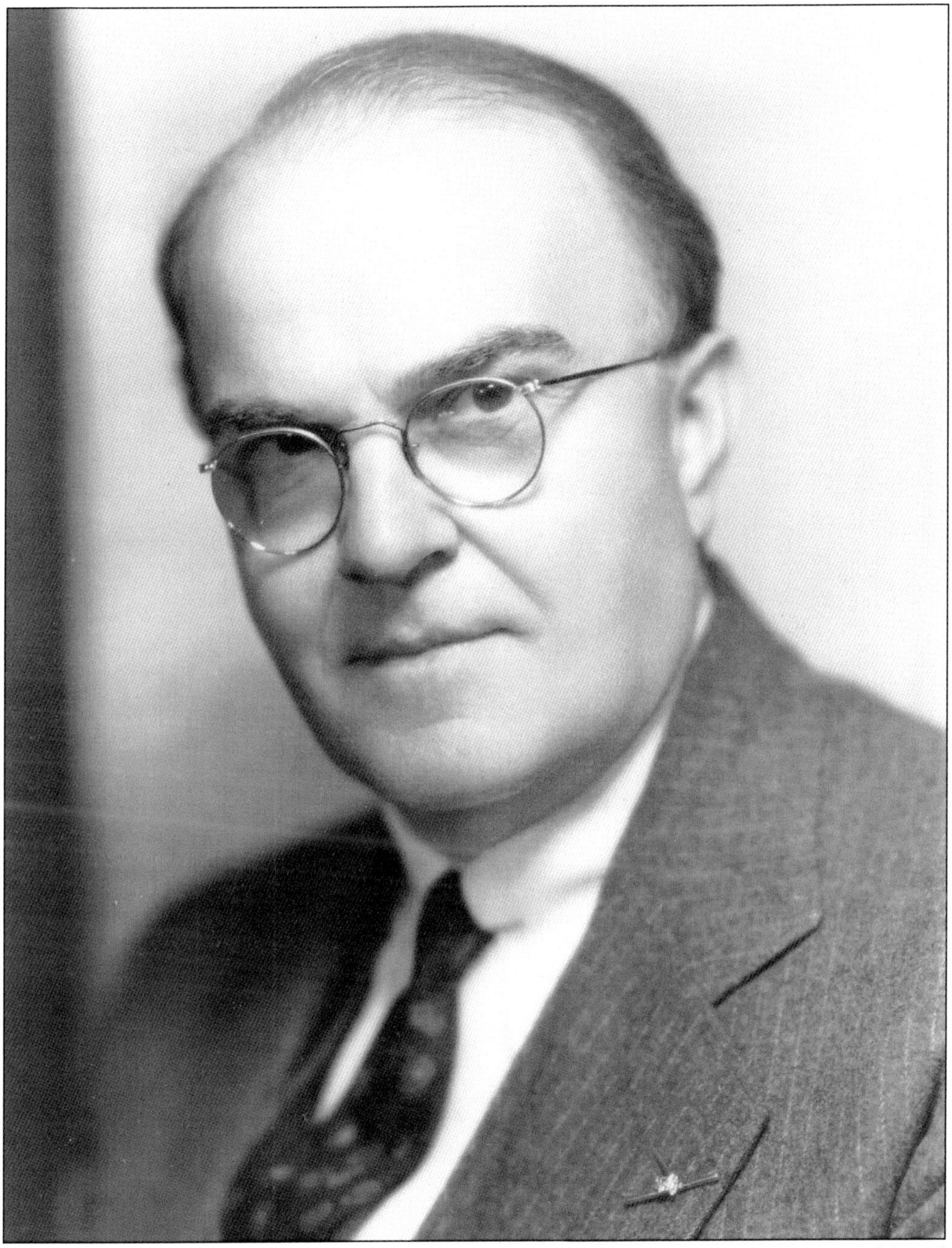

VICTOR MOORE (1876–1962). A durable American stage and screen actor, Victor Moore debuted in 1915 and had a career that spanned 50 films and 21 Broadway shows alongside many greats in the entertainment field. On Broadway, Moore worked closely with director Cecil B. DeMille, George M. Cohan, George Gershwin, Irving Berlin, and Cole Porter. In Hollywood, he was in films that starred Fred Astaire and Ginger Rodgers and Bob Hope. Moore makes a cameo appearance as a plumber alongside Marilyn Monroe and Tom Ewell in *The Seven Year Itch* (1955). Ever versatile, he was even a voice for Daffy Duck. The Victor Moore Arcade bus terminal was named after him.

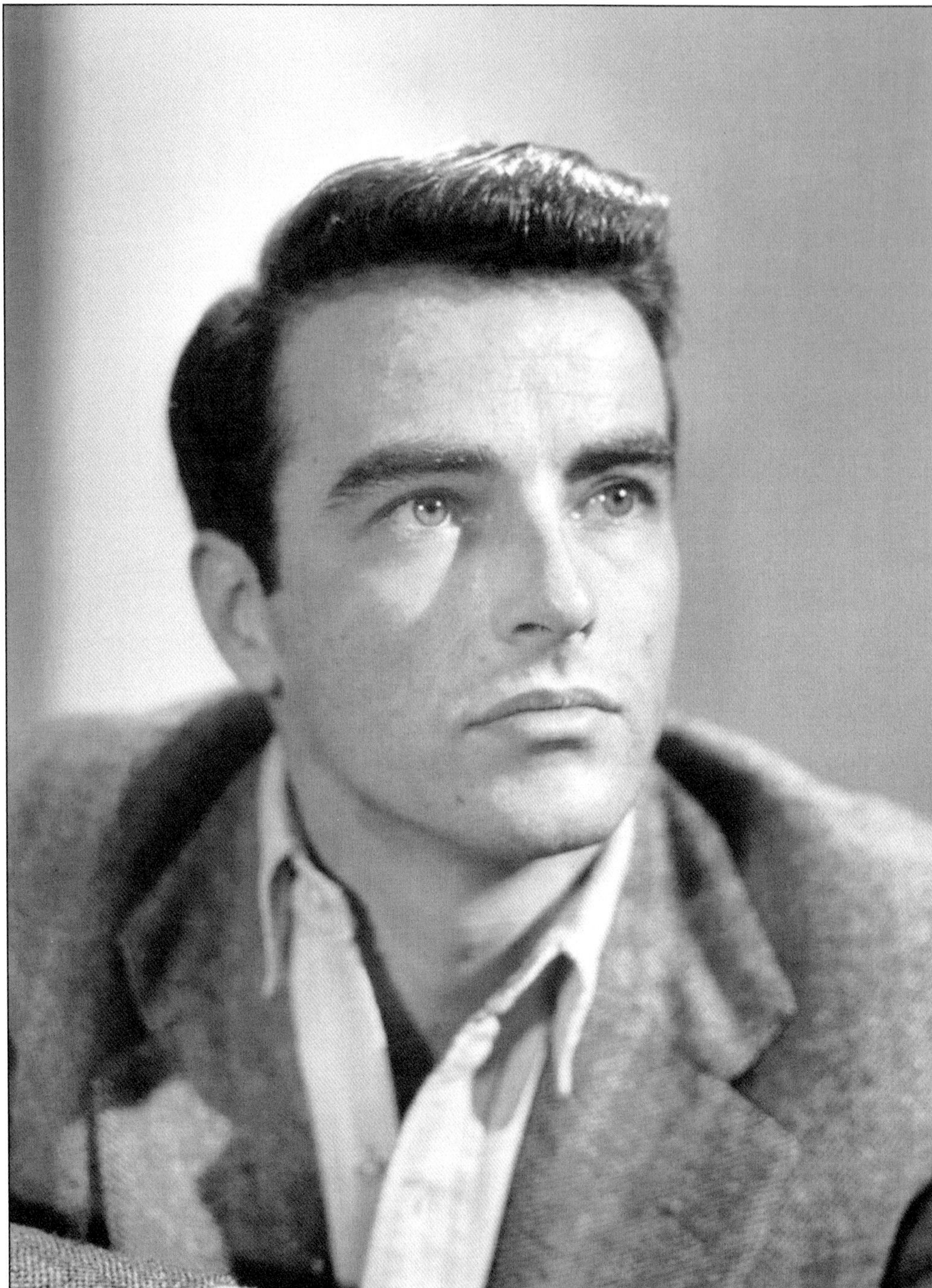

MONTGOMERY CLIFT (1920–1966). Critically acclaimed actor Montgomery Clift was known for his roles as the archetypal "victim hero." Born in Nebraska, Clift came to New York and resided in The Chateau as a youth, when he landed roles on Broadway before moving on to Hollywood stardom. He is perhaps best known for his role as Pvt. Robert E. Lee "Prew" Prewitt in the 1953 classic *From Here to Eternity*, starring Burt Lancaster and Frank Sinatra.

CHESTER CARLSON (1906–1968). Patent attorney and inventor Carlson is the father of xerography. Here, he is demonstrating the chemical reaction that made "10-22-38 Astoria" appear on paper, the phrase being the first dry (or Xerox) copy ever made.

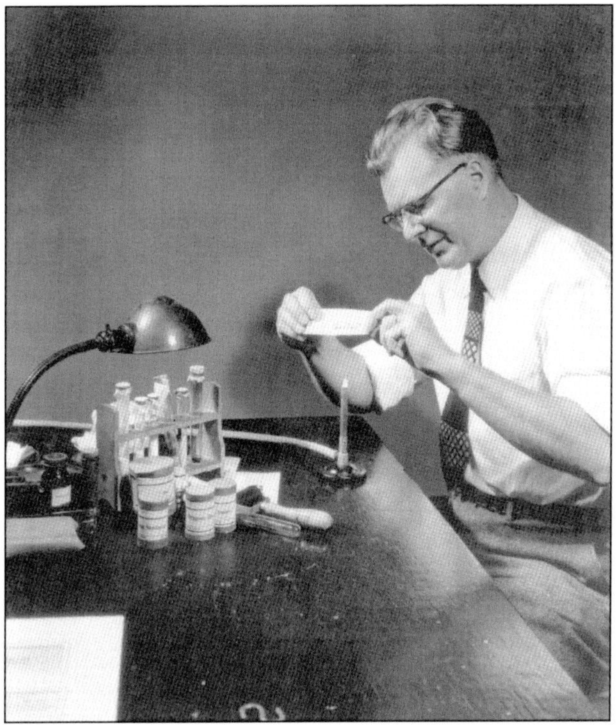

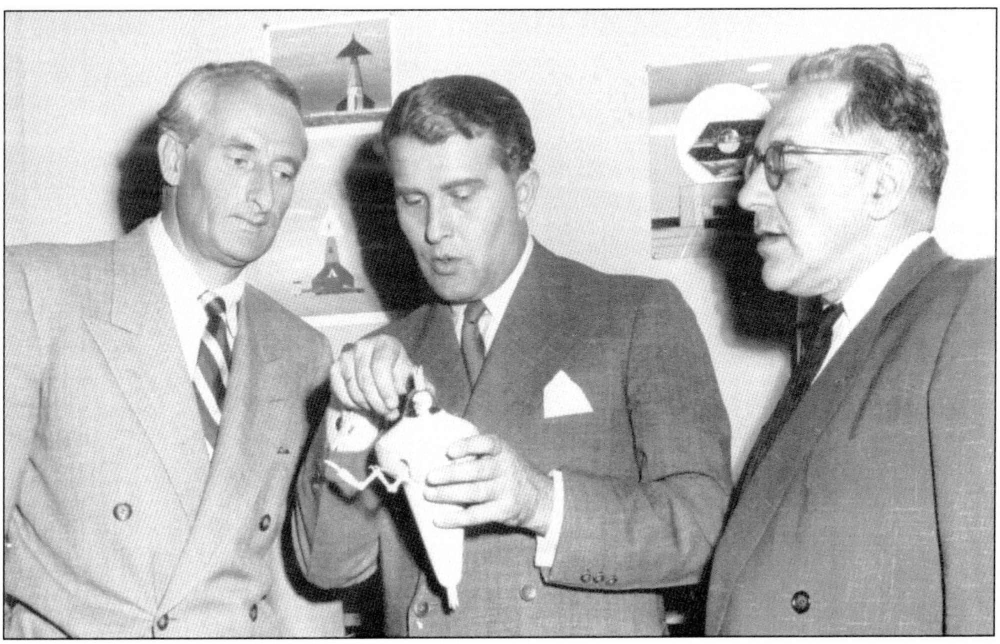

WILLY LEY (1906–1969). Seen on the right with German physicist Heinz Haber (left) and rocket scientist Wernher von Braun (center), Willy Oskar Otto Ley was a historian, proponent of spaceflight, and helped to popularize rocketry, spaceflight, and natural history in his native Germany and in the United States. He lived in Jackson Heights from the mid-1950s until his death in 1969, a month before Apollo 11 successfully landed on the Moon. The crater Ley located on the far side of the Moon is named in his honor.

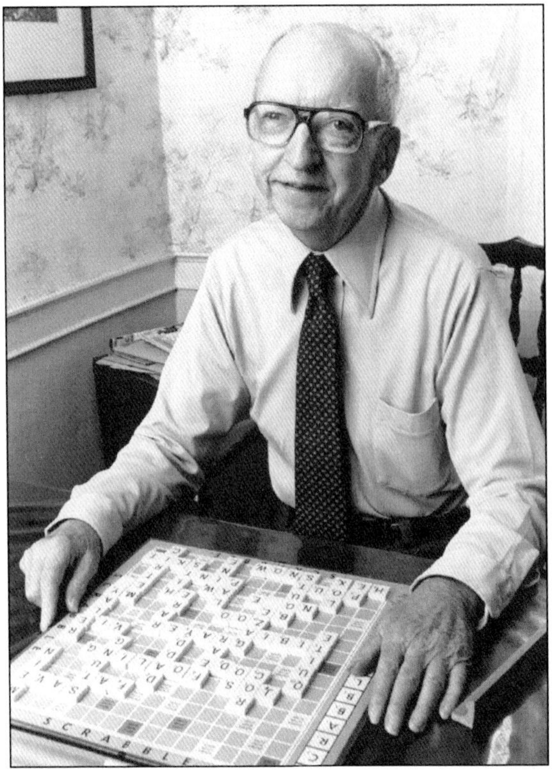

Alfred Mosher Butts (1899–1993). Finding himself unemployed in the early 1930s, Butts, an architect by profession, set out to design a board game that he eventually perfected at the Community Methodist Church. He considered calling his creation "Lexiko," "Criss Cross Words," and even "It" before settling on Scrabble (a word of Dutch derivation that means "to grab"). It is said that Butts looked to the *New York Times* to calculate how frequently a given letter would be used in the game. He included only four S tiles amid the rest to ensure that the ability to make words plural was limited. (Courtesy of the *Chicago Tribune*.)

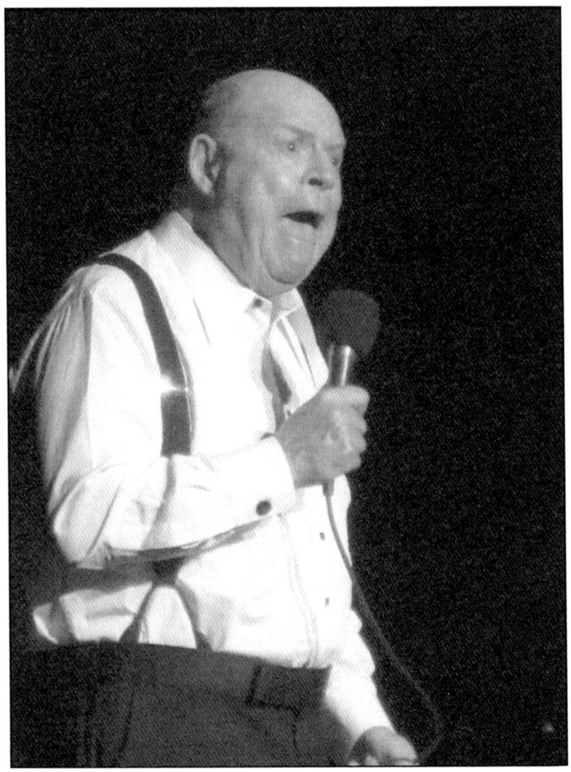

Don Rickles. Known as "Mr. Warmth," Rickles is an insult comedian par excellence. It has been said that being insulted by Rickles is a badge of honor, and his fans are legion. Rickles has appeared in many motion pictures, including *Casino* (1995), directed by Martin Scorsese, another Queens resident.

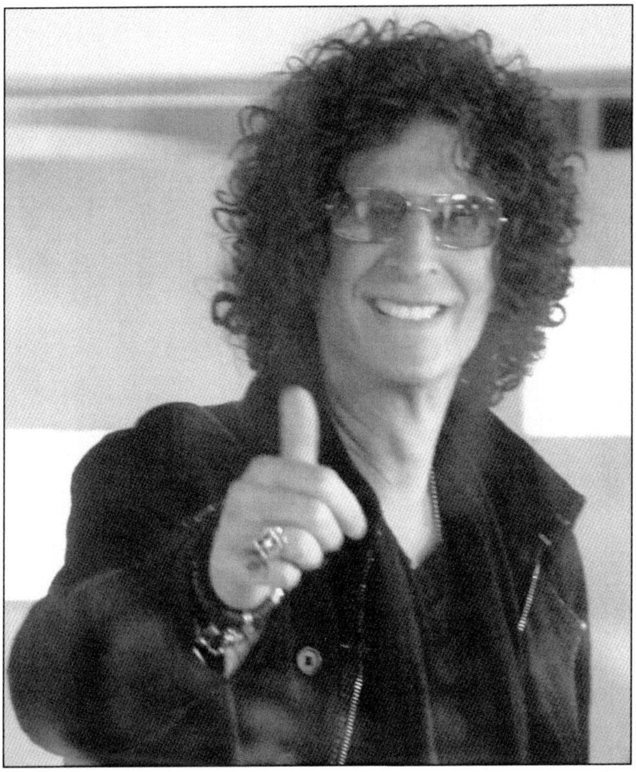

Howard Stern. The outspoken radio personality whose controversial style has earned him the place as America's top "shock jock" also called Jackson Heights his home.

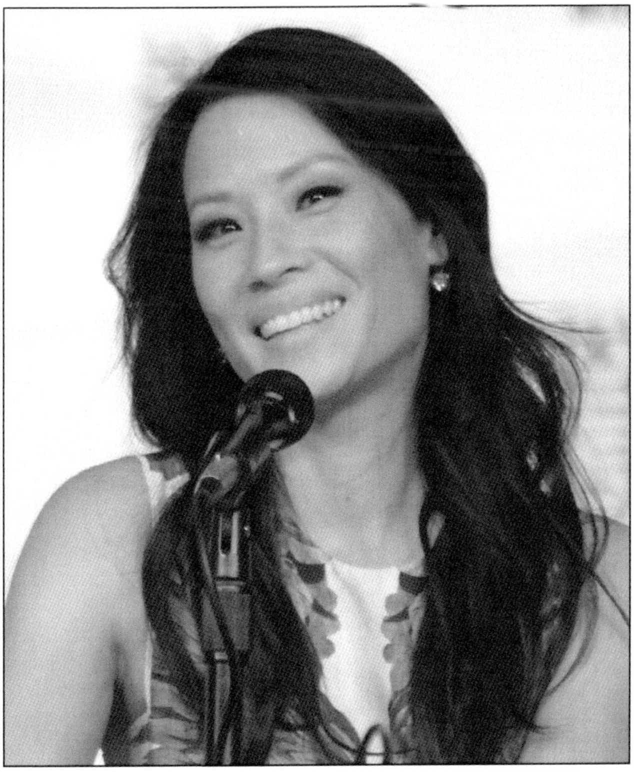

Lucy Liu. Actress, narrator, and film producer, Liu is known for her role as Ling Woo in the television series *Ally McBeal* (1998–2002) for which she was nominated for a primetime Emmy Award and a Screen Actors Guild Award. Liu was born in Jackson Heights on December 2, 1968. She attended middle school at Public School/Intermediate School No. 145. In 2012, Liu joined the cast of *Southland* in the recurring role of Jessica Tang, a role that landed her a Critics' Choice Television Award. Liu has taken on many causes, among which are the abolition of human trafficking and finding a cure for breast cancer.

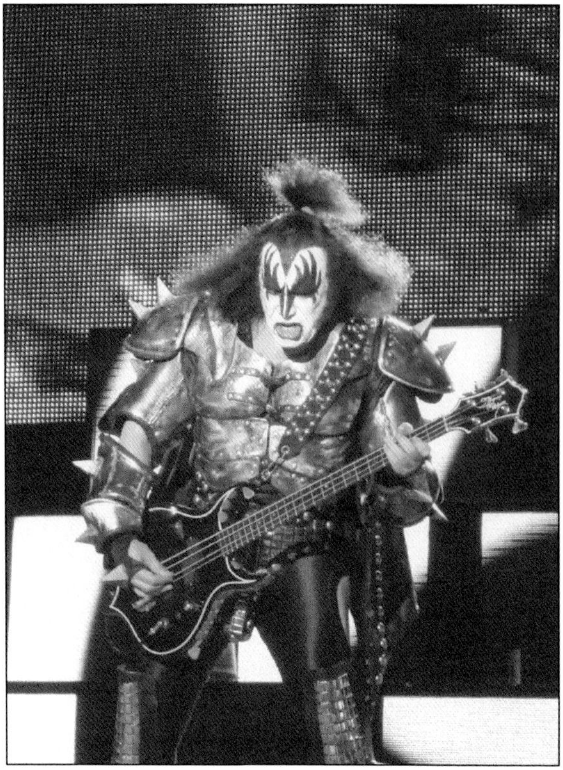

Gene Simmons. Born Chaim Weitz in 1949, Simmons is the cofounder, bassist, and co-vocalist of the renowned hard rock band Kiss. With Kiss, Simmons, known as "The Demon" onstage, has sold more than 100 million albums worldwide.

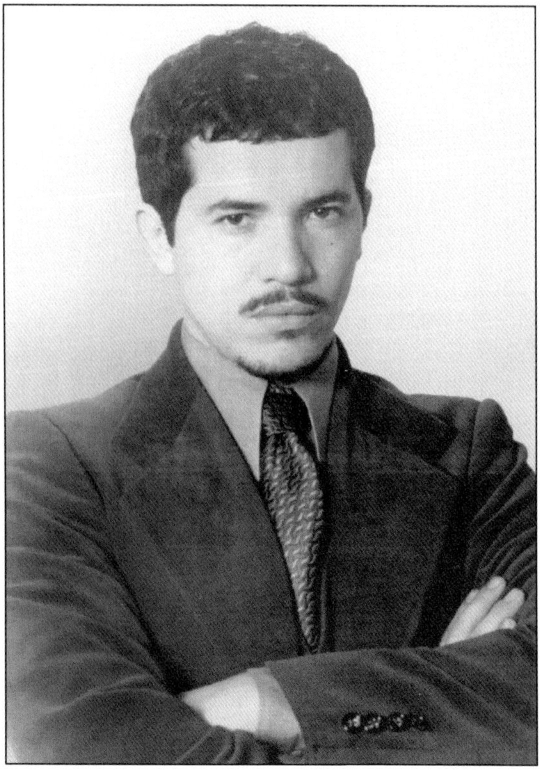

John Leguizamo. Originally born in Bogota, Colombia, comedian and actor Leguizamo came to Jackson Heights when he was four. The *Carlito's Way*, *Romeo + Juliet*, and *Moulin Rouge!* star credited growing up in the neighborhood as the basis for his success as a comedian. "It was tough. There were lots of fights. I would walk through a park and be attacked, and I had to defend myself all the time. But this helped me to become funny so that I wouldn't get hit," said Leguizamo. He attended Public School/Intermediate School No. 145, the same as Lucy Liu.

THE WRONG MAN. A rash of local robberies eventually led to the wrongful arrest of Christopher "Manny" Balestrero in a case of mistaken identity. A mild-mannered bassist at the Stork Club in Manhattan, Balestrero was picked up at 5:30 p.m. on January 14, 1953, by two detectives from the 110th Precinct just as he was about to enter his home at 41-30 Seventy-third Street. Based on circumstantial evidence, he was booked and imprisoned for robbing the Prudential loan office inside the Victor Moore Arcade building. Balestrero's plight inspired Alfred Hitchcock's classic film noir *The Wrong Man* (1956) starring Henry Fonda. (Courtesy of Time-Life.)

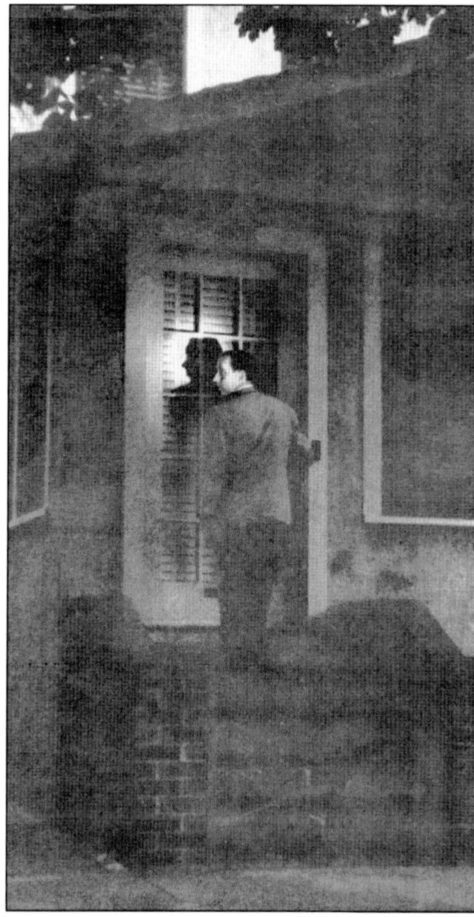

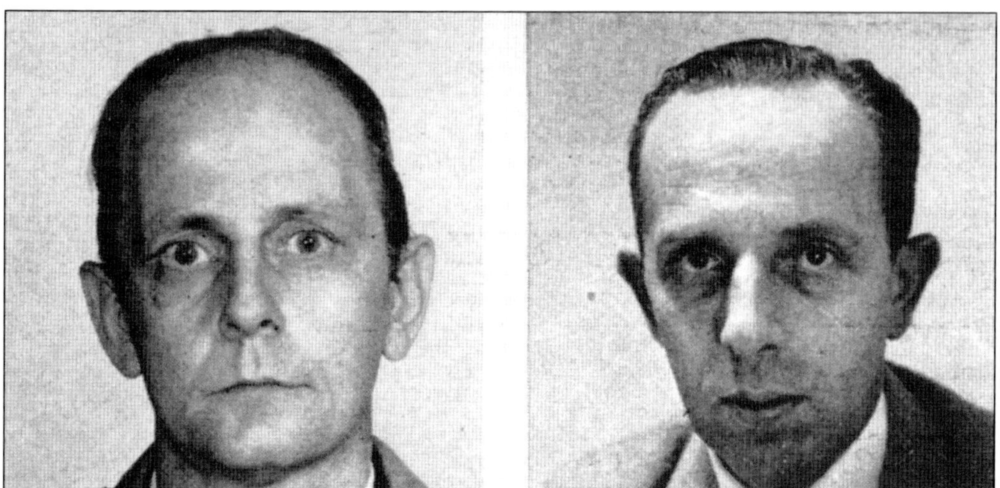

MISTAKEN IDENTITY. Will the real Christopher "Manny" Balestrero please stand up? Balestrero (right) himself was exonerated as Charles J. Daniell (left), an unemployed plastics molder, later confessed to the crimes he was accused of committing. "Name any stickup in Jackson Heights and I did it," boasted Daniell during his confession. Balestrero died in 1998. (Courtesy of Time-Life.)

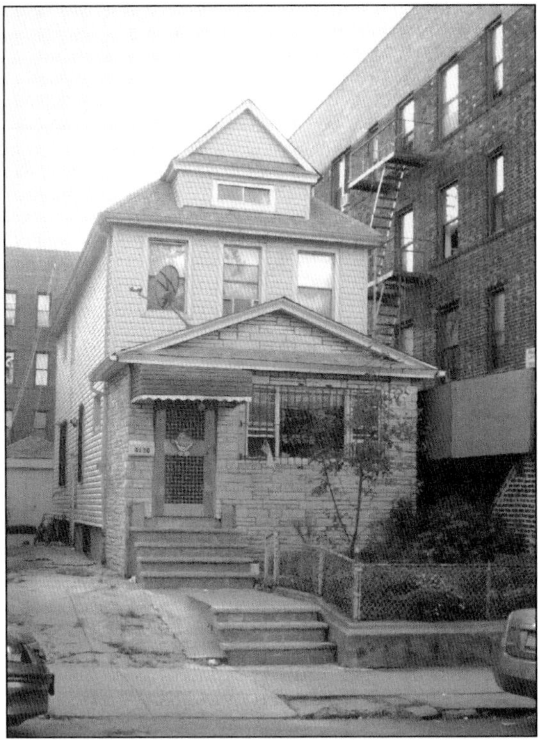

FILMING *THE WRONG MAN*. Alfred Hitchcock filmed the screen version of Balestrero's ordeal on the streets of Jackson Heights and throughout Queens. Many of the real locations were used, including the various mom-and-pop grocery shops in Jackson Heights that were held up as well as the loan office inside of the Victor Moore Arcade building. At left, the Balestrero home still stands today. In the photograph below, Henry Fonda is in the IRT subway with a sign in the background that reads, "Roosevelt Avenue/Jackson Heights." The headline on the cover of the mock-up *Daily News* reads, "Queens Holdup." Hitchcock relied on absolute authenticity for this production. (Below, Culver Pictures Archives.)

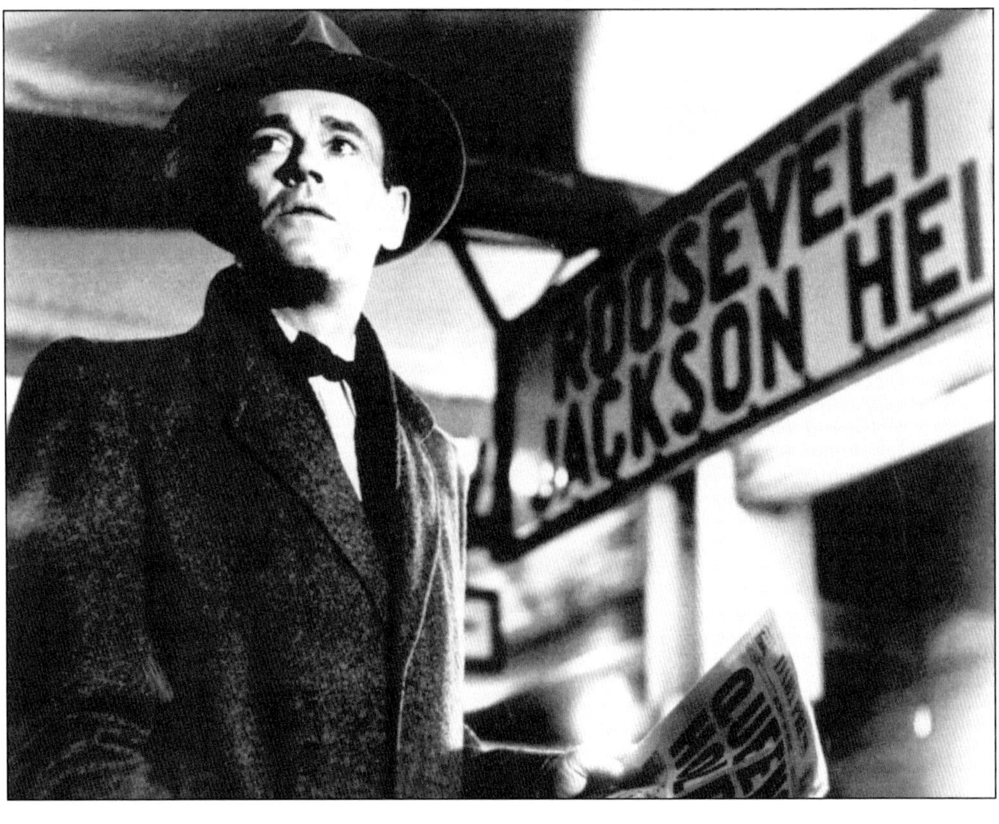

Five

Community Life

By the mid-20th century, the evolution of Jackson Heights went beyond the exclusive garden apartment ideal that Edward A. MacDougall and the Queensboro Corporation established.

When Jackson Heights finally met its physical capacity, the land once reserved for tennis courts and golf was developed for additional housing. Little construction took place between the 1950s and 1980s.

As a result of the booming population and changing times, Jackson Heights progressed from the former restricted community that excluded Jews, Catholics, and African Americans to become a reflection of the diverse city that surrounds it.

No longer a haven for the well-to-do and social elite, Jackson Heights became more of a working-class neighborhood. What began as isolated farmland, Jackson Heights experienced an array of social change reflective of 20th-century America.

As one walks through Jackson Heights, among the historic buildings that were once meant to house wealthy patrons, one encounters people from all walks of life creating a tapestry that includes immigrants from across the ocean and transplants from other parts of the country—all in search of a better way of life.

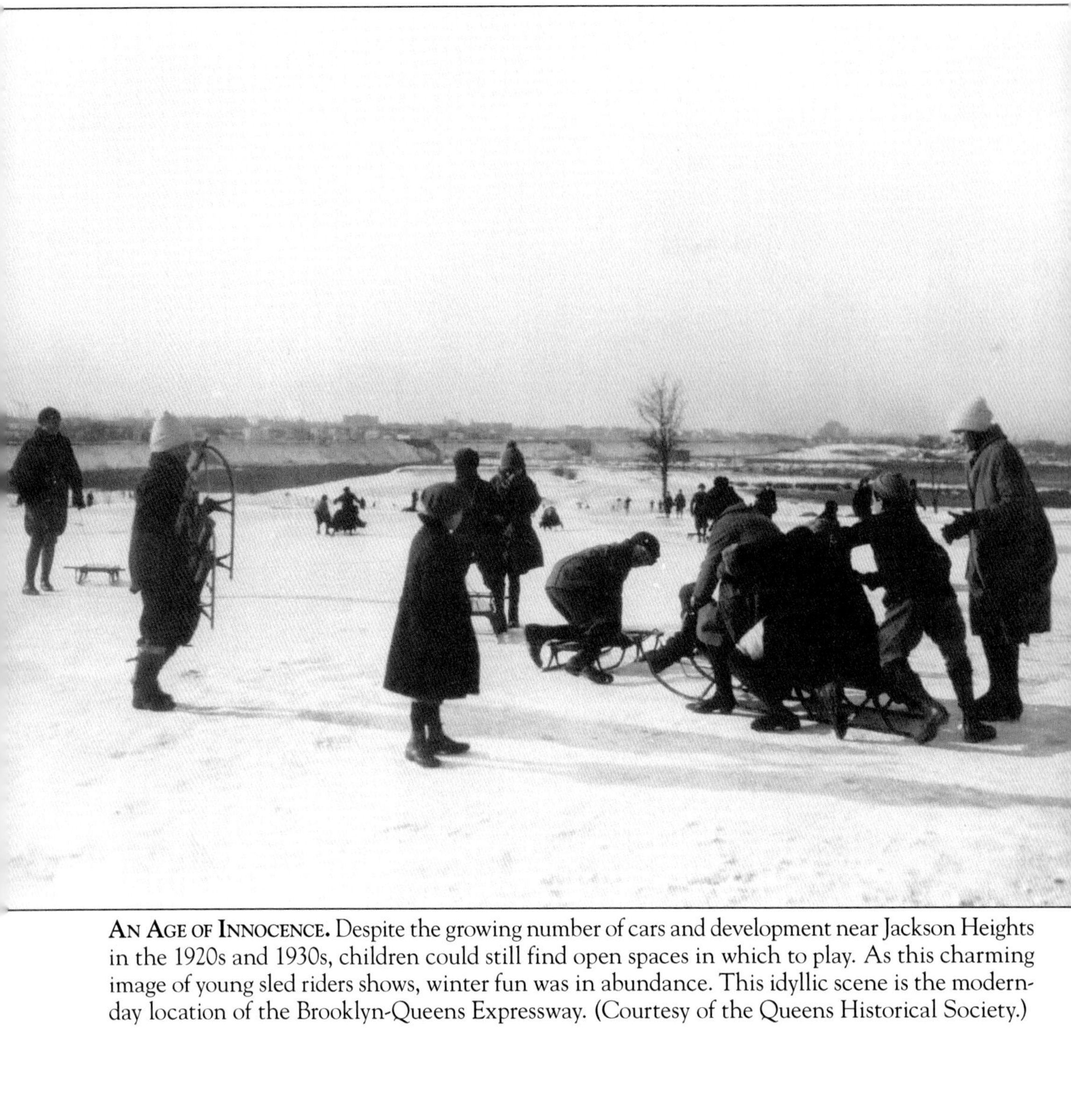

An Age of Innocence. Despite the growing number of cars and development near Jackson Heights in the 1920s and 1930s, children could still find open spaces in which to play. As this charming image of young sled riders shows, winter fun was in abundance. This idyllic scene is the modern-day location of the Brooklyn-Queens Expressway. (Courtesy of the Queens Historical Society.)

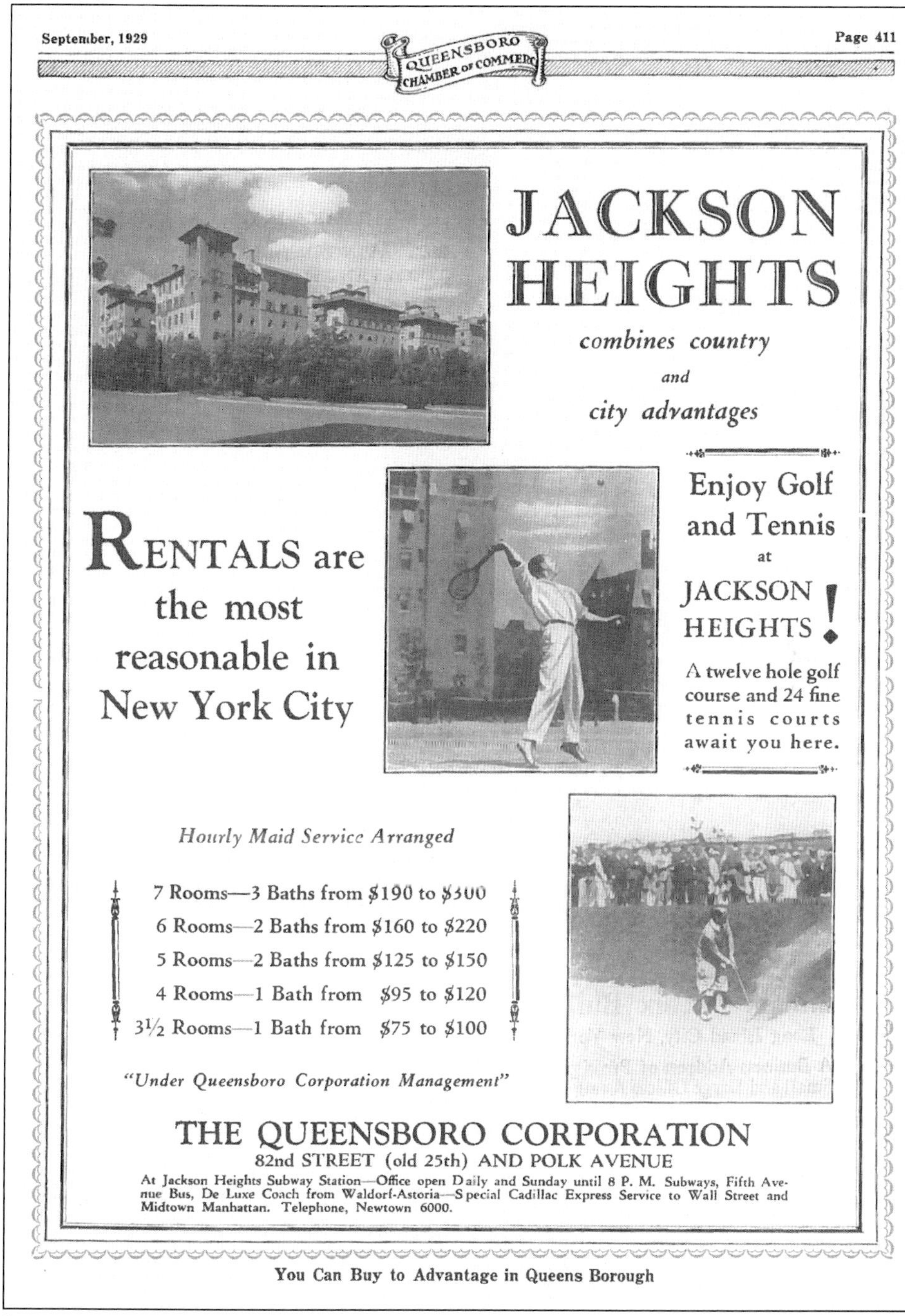

September, 1929 QUEENSBORO CHAMBER OF COMMERCE Page 411

JACKSON HEIGHTS

combines country and city advantages

RENTALS are the most reasonable in New York City

Enjoy Golf and Tennis at JACKSON HEIGHTS!

A twelve hole golf course and 24 fine tennis courts await you here.

Hourly Maid Service Arranged

7 Rooms—3 Baths	from $190	to $300
6 Rooms—2 Baths	from $160	to $220
5 Rooms—2 Baths	from $125	to $150
4 Rooms—1 Bath	from $95	to $120
3½ Rooms—1 Bath	from $75	to $100

"Under Queensboro Corporation Management"

THE QUEENSBORO CORPORATION

82nd STREET (old 25th) AND POLK AVENUE

At Jackson Heights Subway Station—Office open Daily and Sunday until 8 P. M. Subways, Fifth Avenue Bus, De Luxe Coach from Waldorf-Astoria—Special Cadillac Express Service to Wall Street and Midtown Manhattan. Telephone, Newtown 6000.

You Can Buy to Advantage in Queens Borough

A Country Setting with City Advantages. Amenities such as golf and tennis were selling points made by the Queensboro Corporation. Allusions to health and leisure are evident in its advertising campaigns, such as this *Queensborough* magazine advertisement in September 1929, right before the stock market crash that ushered in the Depression. Aimed at prospective renters, this advertisement provides the monthly rent costs, which ranged from $75 to $300 (roughly $1,000 to $4,000 in 2011 dollars). Hourly maid service was also available. (Courtesy of the Queens Chamber of Commerce.)

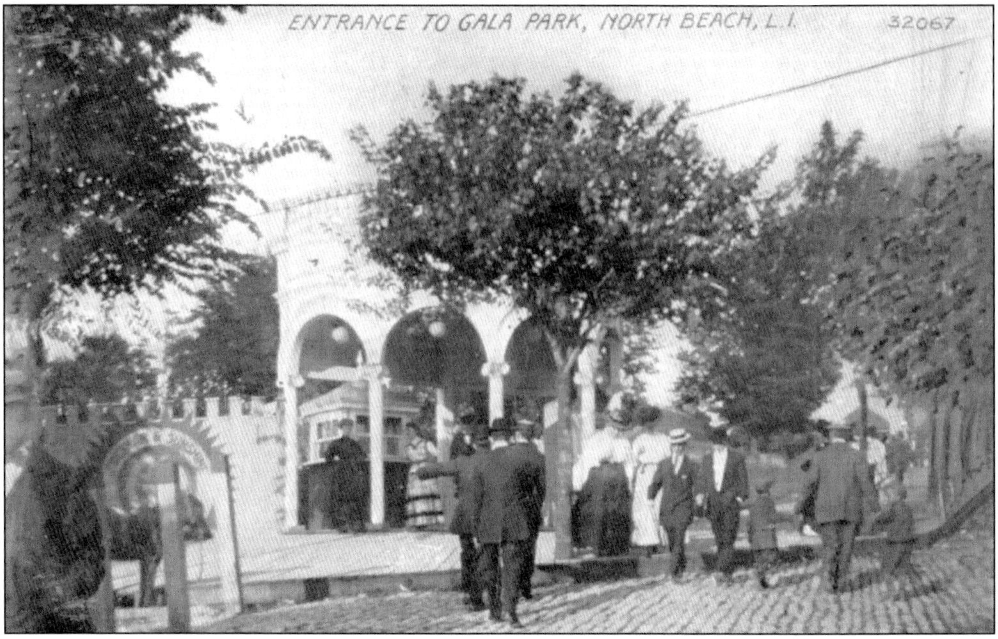

North Beach Fairgrounds. Situated on a peninsula overlooking Flushing Bay (or Bowery Bay, as it was originally called), the amusement park at North Beach was created by brewer George Ehret and piano manufacturer William Steinway in 1886. The park featured a merry-go-round, a steam-powered roller coaster, a silent movie theater, a bathing beach, and an enormous dining and dance pavilion, where Ehret's beer flowed daily. More than 10,000 visitors came from different parts of the city, including nearby Flushing, Newtown, and Trains Meadow. The park featured one of the first Ferris wheels in the United States. The passage of the Volstead Act prohibiting the sale of alcohol forced the park into bankruptcy. It closed in 1920.

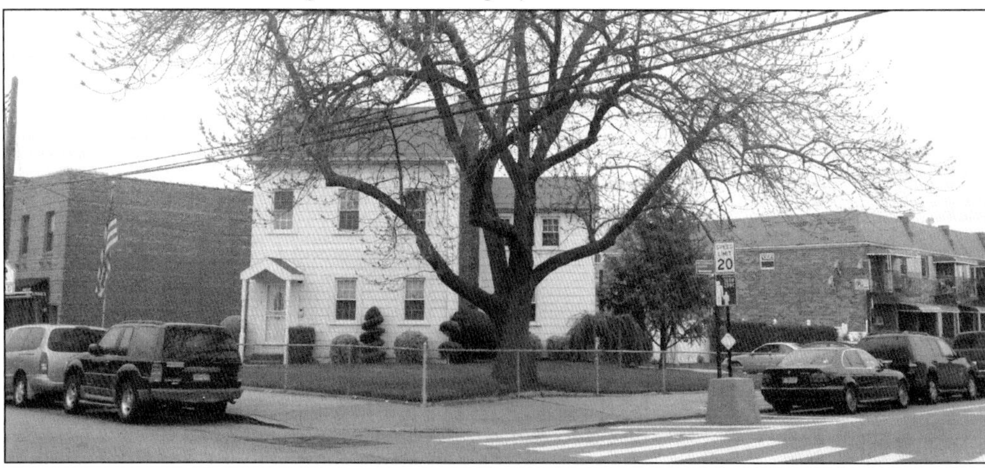

A Relic of the Past. Located on the northwest corner of Thirty-first Avenue and Eighty-first Street remains the last vestige of the former Trains Meadow. This yellow clapboard home stands at an angle as opposed to the other homes, which stand in rows. This is because the old Trains Meadow Road ran adjacent to the property. By 1920, Trains Meadow Road, which ran in a diagonal and sometimes crisscrossed path, was decimated and disappeared from the map when developers laid out the grid of cross streets. According to records, the home, now a private residence, was once used as an inn.

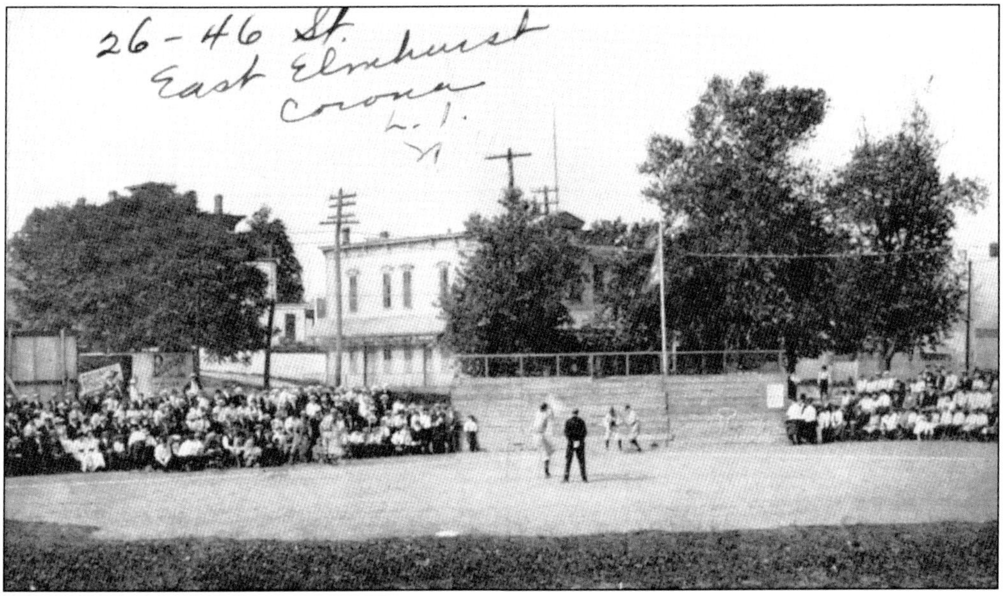

"Play Ball!" Baseball officially became known as the national pastime by the early 20th century. Various neighborhoods in Queens had their own local clubs that, with much fanfare, competed against rivals from other local towns or teams from as distant as Brooklyn and Manhattan. In this postcard image dated 1914, residents from Trains Meadow, Corona, and Newtown watch a Sunday afternoon ball game (similar to those played by the Jackson Baseball Club) at the northeast corner of Northern Boulevard and 100th Street, near the border of Corona and Jackson Heights.

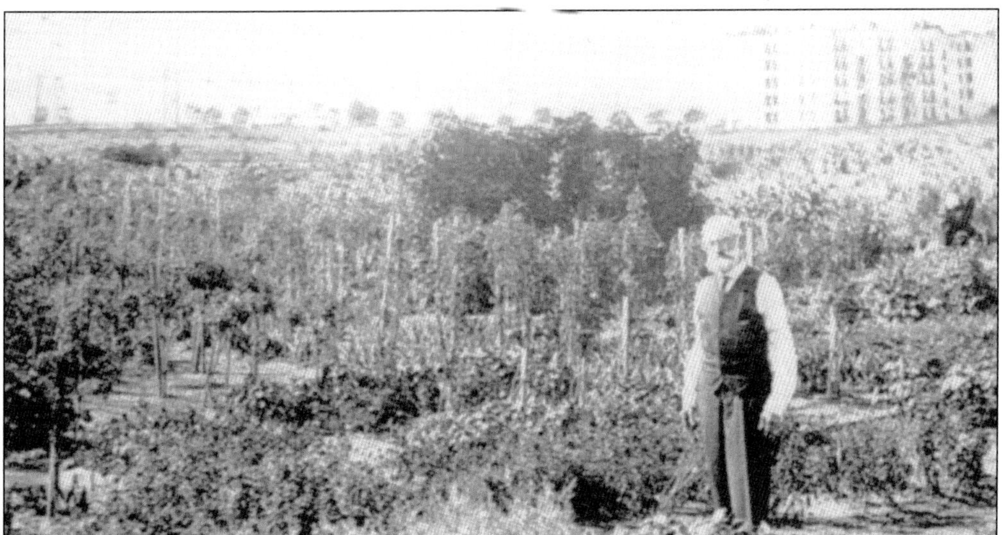

Victory Garden. With America's entry into World War I, the community of Jackson Heights was very active in the war effort. A Red Cross branch was established near Eighty-second Street and Roosevelt Avenue. Another means of support were victory gardens, which were vegetable, fruit, and herb gardens planted to reduce the pressure on the public food supply brought on by the war. Charles Lathrop Pack organized the National War Garden Commission and launched the war garden campaign in March 1917. In this photograph, an elderly gentleman tends to his victory garden. Oban, Penrhyn, and Laurel Courts can be seen in the distance.

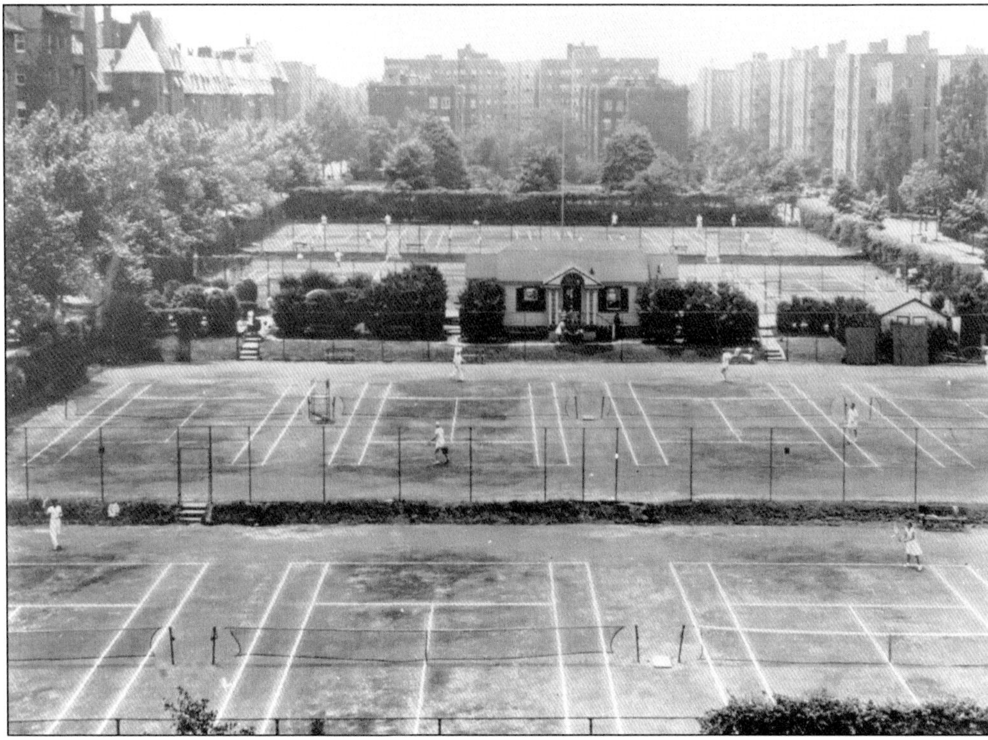

TENNIS. Shown here is the Jackson Heights Tennis Club at the height of its popularity. Opened in 1922, between Seventy-ninth and Eightieth Streets and Thirty-fourth Avenue and Northern Boulevard, the club began with eight clay courts; by 1930, a total of 16 courts were installed. Many championships were held here, including the Eastern Clay Court Tournaments. Tennis great Bill Tilden also made an appearance. (Courtesy of the Queens Historical Society.)

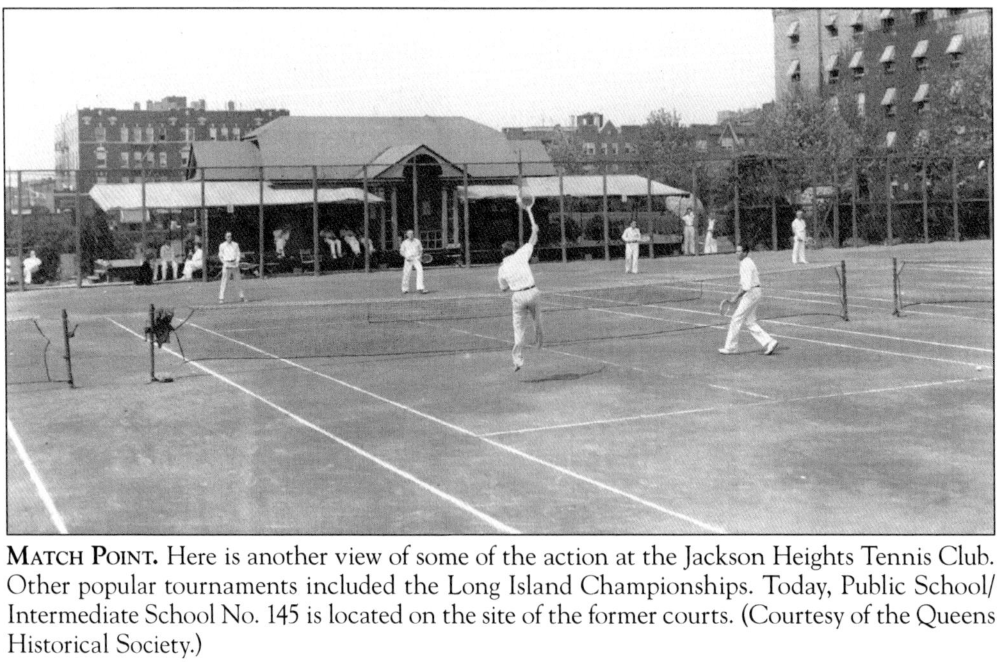

MATCH POINT. Here is another view of some of the action at the Jackson Heights Tennis Club. Other popular tournaments included the Long Island Championships. Today, Public School/ Intermediate School No. 145 is located on the site of the former courts. (Courtesy of the Queens Historical Society.)

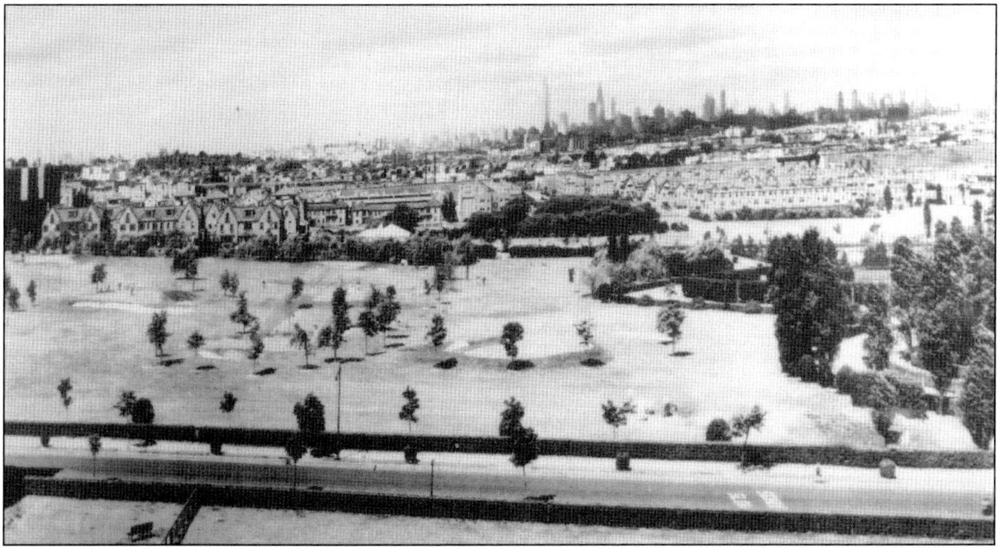

A Manhattan Bedroom Community, c. 1930. This sprawling view shows the Manhattan skyline in the distance. The Empire State Building is clearly visible, and the Jackson Heights Golf Course is in the foreground, with Seventy-ninth Street crossing at the bottom of the photograph. The English Garden homes are to the left. The golf course that dominates the center of the landscape was designed by A.W. Tillinghast and was expanded several times during the 1920s. (Courtesy of the Queens Historical Society.)

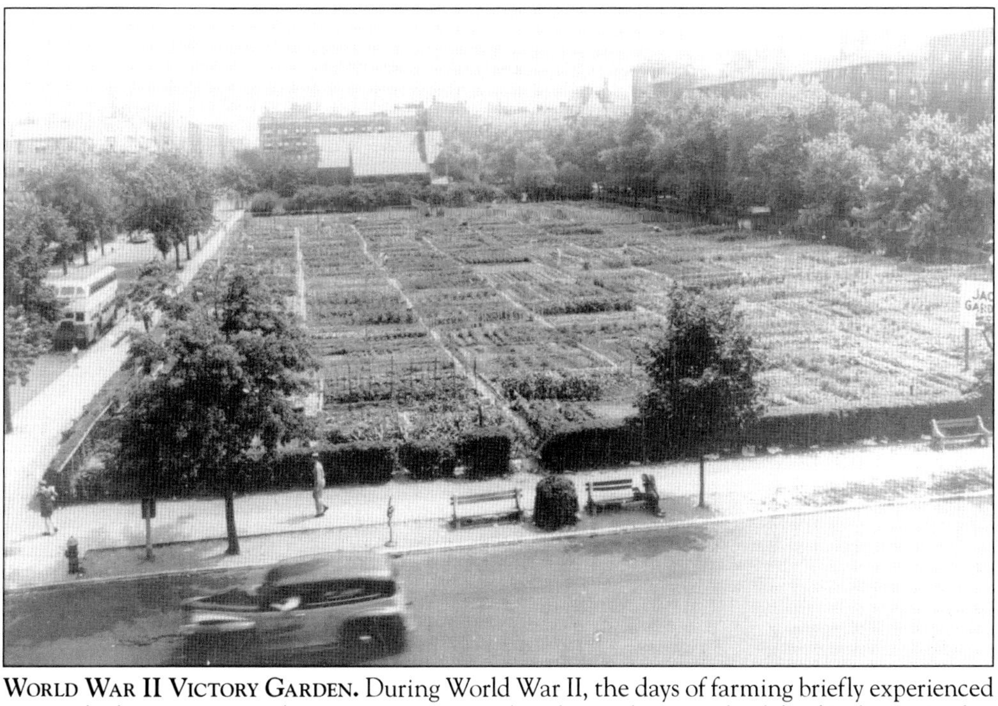

World War II Victory Garden. During World War II, the days of farming briefly experienced a revival when victory gardens were again introduced into the everyday life of Jackson Heights residents to help support the war effort. This immense garden was located between Eighty-first and Eighty-second Streets, south of Northern Boulevard. (Courtesy of the Queens Borough Public Library, Long Island Division, Thomas Langdon Collection.)

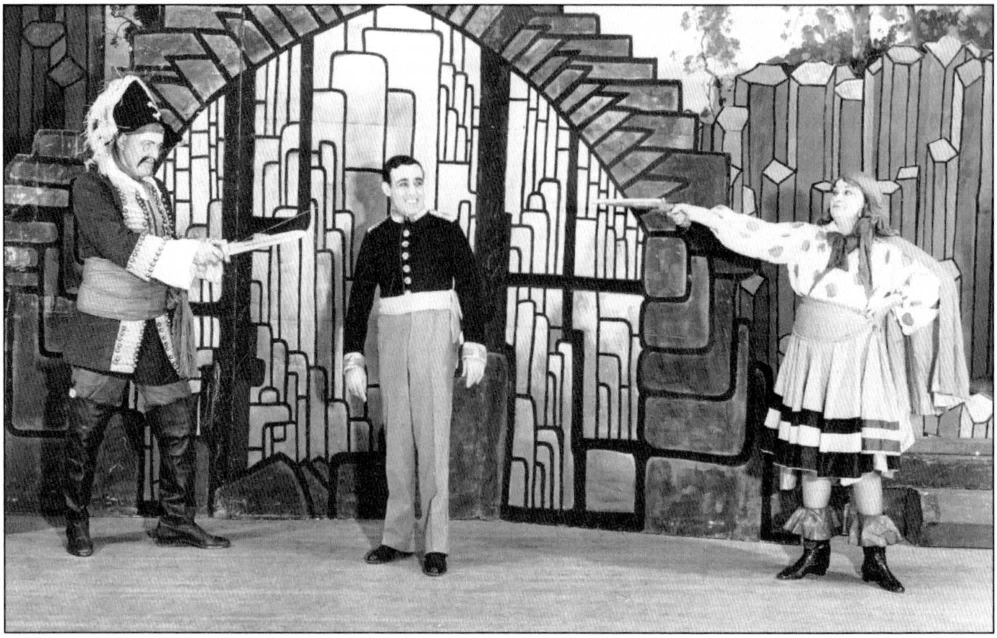

Pirates of Penzance. A community theater was established in Jackson Heights in the 1920s. Seen here is a performance of *The Pirates of Penzance* by members of the Jackson Heights Community Playhouse. (Both, courtesy of the Queens Borough Public Library, Long Island Division.)

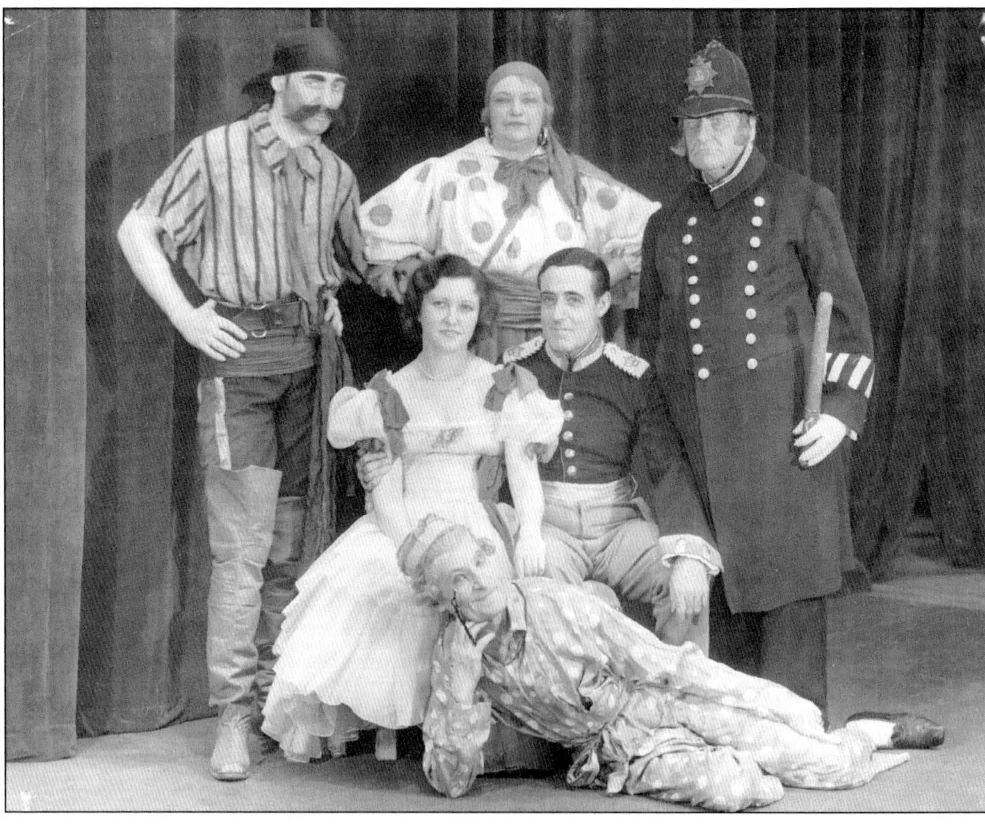

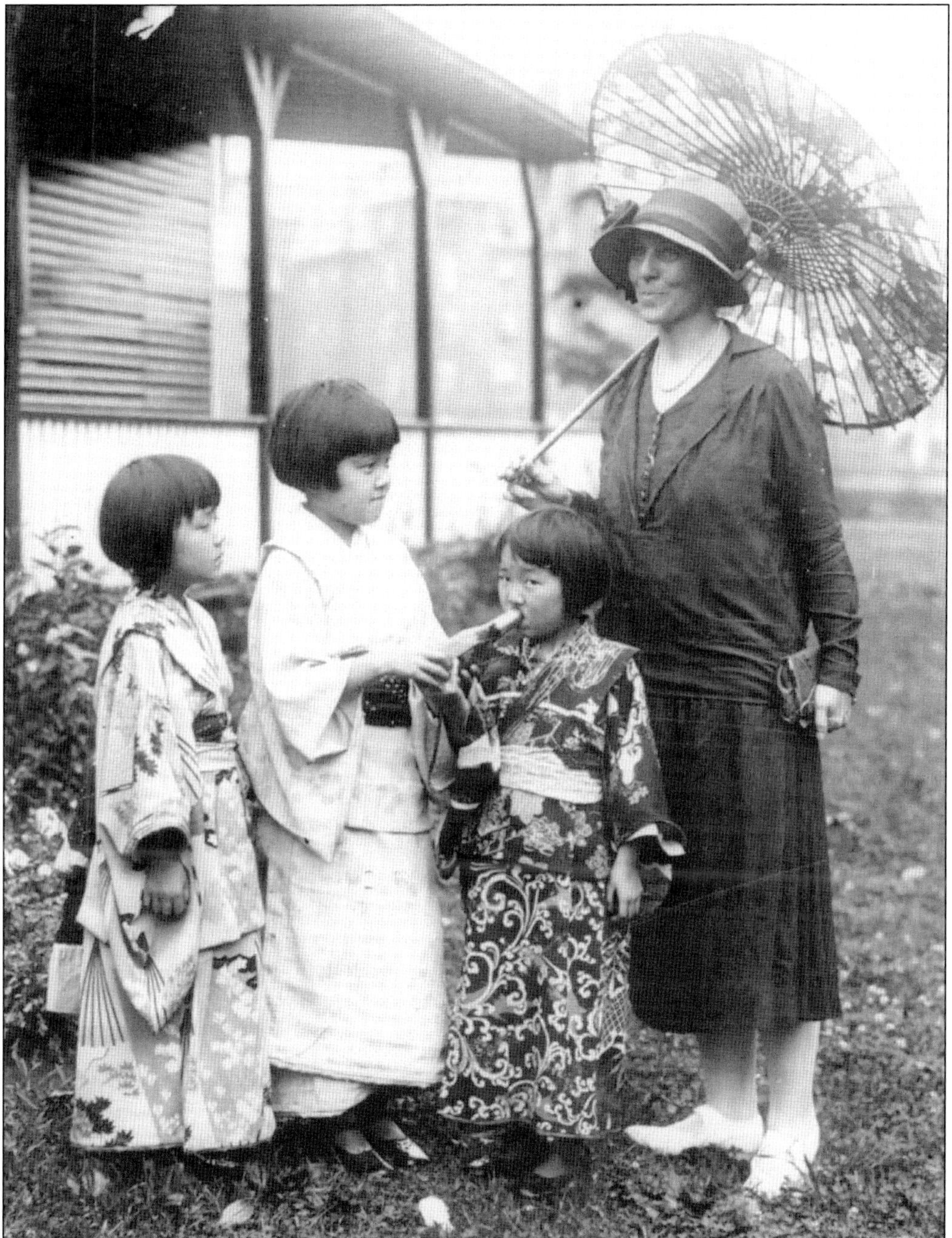

JAPANESE PARTY. On July 25, 1925, the community hosted a Japanese garden party to help benefit the Tsuda College for Women of Tokyo, destroyed two years earlier in an earthquake. Attracting more than 500 people, the party (held in the garden courtyard of The Towers) was inspired by the wife of financier Frank A. Vanderlip, who held a similar fundraiser in Manhattan the year before. The festivities she organized included tennis matches with the Japanese Davis Cup team, floral exhibits, Japanese dancing, and a demonstration of martial arts. Here, Narcissa Cox Vanderlip poses with three children dressed in kimonos. (Courtesy of the New-York Historical Society.)

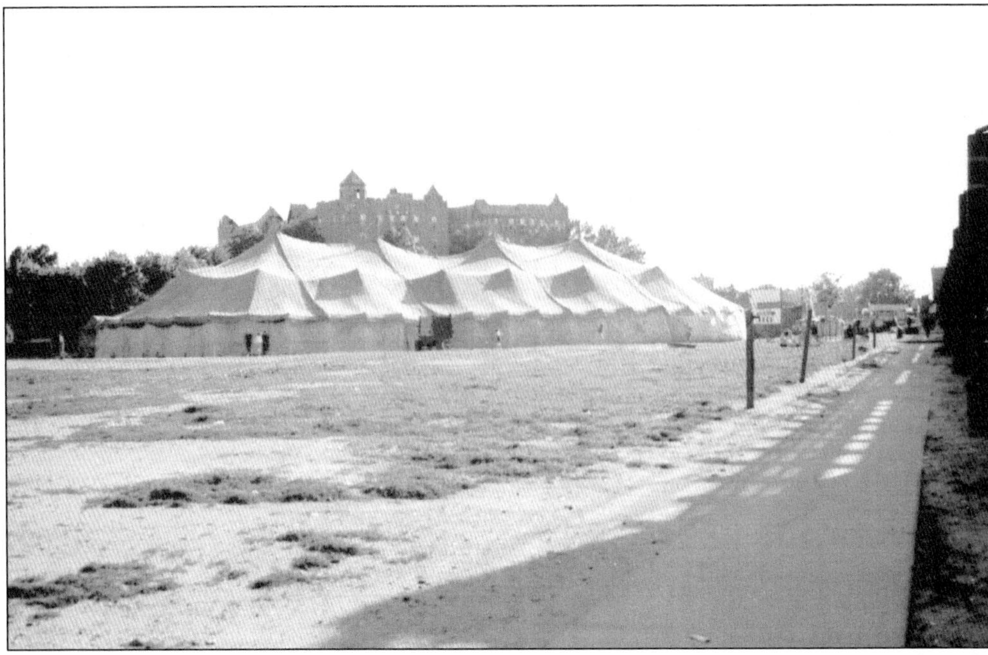

THE CIRCUS IN TOWN. With available space still in existence, large-scale diversions, such as the circus, were held in open lots like this just off Roosevelt Avenue. In the background is the Spanish Gardens. (Courtesy of the Queens Historical Society.)

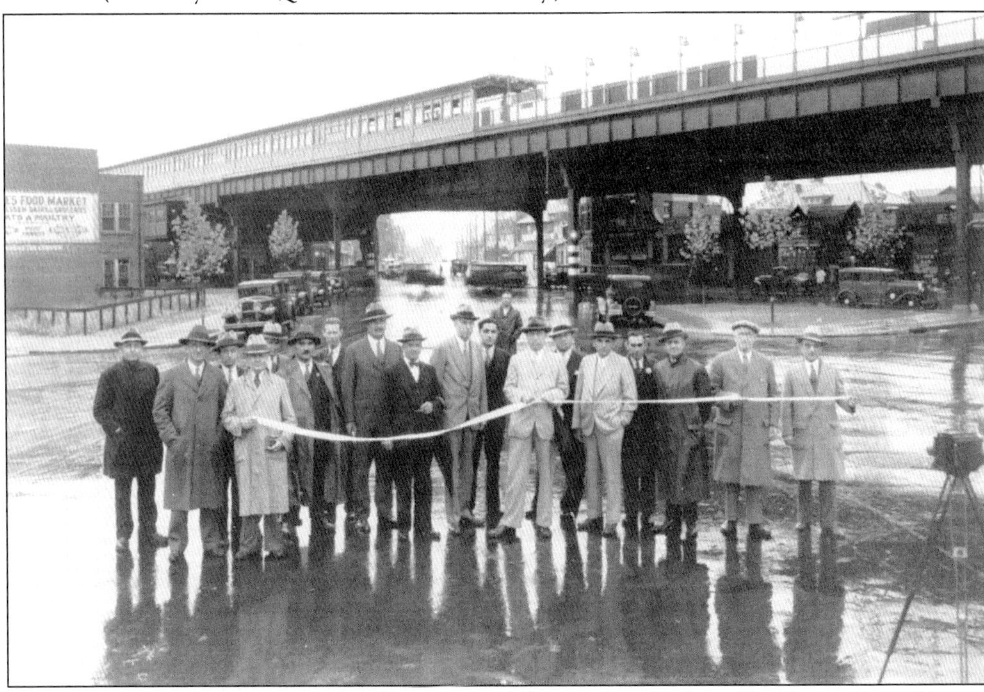

MAKING THE CONNECTION. On October 6, 1932, delegates from Jackson Heights and neighboring Woodside join at the intersection of Broadway and Roosevelt Avenue to officially open the last station between Woodside Avenue and Broadway. The IRT No. 7 tracks are seen in the background of this view looking north. (Courtesy of the Queens County Topographical Bureau.)

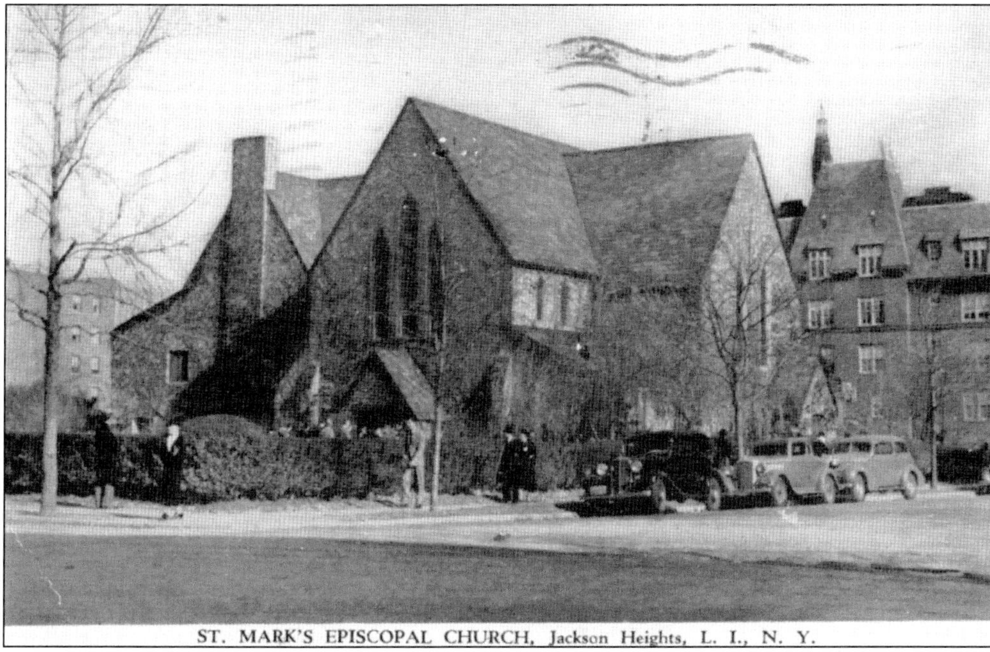

ST. MARK'S EPISCOPAL CHURCH. With the help of the Church Building Fund, St. Mark's Episcopal Church opened on Christmas Eve 1927. Located on the northeast corner of Eighty-first Street and Thirty-fourth Avenue, the church was designed by Robert Tappan. A parish house was added in 1948.

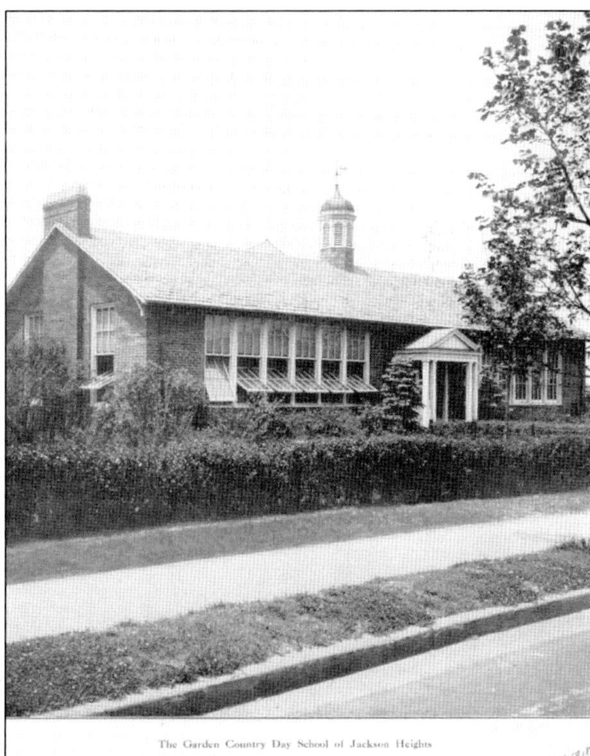

A NEW TYPE OF "GARDEN." Many received a first-class education at the Garden Country Day School. The private school is shown just after construction was completed in the late summer of 1928. This advertisement announces its opening on September 17. (Courtesy of the Queens Historical Society.)

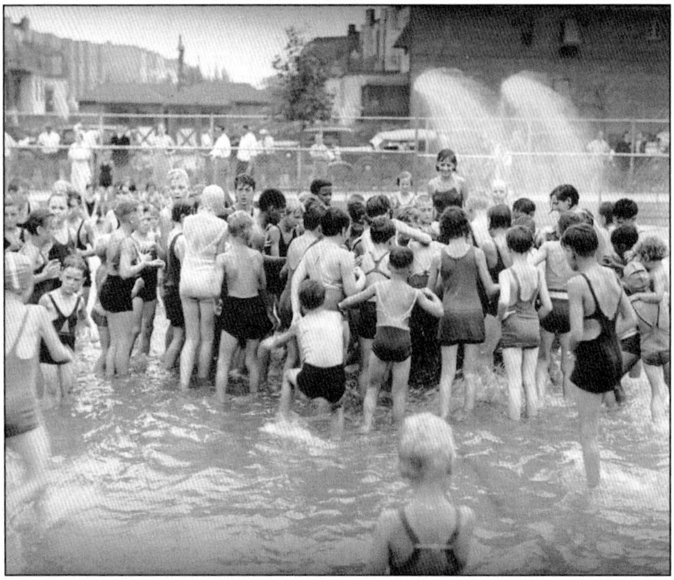

A Refreshing Escape. On August 11, 1934, one of the first wading pools in the city opened at what is now the Dennis P. Gorman Memorial Playground at Thirtieth Avenue, between Eighty-fourth and Eighty-fifth Streets. Such innovations helped provide relief from summer heat. Gorman was a notable Jackson Heights resident instrumental in improving bus service to the community. (Courtesy of Max Ulrich/New York City Park Photograph Dennis P. Gorman Archive.)

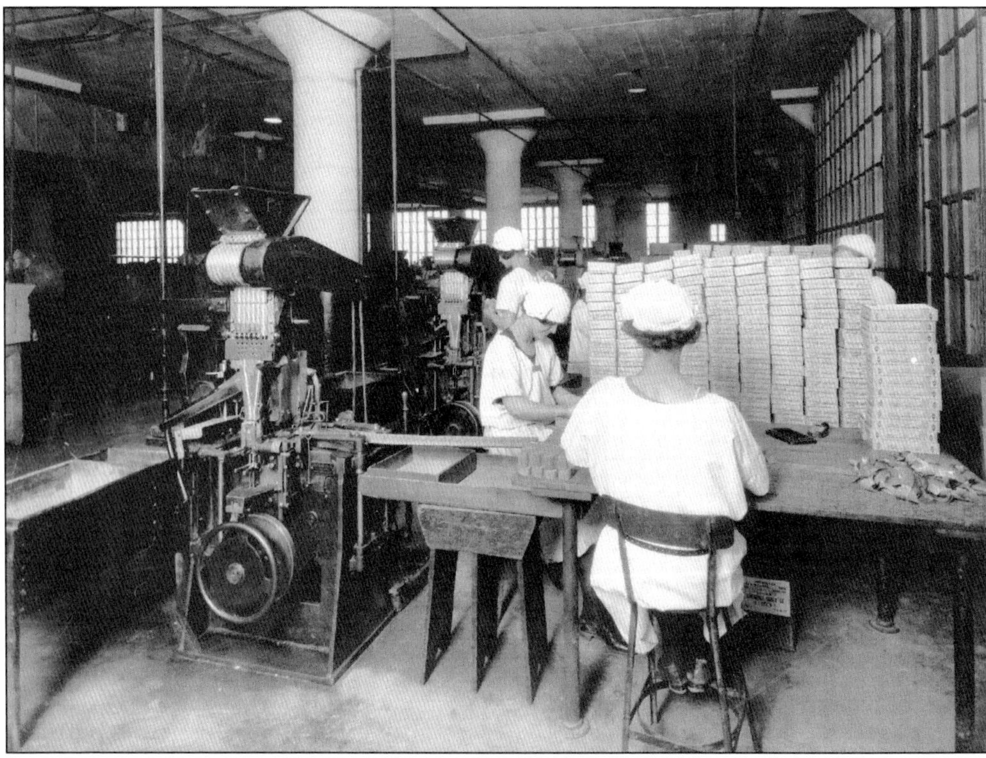

An Honest Day's Work. The American Chicle Company opened its chewing gum factory in neighboring Long Island City in 1919. Constructed and designed by the Ballinger Company, the facility produced the popular Chiclets and Dentyne brands of chewing gum. Part of the Degnon Terminal manufacturing complex, the factory employed many workers from western Queens, Brooklyn, and Jackson Heights. The factory, which also produced Certs breath mints and Trident gum, was taken over by the Adams Chewing Gum Company. In November 1976, an explosion injured and killed several employees and destroyed much of the building.

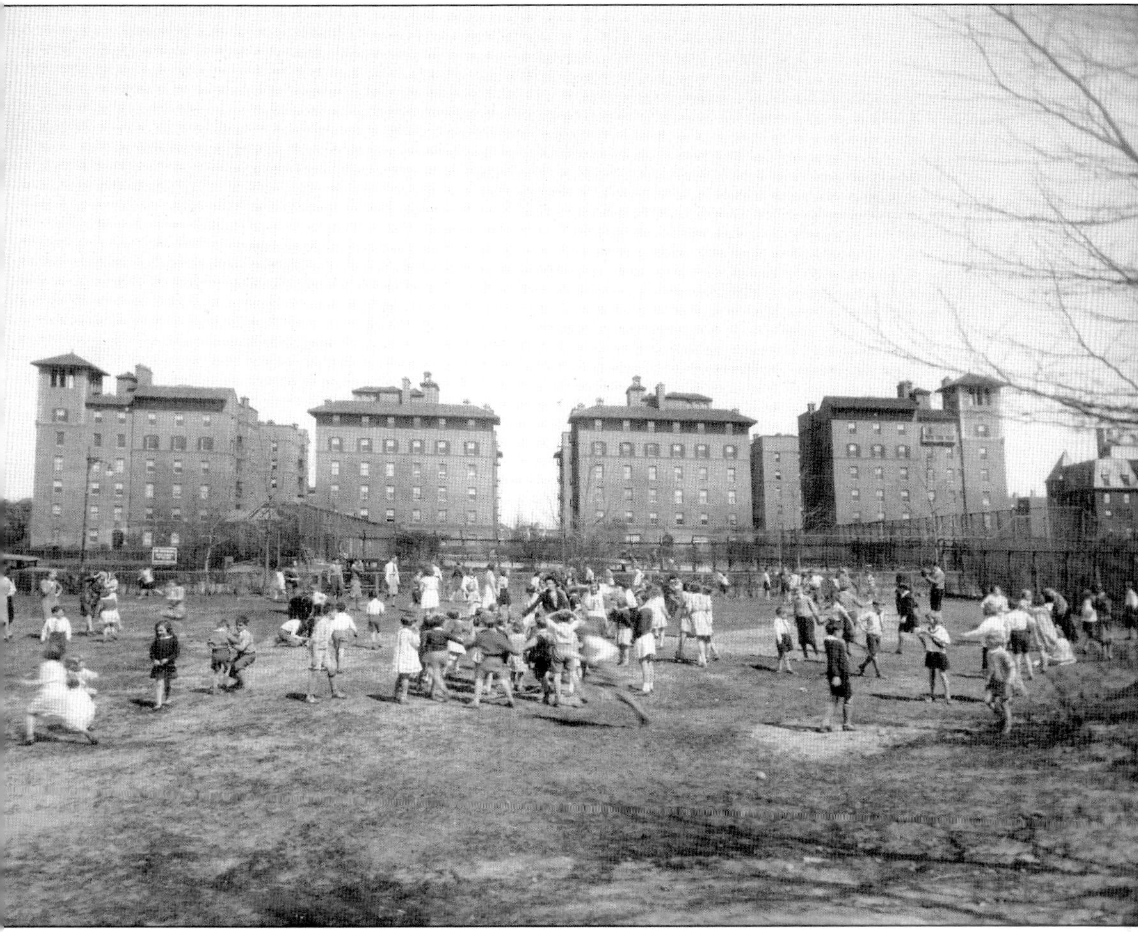

A Time for Recess. Here, children and teachers at the newly formed Garden Country Day School play ring-around-the-rosy in the shadow of The Towers in the spring of 1930. Note the tennis courts behind them. (Courtesy of the Garden Country Day School.)

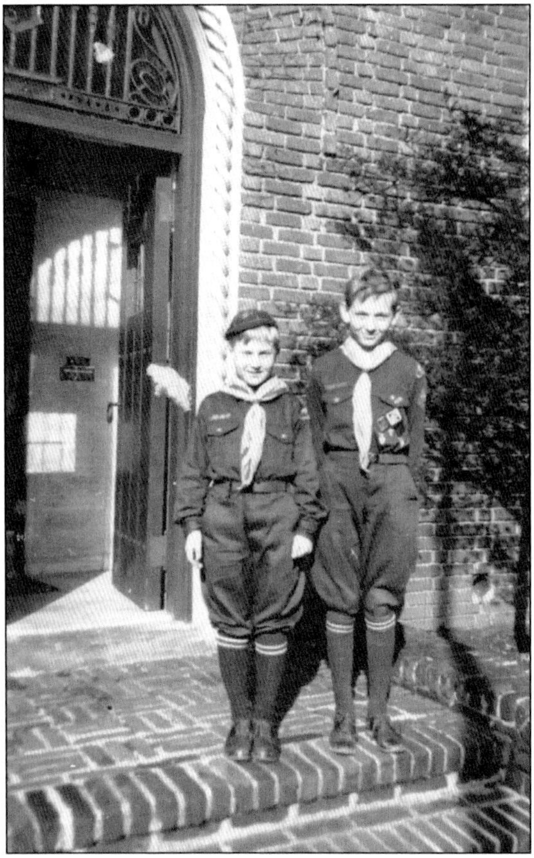

A Couple of Good Scouts. Two dutiful Boy Scouts are in full uniform outside of Linden Court. The Boy Scouts of America has its origins in Queens, in particular the Flushing home of Daniel Carter Beard, who held the first meeting in 1910.

Working in the Garden. Gardening was not only a favorite pastime for Jackson Heights adults but also for neighborhood youngsters.

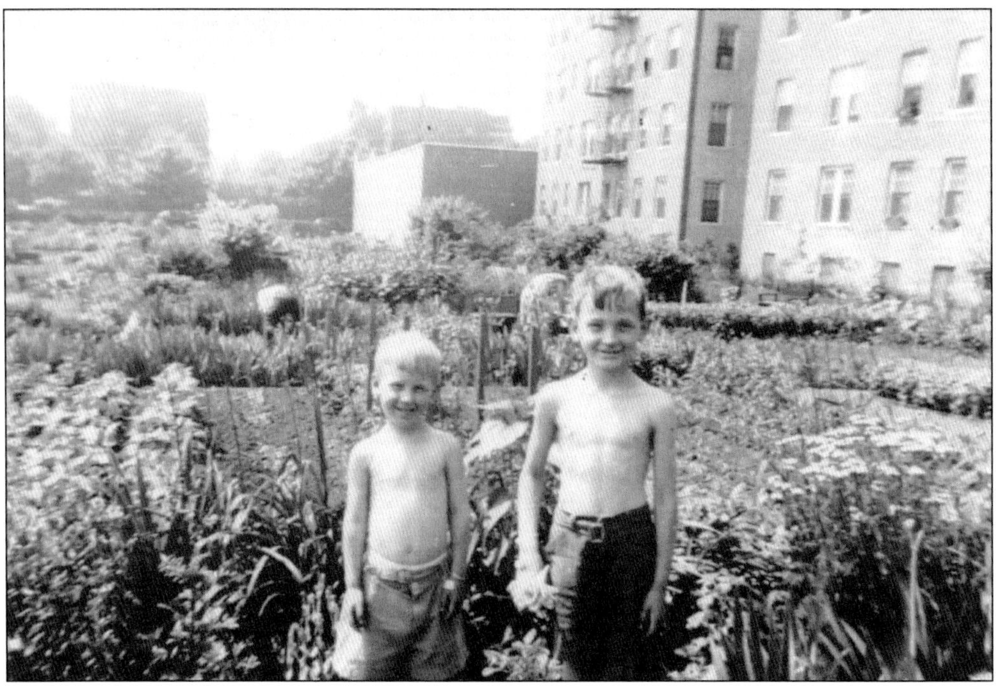

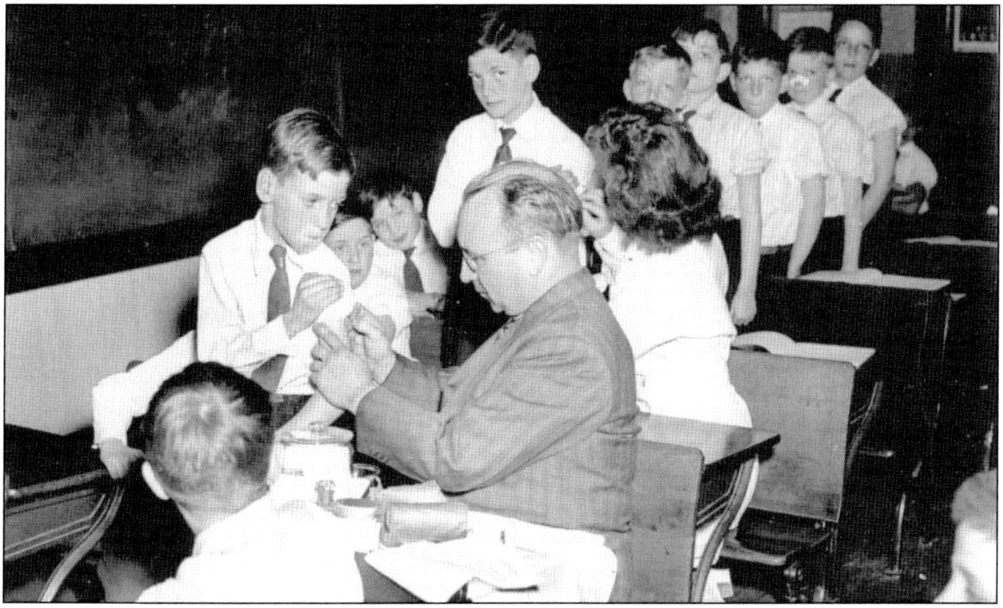

Medication Time. It is April 1947, and a threat of smallpox has descended on Queens. The department of health took active measures to thwart a possible epidemic by vaccinating the young and the elderly. Eight-year-old Joseph Burns grimaces while a doctor vaccinates him at St. Joan of Arc Parochial School. (Courtesy of the *Chicago Tribune*.)

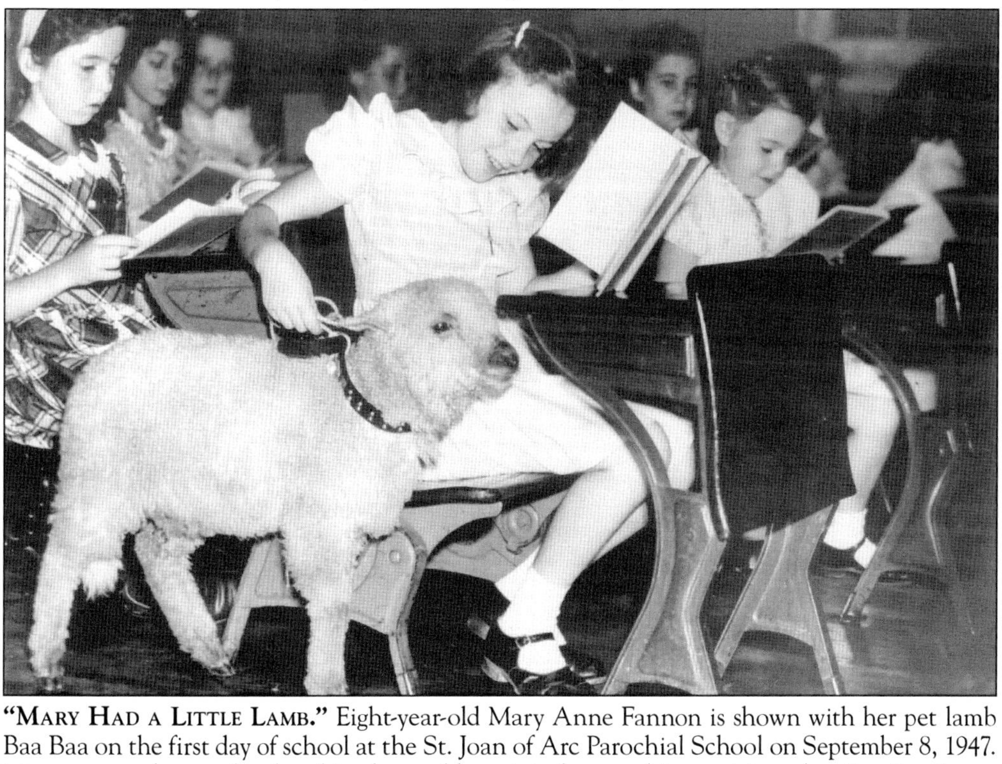

"Mary Had a Little Lamb." Eight-year-old Mary Anne Fannon is shown with her pet lamb Baa Baa on the first day of school at the St. Joan of Arc Parochial School on September 8, 1947. Mary appears happy that her friend was able to join her on this auspicious day; Baa Baa is not so sure.

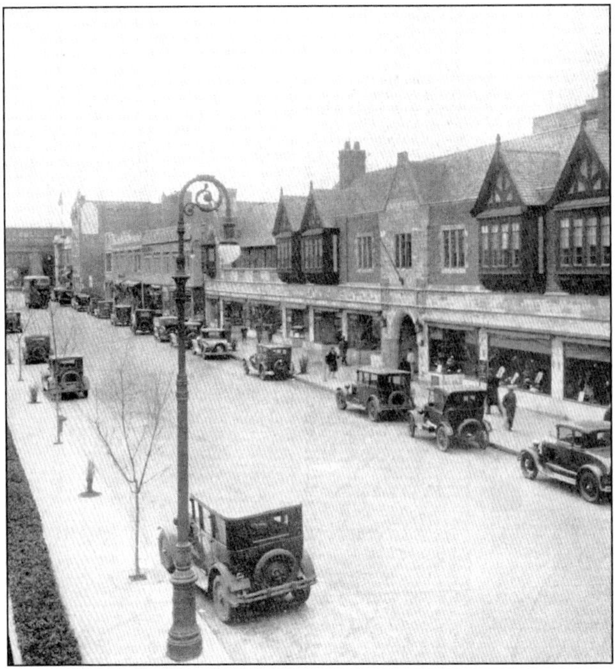

Shopping along Eighty-second Street. As the Jackson Heights neighborhood grew, so did local commerce. Built in the Neo-Tudor style, the Gables, along Eighty-second Street between Thirty-seventh and Roosevelt Avenues, featured stores from clothing boutiques to bookstores. Period cars line the street in this picture taken at the height of the 1929 Christmas shopping season. (Courtesy of the Queens Borough Public Library, Long Island Division, Illustrations Collection–Jackson Heights.)

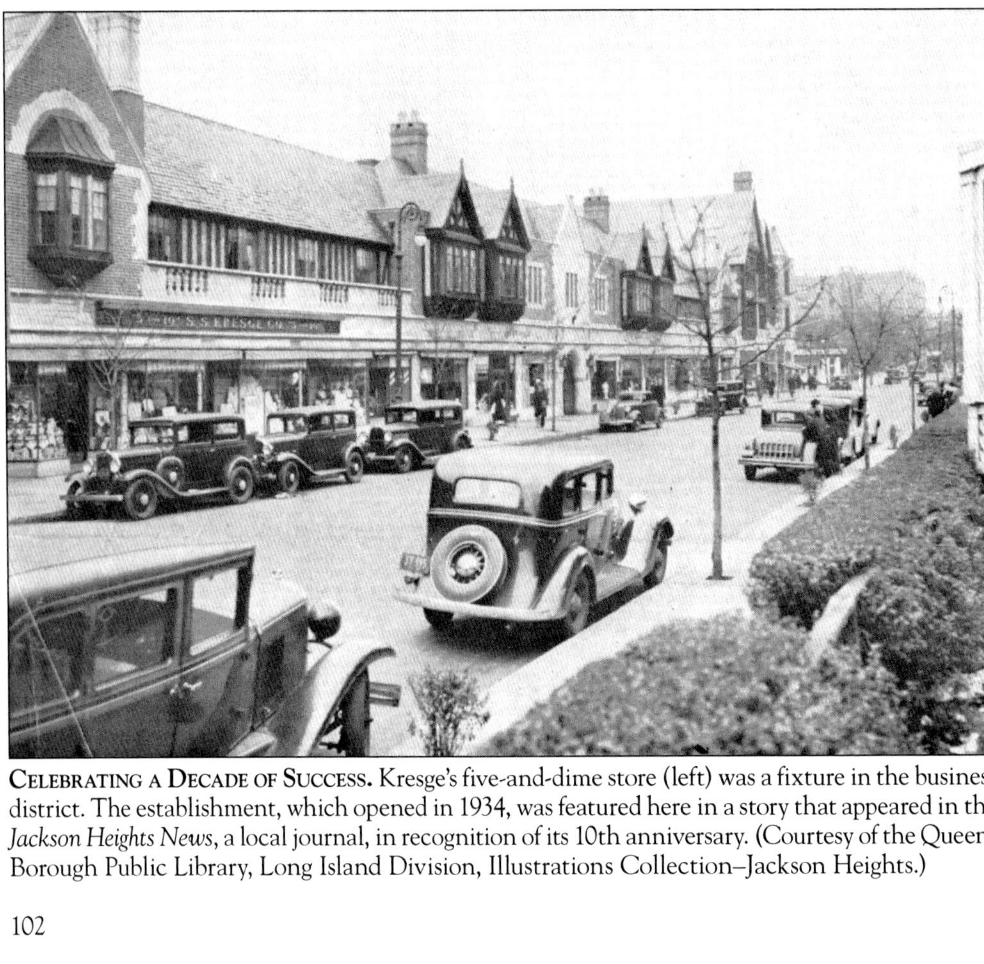

Celebrating a Decade of Success. Kresge's five-and-dime store (left) was a fixture in the business district. The establishment, which opened in 1934, was featured here in a story that appeared in the *Jackson Heights News*, a local journal, in recognition of its 10th anniversary. (Courtesy of the Queens Borough Public Library, Long Island Division, Illustrations Collection–Jackson Heights.)

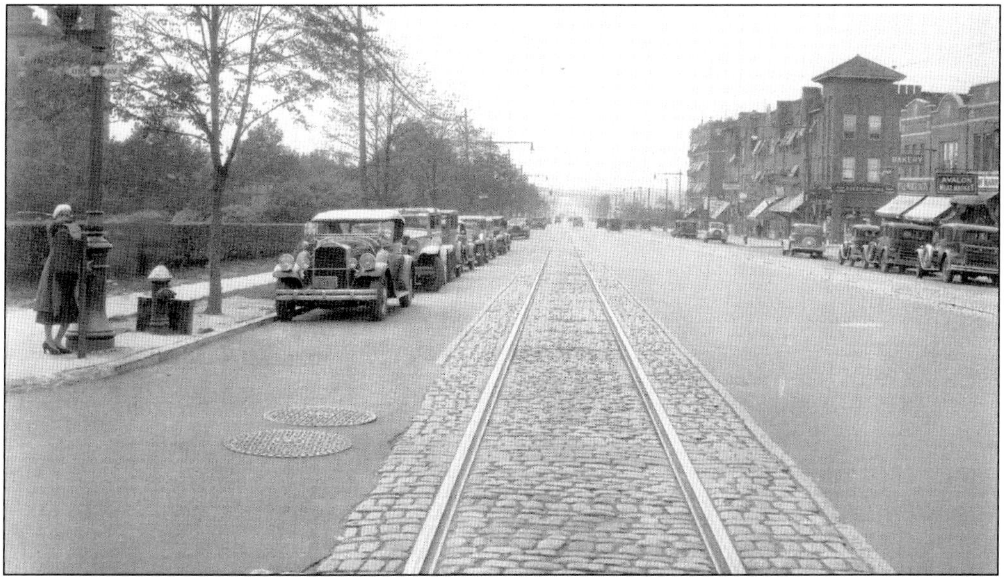

Business and Community Growth. A view looking west on Northern Boulevard at Eighty-fourth Street shows newly developed businesses and sidewalks. The street was much narrower when this image was taken on November 4, 1926. Trolley tracks of the Queens County Railway can be seen at right, and the shops, which included drugstores, hardware stores, ice cream parlors, and delicatessens, are below grade level. In the late 1930s, the boulevard was widened to accommodate more vehicular traffic. This eliminated the depressed sidewalks and brought the shops to street level.

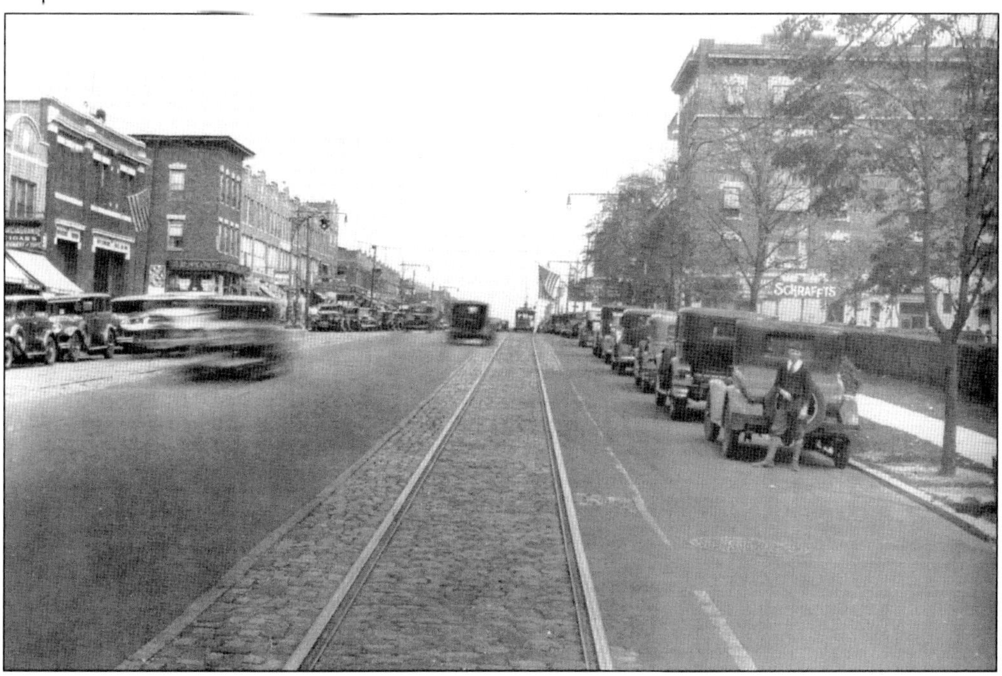

Looking East. This photograph was taken from the same spot, but facing east along Northern Boulevard heading toward Corona. The FDNY firehouse for Engine No. 307, Ladder No. 154, 14th Division is to the left.

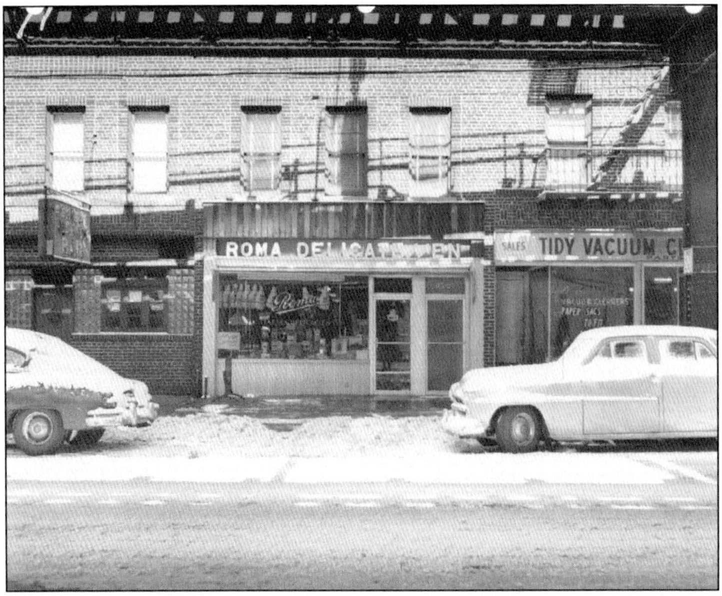

"VIVA ITALIA!" The Roma Delicatessen at 9527 Roosevelt Avenue sits in the shadow of the elevated roadway in this 1956 photograph. The Roma was a reflection of the Italian community's presence in the neighborhood, one of the many cultures that began to move into the area in the mid-20th century. The Tidy Vacuum Cleaner store is to the right. (Courtesy of the Queens Borough Public Library, Long Island Division.)

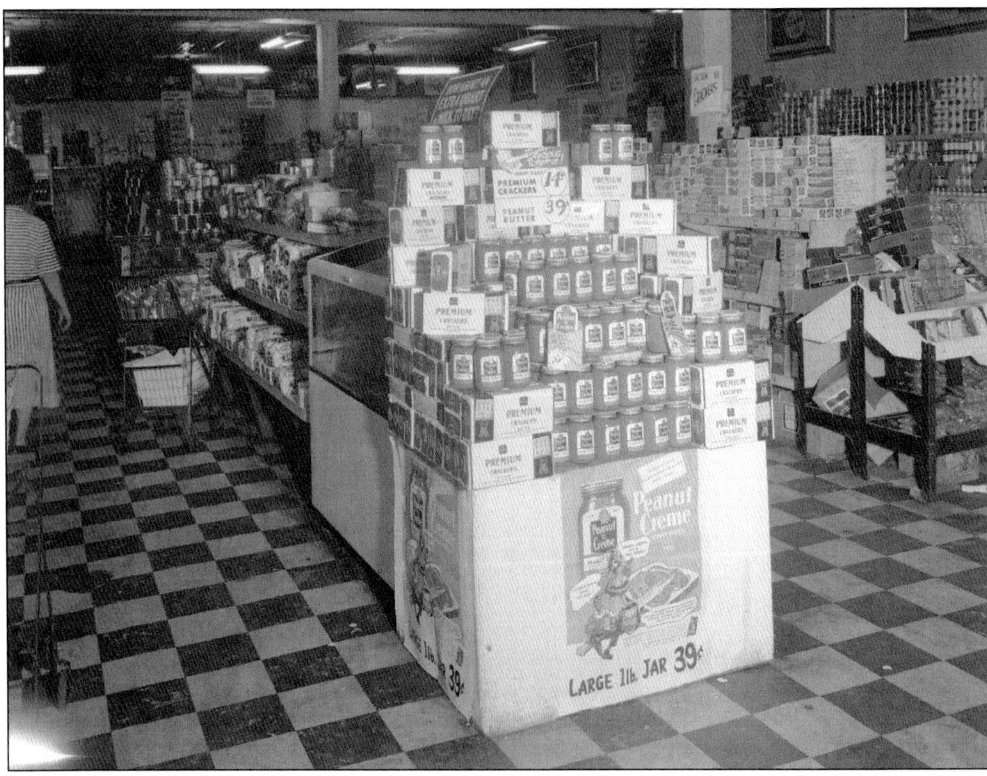

PEANUT CREME. In this photograph, dated July 25, 1947, patrons of Huberts Grocery Store are greeted by the sight of this display stand showing Peanut Creme on sale for 39¢. Other products include Nabisco Premium Crackers for just 14¢. Behind the display stand to the left are shelves of Silver Cup white bread produced at the Silver Cup wholesale bakery just a few miles down Northern Boulevard in Long Island City. (Courtesy of the Queens Borough Public Library, Long Island Division.)

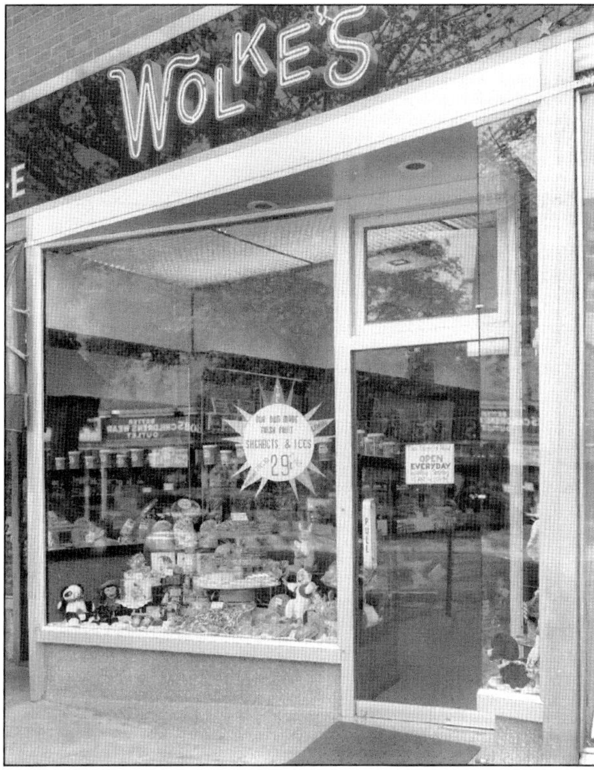

Wolke's. For anyone with a sweet tooth living in the vicinity of Ninetieth Street between Thirty-seventh and Roosevelt Avenues, Wolke's candy shop and ice cream parlor proved irresistible. Many patrons will recall the homemade sherbet and ices with lemon, lime, raspberry, orange, and strawberry, all served by the ever patient Mrs. Wolke. (Courtesy of the Queens Bourgh Public Library, Long Island Division.)

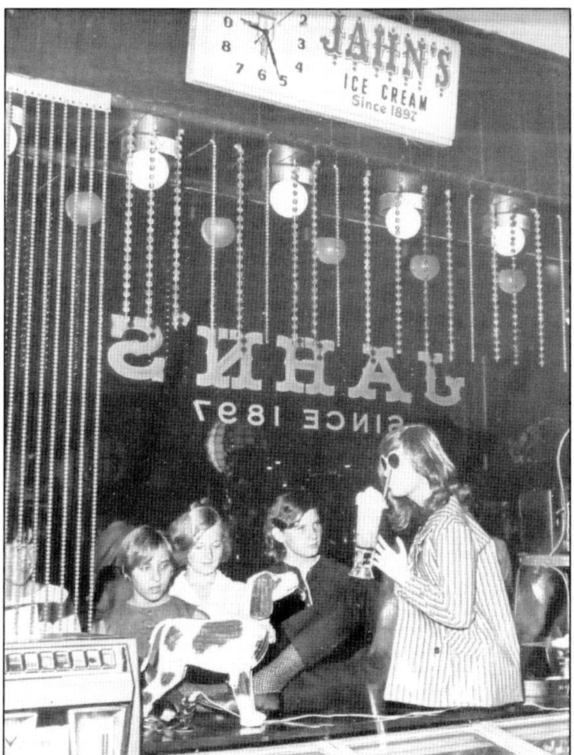

Jahn's Ice Cream Parlor. Deeply rooted in local tradition and history for nearly 120 years, Jahn's Ice Cream Parlor satisfied millions of people of all ages with its delicious ice cream creations. Its first location opened in 1897 by John Jahn at 138th Street and Alexander Avenue in the Mott Haven section of the Bronx. By 1918, he opened up three more locations in Queens, one for each of his children: Elsie (in Jamaica), Frank (in Richmond Hill), and Howard (in Flushing). With other locations throughout the nation, the legacy almost ended in December 2007, when the Richmond Hill location closed. Jahn's arrived at 81-04 Thirty-seventh Avenue in the early 1950s. The Jahn's in Jackson Heights is the only one left in operation. (Courtesy of Jahn's Ice Cream Parlor.)

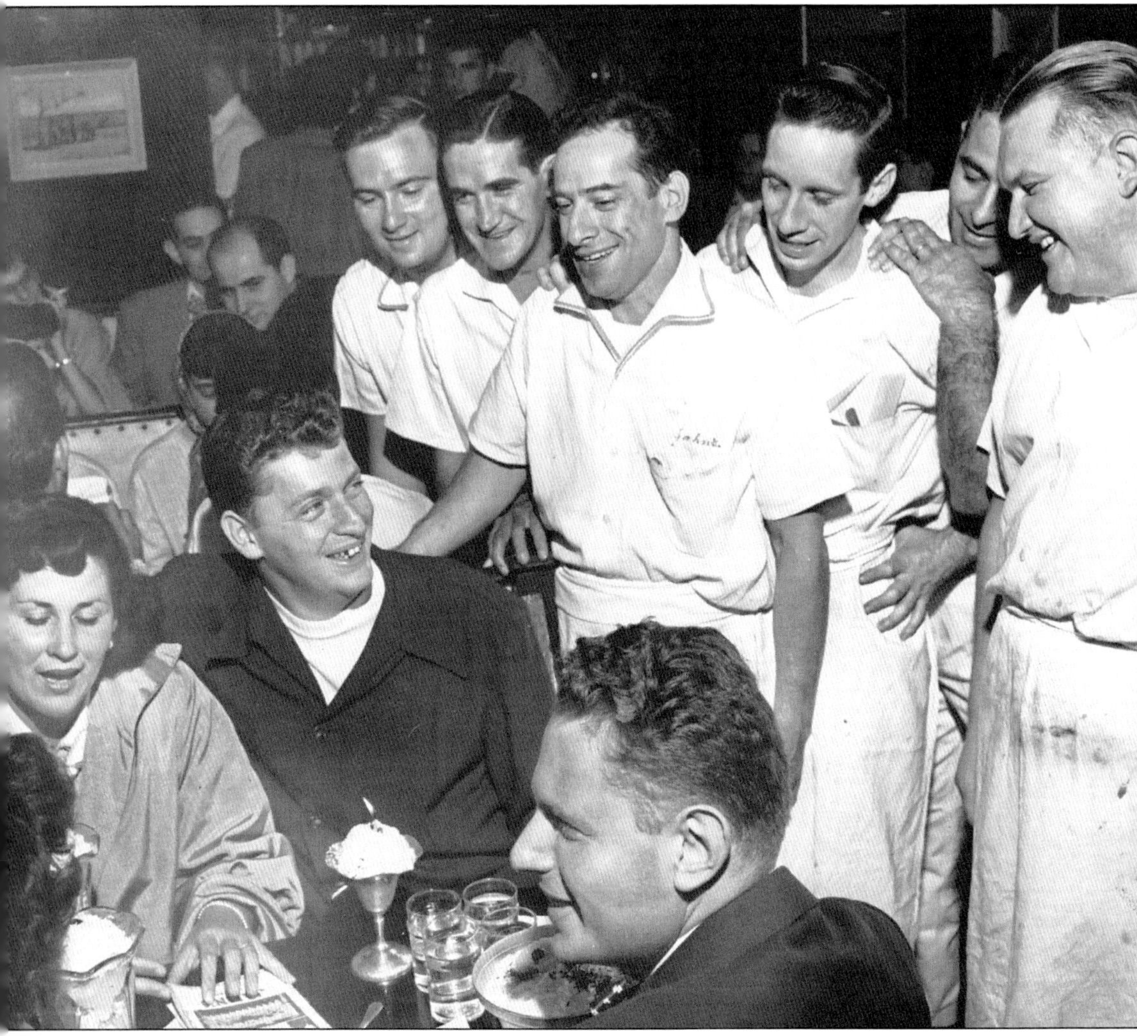

A Special Birthday Treat. Always aiming to please, waiters at the Jackson Heights Jahn's sing "Happy Birthday" to an unidentified man as they present him with a complimentary birthday sundae. The 2012 menu still features old-time classics including the Kitchen Sink that will feed eight. The Banana Royal comes with three large scoops of ice cream, a whole banana, hot fudge, whipped cream, and several maraschino cherries, while other concoctions include Super Duper, Shissel, Bombshell, Tall in the Saddle, Flaming Desire, and Brooklyn Kibitzer.

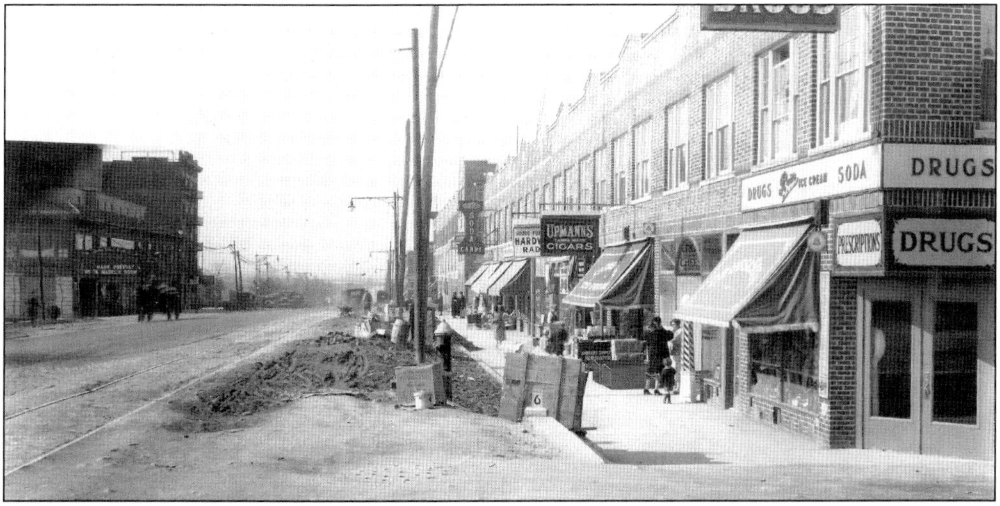

NORTHERN BOULEVARD AND EIGHTY-FOURTH STREET. Shops between Eighty-third and Eighty-fourth Streets on the north side of Northern Boulevard included drugstores, candy shops, and delicatessens. Of interest in this photograph is the lowering of the grade level. If one looks close enough, the shops along Northern Boulevard are below the street level and will soon be at the same level as the roadway once this project was completed. This photograph is dated November 4, 1926.

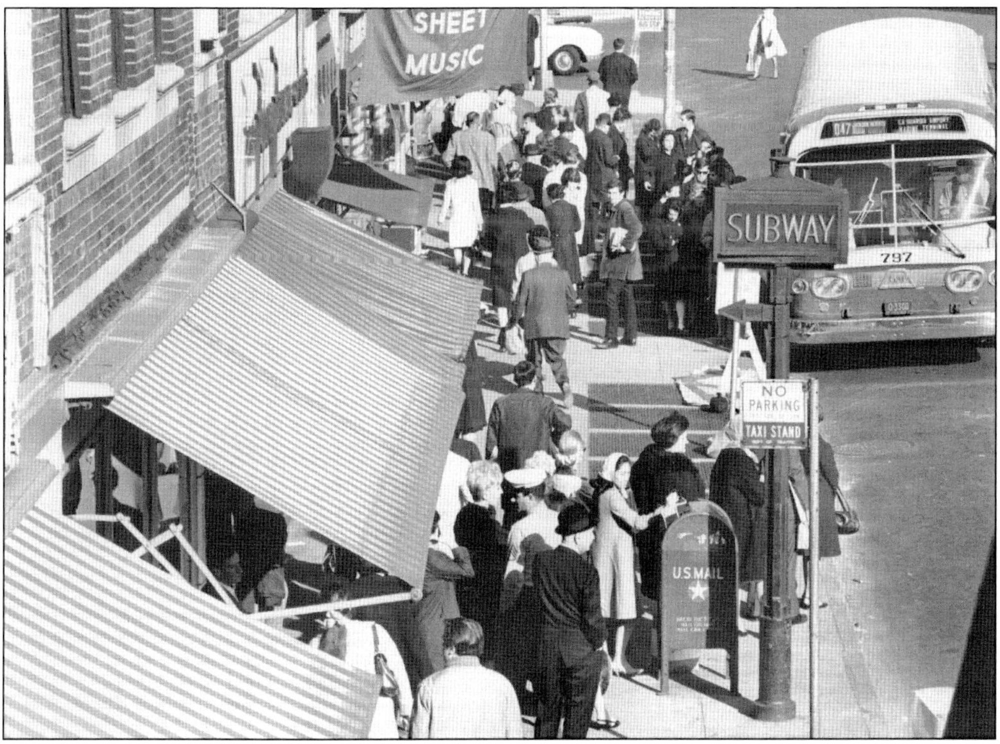

A TYPICAL DAY IN 1963. Pictured is the hustle and bustle along Broadway near Roosevelt Avenue one afternoon in the fall of 1963. On the right, the Q47 bus bound for Elmhurst and the Marine Air Terminal at LaGuardia Airport is seen just as it arrives. People, most likely on their lunch breaks, are window-shopping, mailing letters, and performing other daily errands.

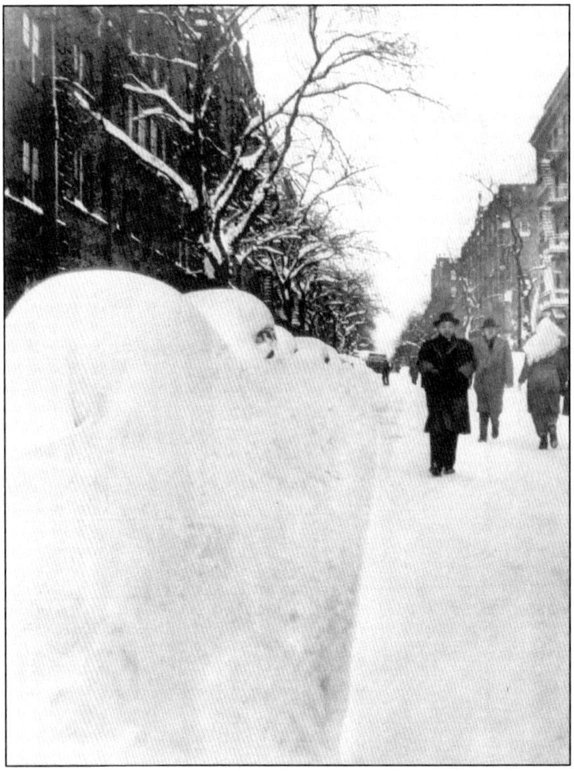

Buried. A memorable winter snowstorm hit the metropolitan area on December 27, 1947, dumping several feet of snow. Jackson Heights residents are making do and are walking carefully down Eighty-second Street past cars that are completely buried.

Almost Home. A mother pushes her child in a stroller through melted snow in January 1948. The snow might have melted somewhat a week after the storm hit, but walking still proved to be difficult. (Courtesy of the Queens Borough Public Library, Long Island Division.)

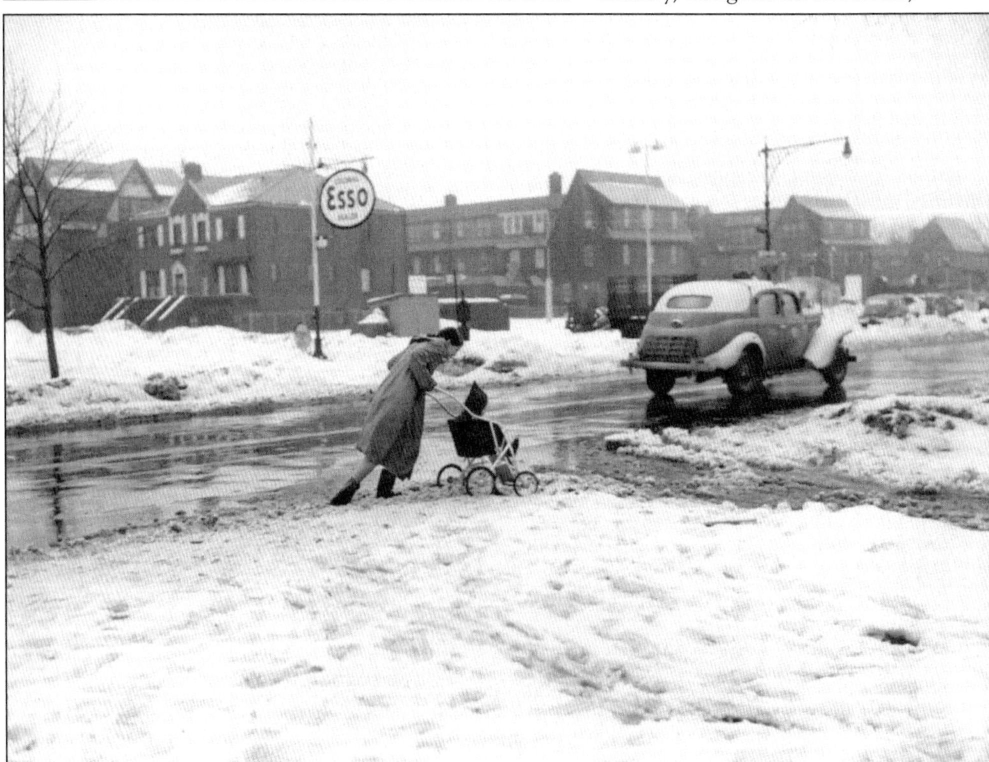

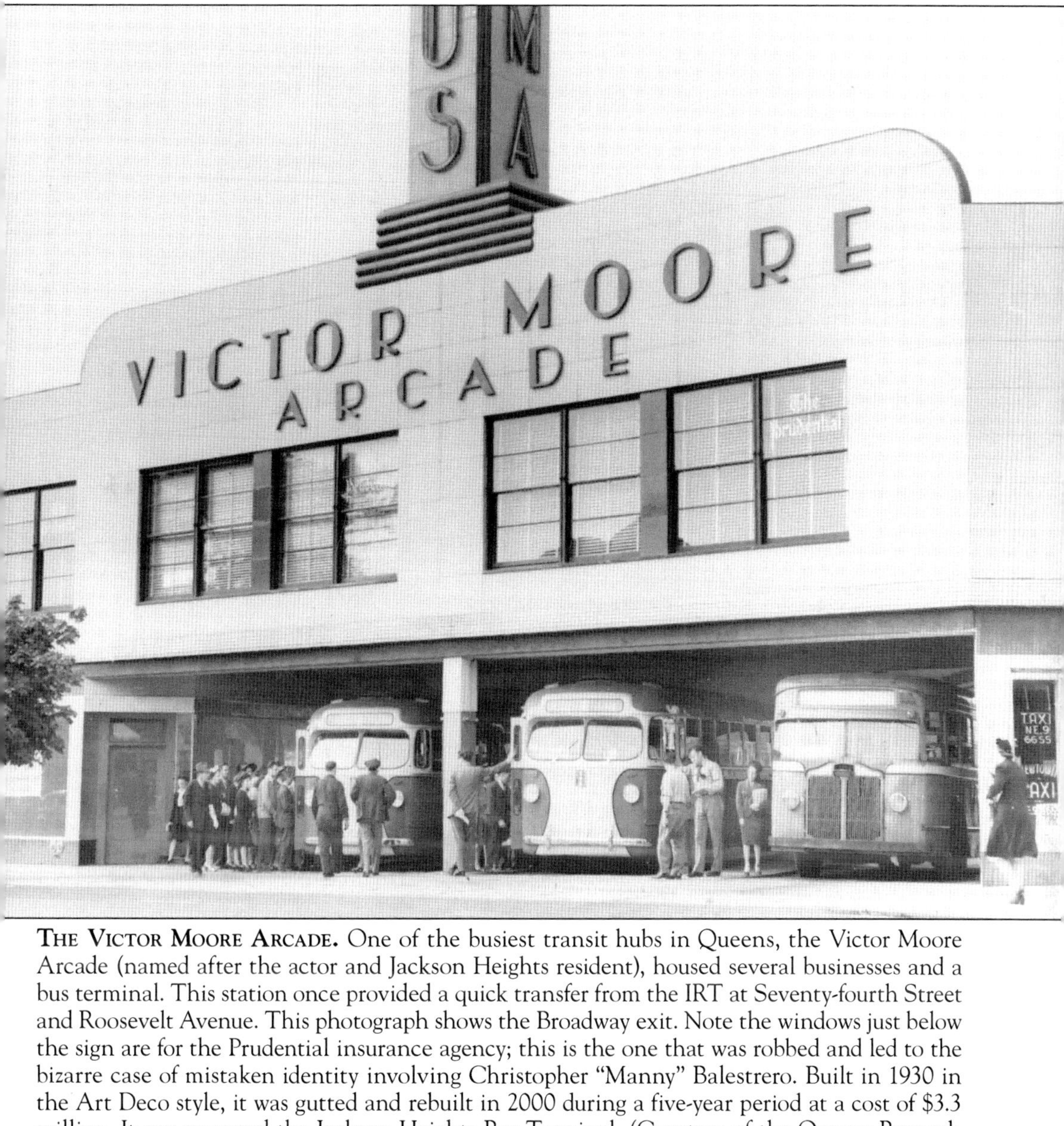

The Victor Moore Arcade. One of the busiest transit hubs in Queens, the Victor Moore Arcade (named after the actor and Jackson Heights resident), housed several businesses and a bus terminal. This station once provided a quick transfer from the IRT at Seventy-fourth Street and Roosevelt Avenue. This photograph shows the Broadway exit. Note the windows just below the sign are for the Prudential insurance agency; this is the one that was robbed and led to the bizarre case of mistaken identity involving Christopher "Manny" Balestrero. Built in 1930 in the Art Deco style, it was gutted and rebuilt in 2000 during a five-year period at a cost of $3.3 million. It was renamed the Jackson Heights Bus Terminal. (Courtesy of the Queens Borough Public Library, Long Island Division.)

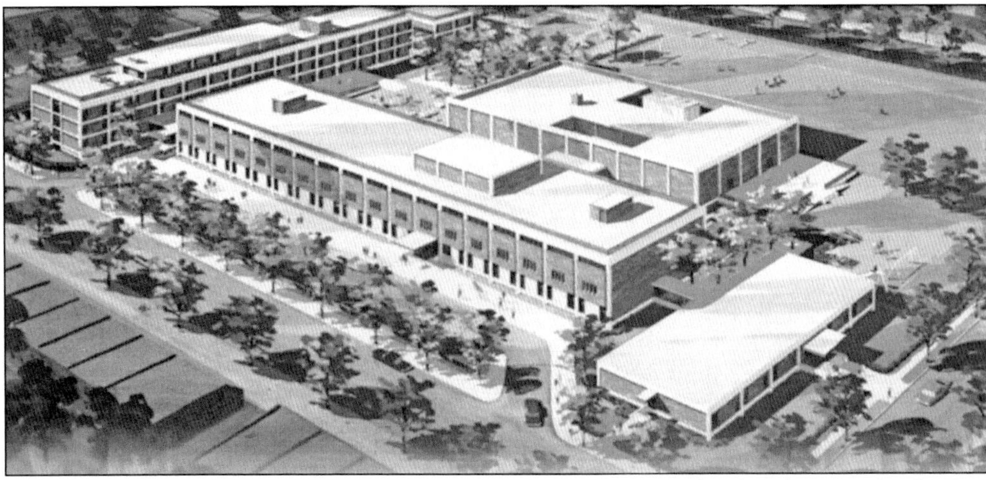

Lexington School and Center for the Deaf. The Lexington School and Center for the Deaf was founded in 1865 and was originally located on Lexington Avenue between Sixty-seventh and Sixty-eighth Streets in Manhattan. On January 8, 1968, Lexington opened its new $9-million, six-acre facility at 26-26 Seventh-fifth Street. Dr. Leo E. Connor was superintendent. The school is comprised of the Lexington School for the Deaf, the Lexington Hearing and Speech Center, Lexington Vocational Services, and Lexington Center for Mental Health. Lexington students come from all over the five boroughs, and a number have other disabilities in addition to deafness, including mobility and mental impairments. The school helps prepare all students to continue on to college, vocational education, job training, or a placement that will support them to live a responsible, productive life. The Lexington School and Center for the Deaf provides education and services to about 2,500 deaf and hard-of-hearing people annually. (Courtesy of the Lexington School and Center for the Deaf.)

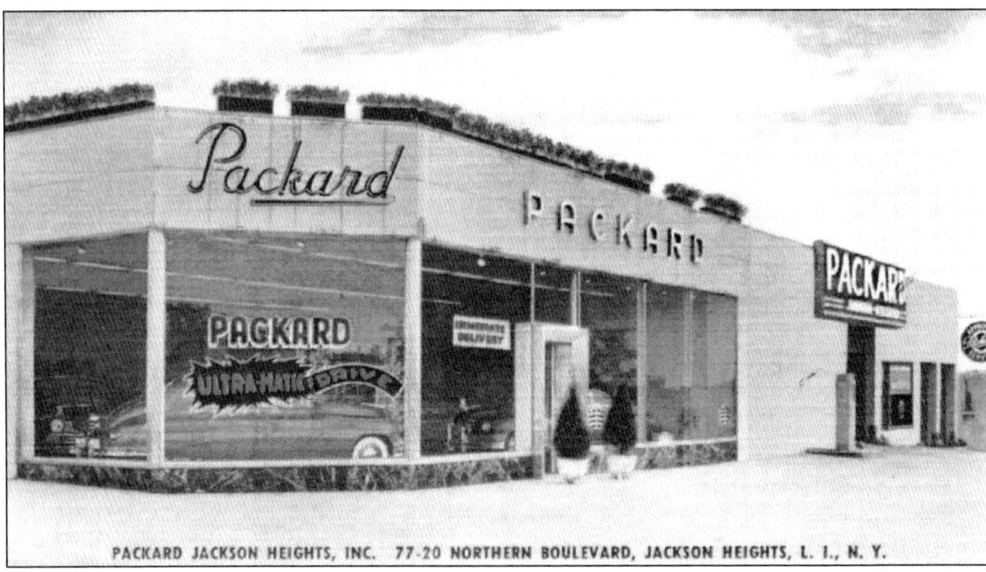

Packard Dealership. Northern Boulevard is home to almost 100 car dealerships along its length from the Queensboro Bridge through Nassau County, Long Island. This Packard dealership was located at 7720 Northern Boulevard. First produced in 1899, the Packard was manufactured by the Packard Motor Car Company in Detroit, Michigan. The company closed in 1958 under the name of the Studebaker-Packard Corporation of South Bend, Indiana.

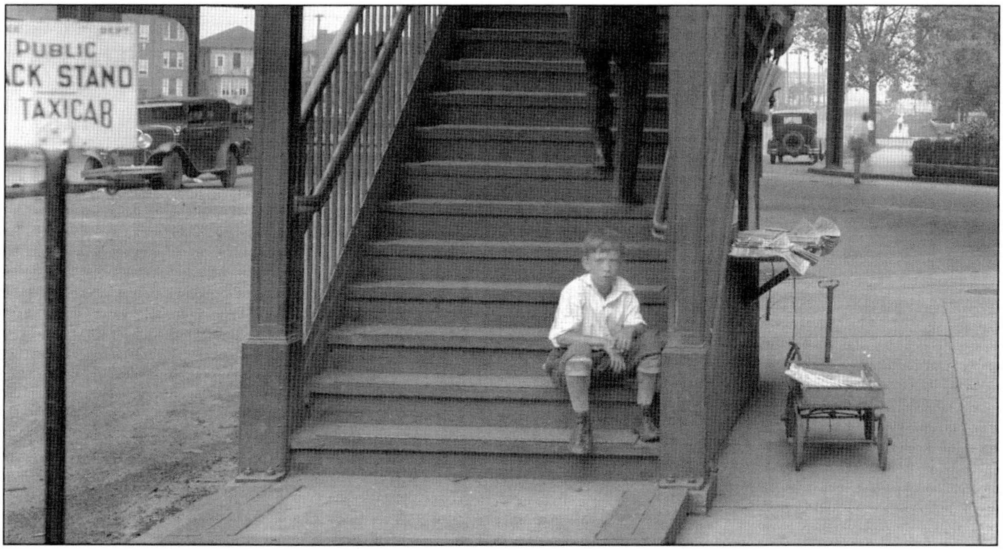

"EXTRA! EXTRA!" Perhaps waiting for the rush hour crowd, or just having experienced it, this solitary paperboy sits at the base of the steps leading from the IRT down to Roosevelt Avenue near Broadway in the 1930s. Note the Radio Flyer cart piled with newspapers for delivery.

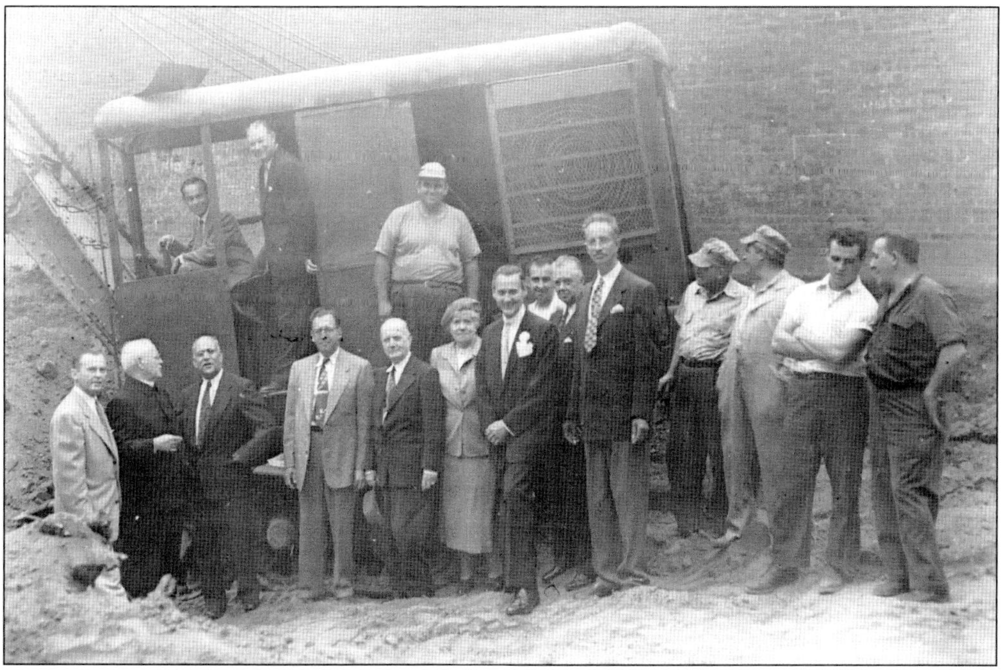

BREAKING NEW GROUND. On September 18, 1952, ground was broken for the Jackson Heights branch of the Queens Borough Public Library. Originally, it opened on April 17, 1917, as a traveling station library, designed to serve the newly developed community. Later, during the 1920s and 1930s, temporary branches were established in storefronts along Thirty-seventh Avenue to serve the growing population. The Jackson Heights Community Federation led an effort to have a library built after World War II, but because of building restrictions and a lack of funds, these efforts were hindered, and the local branch was not finished until 1954. (Courtesy of the Queens Borough Public Library, Long Island Division, Queens Borough Public Library Records.)

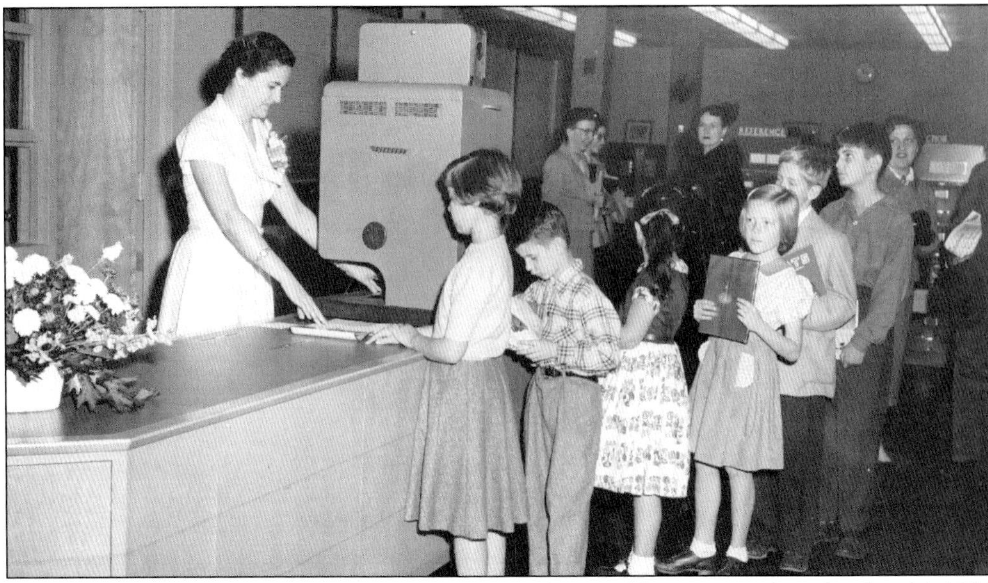

LIBRARY OPENING. After two years of construction, the new library opened on October 26, 1954. Youngsters of Jackson Heights are seen here checking out books during the opening day of the new branch. Extensive renovations occurred in 1970 and again in 1985. An elevator was built and the adult bathrooms were made handicapped accessible in 1999. The branch is now 17,100 square feet. (Courtesy of the Queens Borough Public Library, Long Island Division, Queens Borough Public Library Records.)

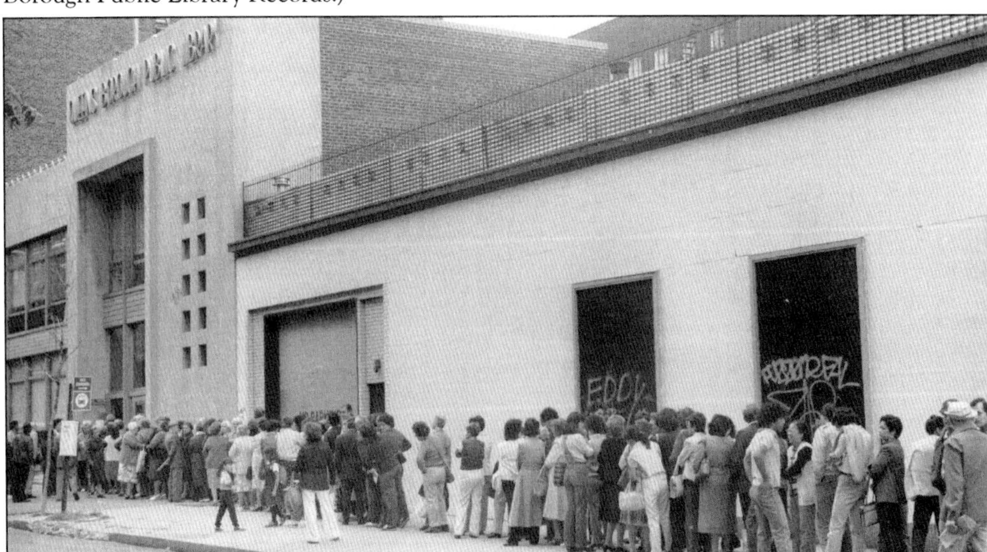

EDUCATION THROUGH UNDERSTANDING. In 1965, the Hart-Celler Act increased immigration, and waves of Asians and Latin Americans entered the United States via New York City. Many settled in Jackson Heights. The Queens Borough Public Library offered free ESOL (English for Speakers of Other Languages) classes for those wishing to learn how to communicate in their new homeland. Seen here is a line of people waiting to be admitted to one of these classes at the Jackson Heights branch in 1980. (Courtesy of the Queens Borough Public Library, Long Island Division, Queens Borough Public Library Records.)

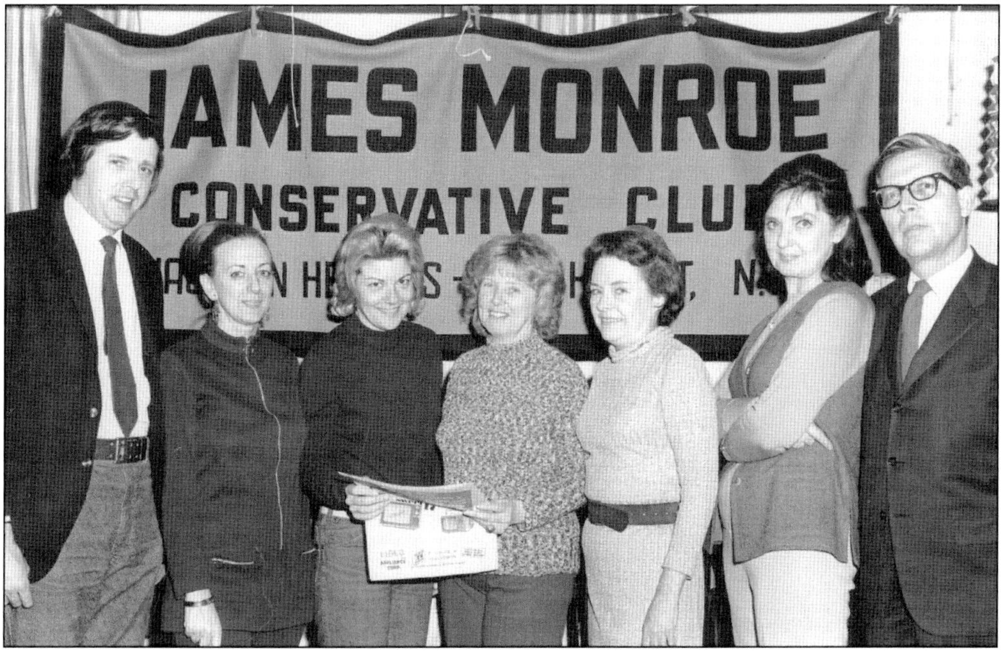

CLUBS AND ORGANIZATIONS. Jackson Heights can boast a long history of community awareness, with many clubs and civic groups having assembled during the past eight decades. Here, members of the James Monroe Conservative Club have gathered at 3540 Eighty-second Street on February 13, 1973. Posing from left to right are publicity chair Emery J. Pristas, secretary Barbara Heyward, vice chair Victoria Harlick, chair Helen Mclane, acting chair Jane Kretzler, committee chair Margaret Brogg, and club president Peter Kolom. (Courtesy of the Queens Borough Public Library, Long Island Division, Joseph A. Ullman Photographs.)

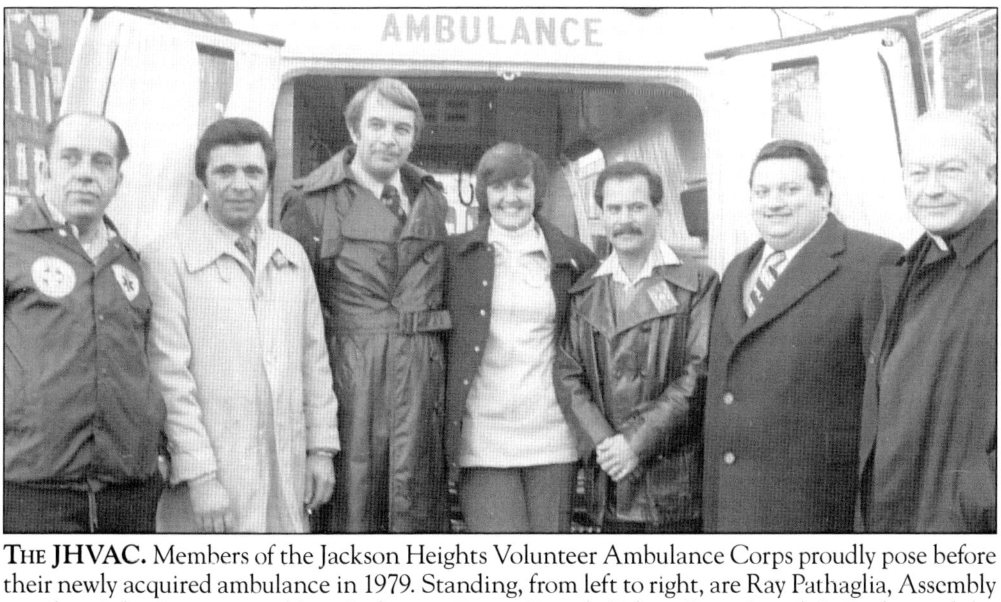

THE JHVAC. Members of the Jackson Heights Volunteer Ambulance Corps proudly pose before their newly acquired ambulance in 1979. Standing, from left to right, are Ray Pathaglia, Assembly members John Lopresto and Ivan Lafayette, Emma Brandt, Fabian Ruez, Joseph LaPoche, and the Reverend Father Eugene F. Donnelly of Church of Our Lady of Fatima. (Courtesy of the Queens Borough Public Library, Long Island Division, Joseph A. Ullman Photographs.)

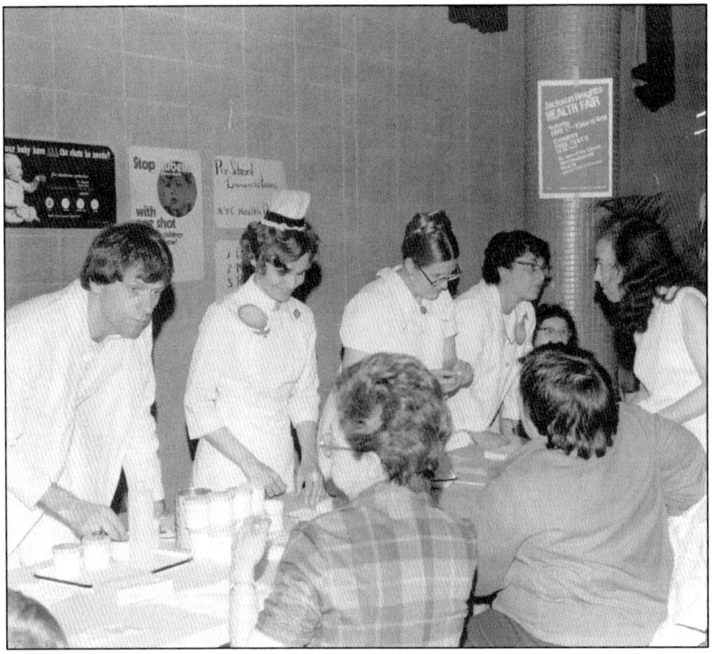

A Lesson in Health. Community members gathered on May 17, 1975, for the annual Jackson Heights Health Fair. Sponsored by the Jackson Heights Federation, the event was held at St. Joan of Arc Roman Catholic Church and helped educate people about healthy eating habits, provided free stress tests, and drew blood from participating donors. (Courtesy of the Queens Borough Public Library, Long Island Division, Joseph A. Ullman Photographs.)

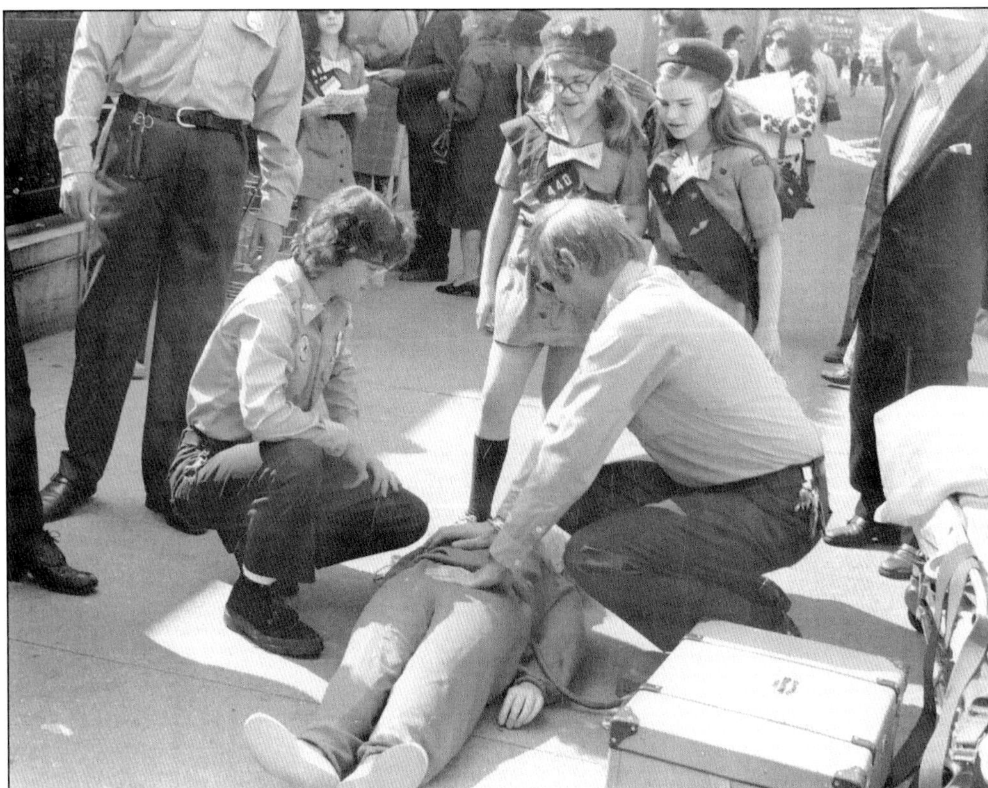

Learning CPR. Other lessons were taught at the health fair, such as lifesaving techniques like CPR. Two girls from Girl Scout Troop No. 40 look on as two men practice on a dummy. (Courtesy of the Queens Borough Public Library, Long Island Division, Joseph A. Ullman Photographs.)

JACKSON HEIGHTS VOLUNTEER AMBULANCE CORPS

80-11 31st AVENUE, JACKSON HEIGHTS, NEW YORK 11370
PHONE 335-3221

Dear Neighbor:

Since the Jackson Heights Volunteer Ambulance Corps began operation in May, we have responded to over 300 calls for assistance. The Jackson Heights Volunteer Ambulance Corps is a community service that provides FREE ambulance service to any person living, working, or visiting in the Jackson Heights area. Why does Jackson Heights need a volunteer ambulance corps?

* All of our services are rendered FREE OF CHARGE. A private ambulance will cost over $50.00 for a trip to the nearest hospital.
* A city ambulance can only take you to a city hospital in an emergency. We offer the patient his choice of hospital... whether it be a local hospital or one in another area.
* We offer routine transport as well as emergency service.
* Our ambulance is fully equipped and all our volunteers are fully trained to handle any medical emergency adequately.

Remember, we are a FREE community service that affects you personally. The only way we can continue this service is through your TAX DEDUCTABLE CONTRIBUTIONS.

Our new extended hours of operation are from 6:00pm to Midnight Monday thru Thursday and 24-Hour weekend service (6:00pm Friday to 6:00am Monday).

PLEASE - HELP US TO HELP YOU

GIVE TO THE JACKSON HEIGHTS VOLUNTEER AMBULANCE CORPS

Thank You

A LETTER TO MEMBERS. The Jackson Heights Volunteer Ambulance Corps (JHVAC) sent this letter explaining the benefits of the new service. Located at 8011 Thirty-first Avenue, the JHVAC provided free ambulatory service to area hospitals, which was available Monday through Friday from 6:00 p.m. to midnight and 24-hour service Friday through Sunday. A private ambulance cost $50.

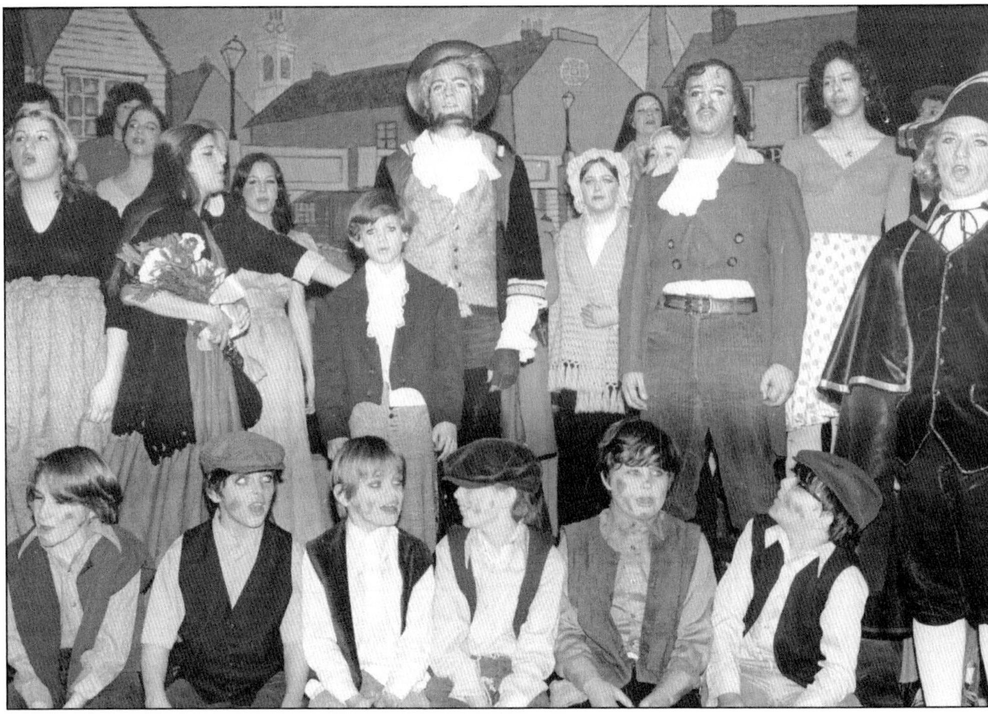

OLIVER! The Teen Club at St. Joan of Arc Roman Catholic Church is seen here in its presentation of *Oliver!* in 1974. (Courtesy of the Queens Borough Public Library, Long Island Division, Joseph A. Ullman Photographs.)

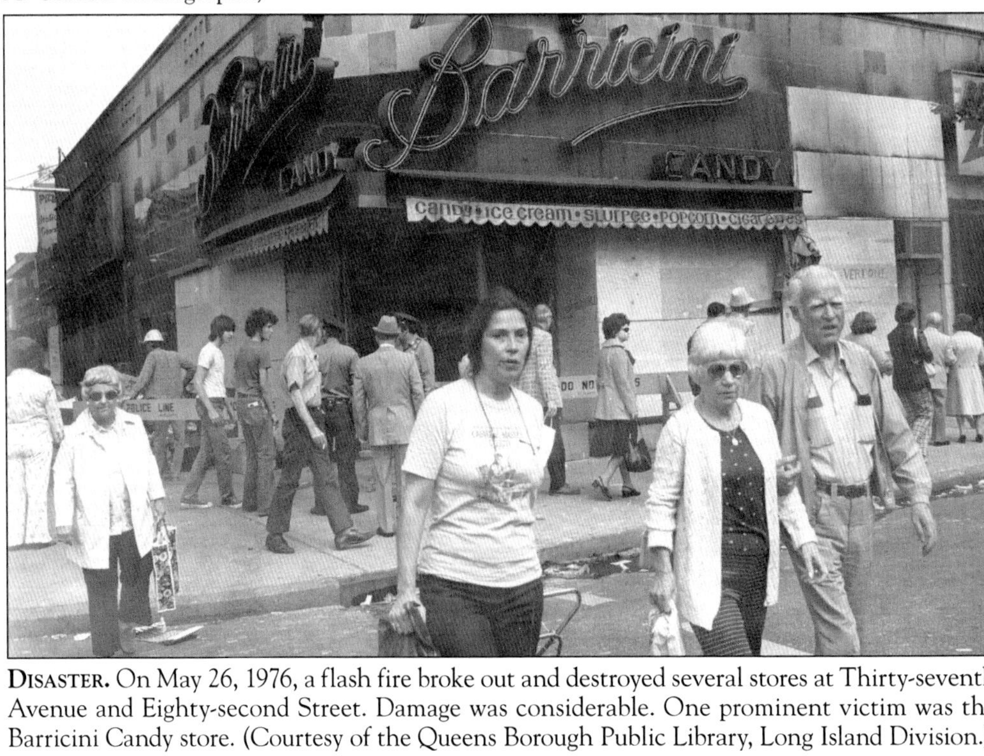

DISASTER. On May 26, 1976, a flash fire broke out and destroyed several stores at Thirty-seventh Avenue and Eighty-second Street. Damage was considerable. One prominent victim was the Barricini Candy store. (Courtesy of the Queens Borough Public Library, Long Island Division.)

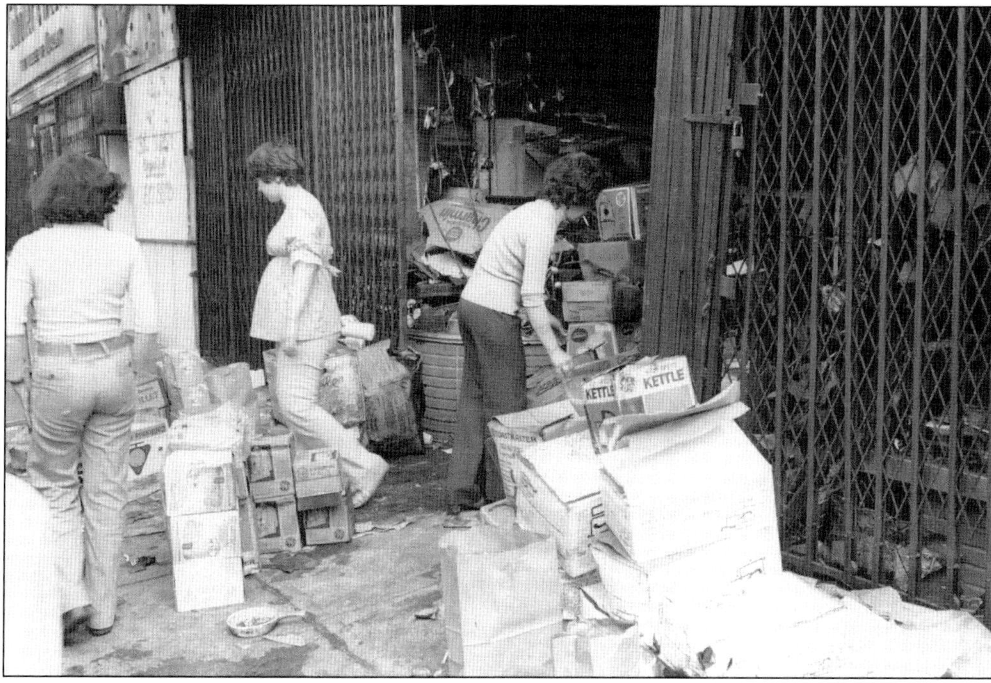

THROWING IT ALL AWAY. The fire devastated the neighboring appliance store. Shown are the owners tossing away charred remains. (Courtesy of the Queens Borough Public Library, Long Island Division.)

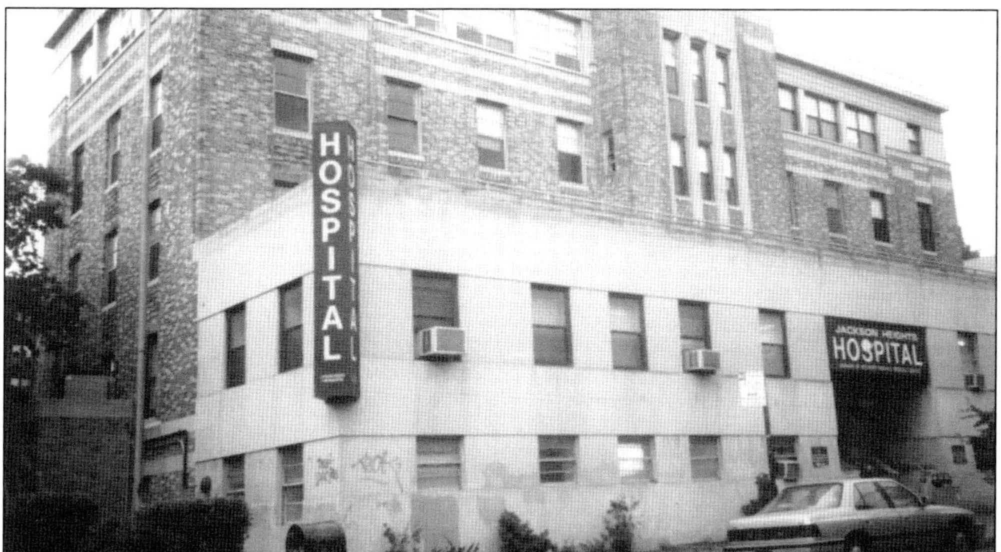

JACKSON HEIGHTS HOSPITAL. This private, nonprofit hospital opened at 3401 Seventy-third Street in 1991. Local residents manned this 83-bed hospital, a division of Wyckoff Heights Medical Center in Bushwick, Brooklyn. Despite an emphasis on one-on-one care, the hospital experienced huge financial losses as cuts in Medicaid and Medicare reimbursements and low patient turnout (there were never more than 20 patients there at a time) took its toll. (Courtesy of the *Queens Gazette*.)

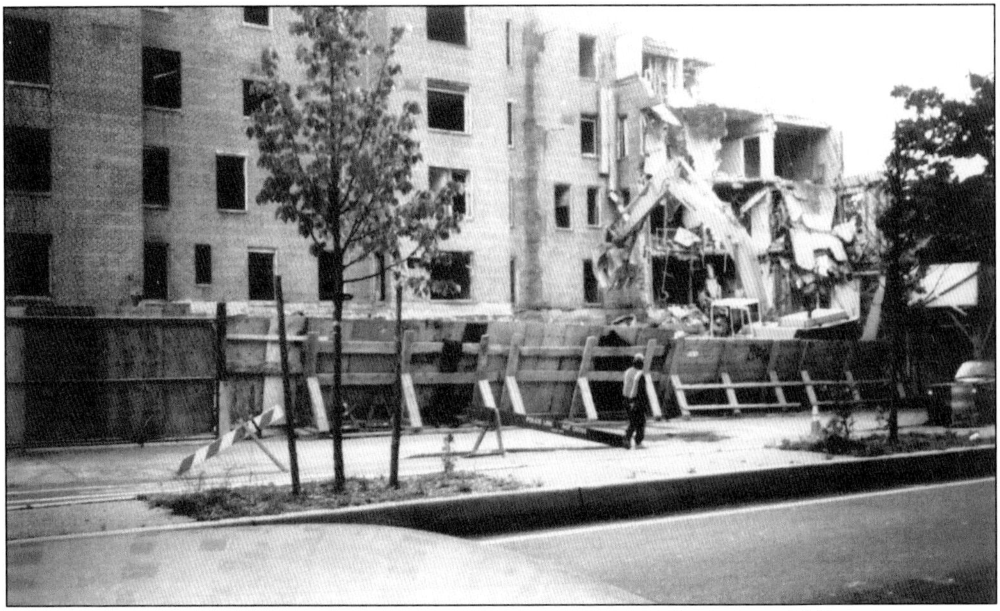

Going, Going, Gone. The hospital fell to the wrecking ball in 1997. It officially closed in December the previous year, laying off 259 employees. (Courtesy of the *Queens Gazette*.)

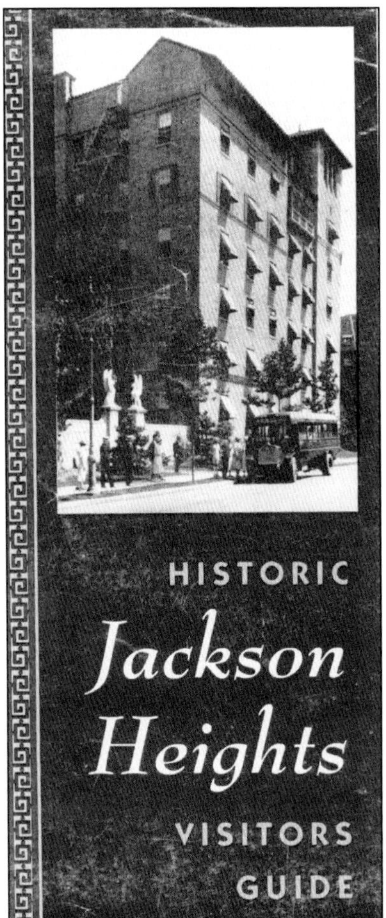

A Historic Proposal. In the 1990s, a campaign was assembled to turn Jackson Heights into a historic district. Brochures, such as this one, were distributed showing points of historic interest. (Courtesy of Sid Potashnick.)

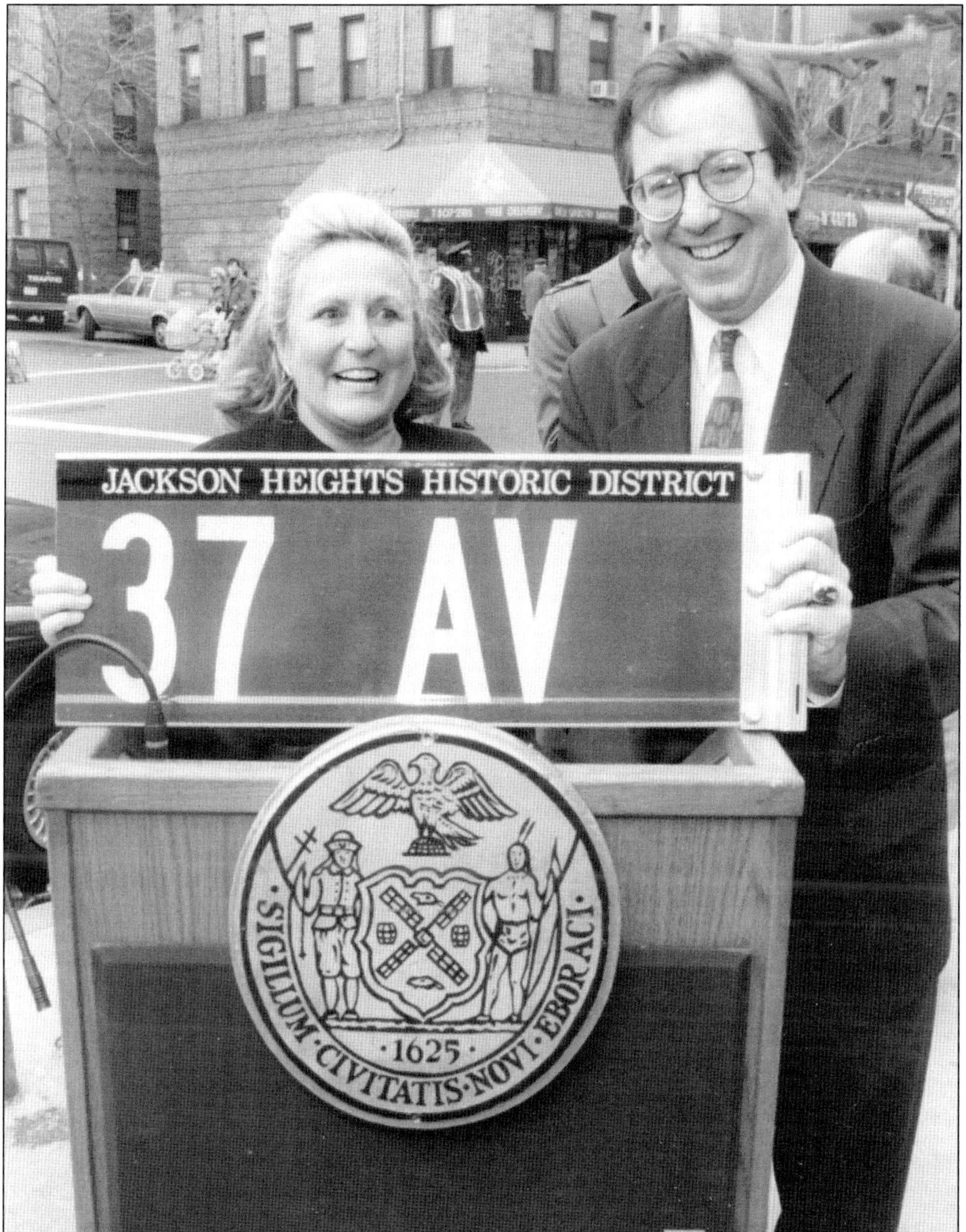

VINDICATION. Jackson Heights, between Seventy-sixth and Eighty-eighth Streets and Roosevelt Avenue and Northern Boulevard, was designated a New York City Historic District on October 19, 1993; this area includes half of the neighborhood. Unlike state and national historic districts, which the neighborhood is also listed as, the local designation came with aesthetic protections. A nationally recognized historic district since 1999, it includes 2,203 contributing buildings within the area as well as 19 contributing sites and three contributing objects. Seen here are former commissioner of the New York City Landmarks Preservation Commission Barbaralee Diamonstein-Spielvogel and council member John Sabini. (Courtesy of the *Queens Gazette*.)

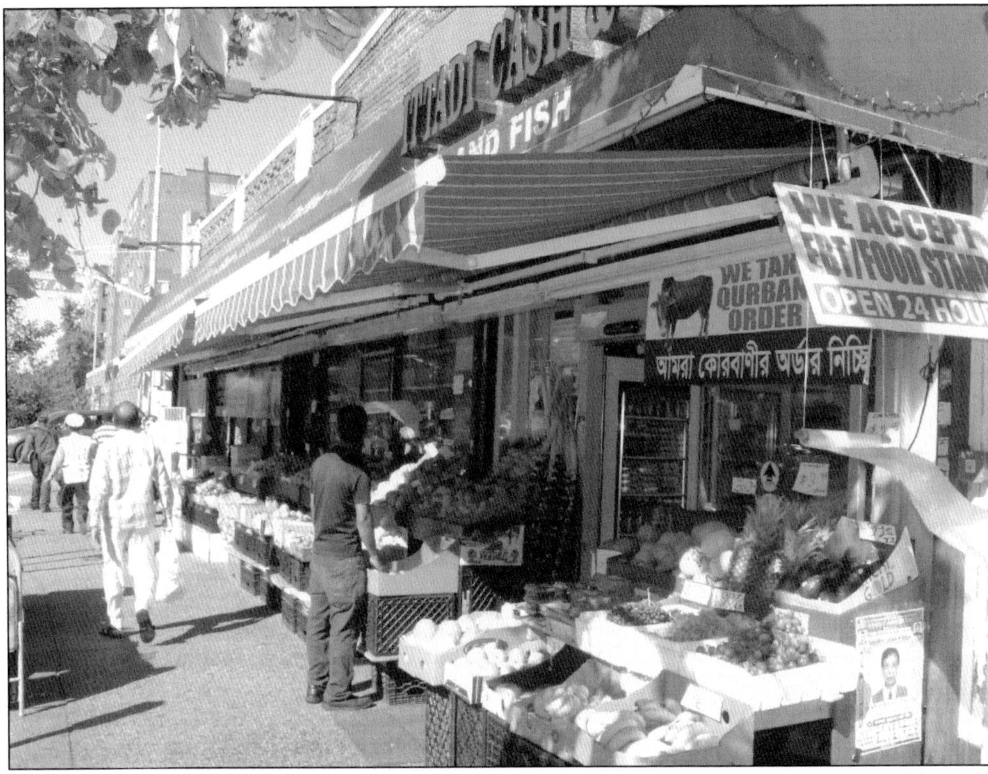

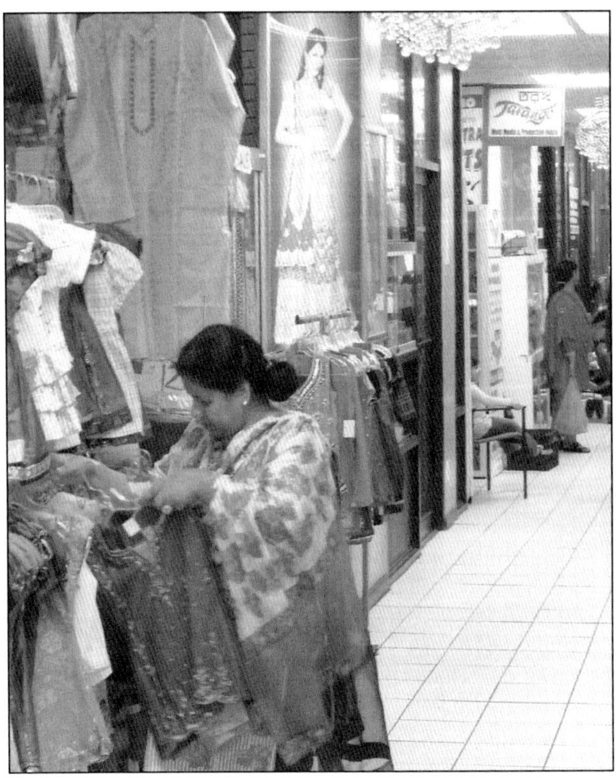

Foods of Bangladesh. This market caters to the Bangladeshi community. Note the sign featuring a cow that reads, "We take Qurbani Orders," above the doorway. Qurbani is the sacrifice of a livestock animal during the Muslim holiday Eid al-Adha (Feast of the Sacrifice), which honors the prophet Abraham.

Shopping in Little India. Jackson Heights is home to a large Indian, Bangladeshi, and Pakistani population. Here, a woman shops for ethnic-style clothing in a store located in Little India along Seventy-fourth Street.

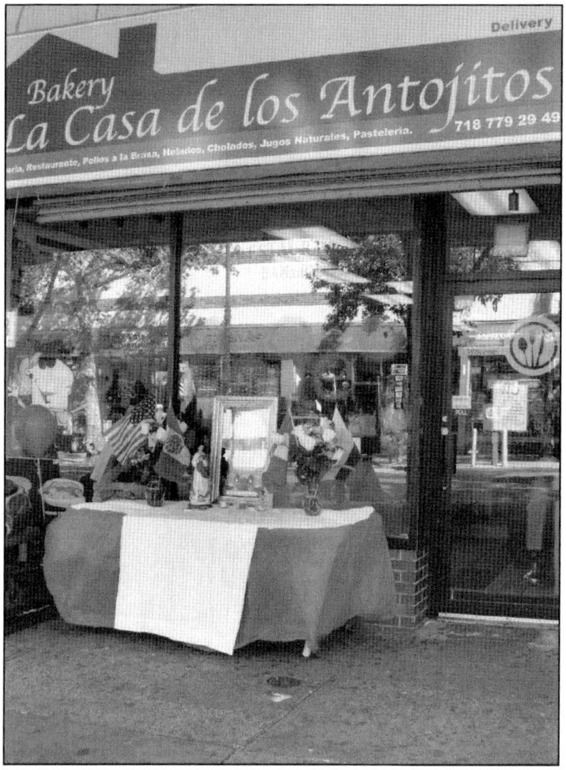

A MULTICULTURAL EXPERIENCE. La Casa de los Antojitos, a Colombian bakery, prominently displays a religious shrine.

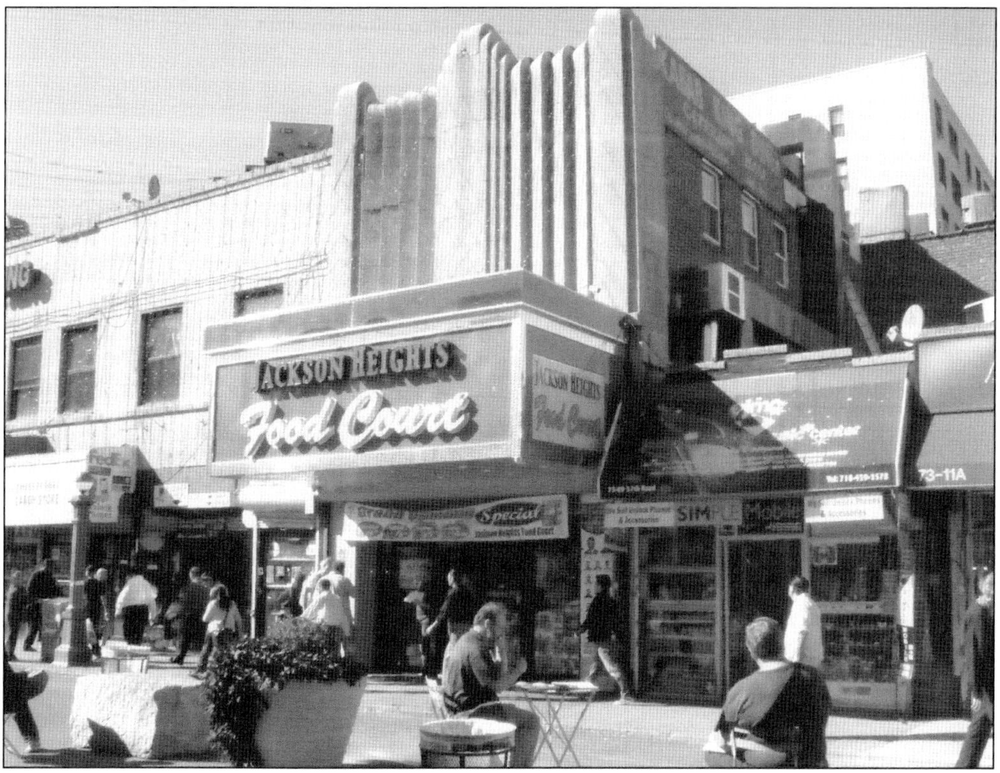

THE JACKSON HEIGHTS PROMENADE. The former Eagle Theatre, an Art Deco theater that most recently screened Bollywood movies from India, is now the Jackson Heights Food Court. Foods from the Middle and Far East can be found inside. Outside, city officials turned Thirty-seventh Road near Seventy-fourth Street into a promenade where people can sit and enjoy the food and do some people watching.

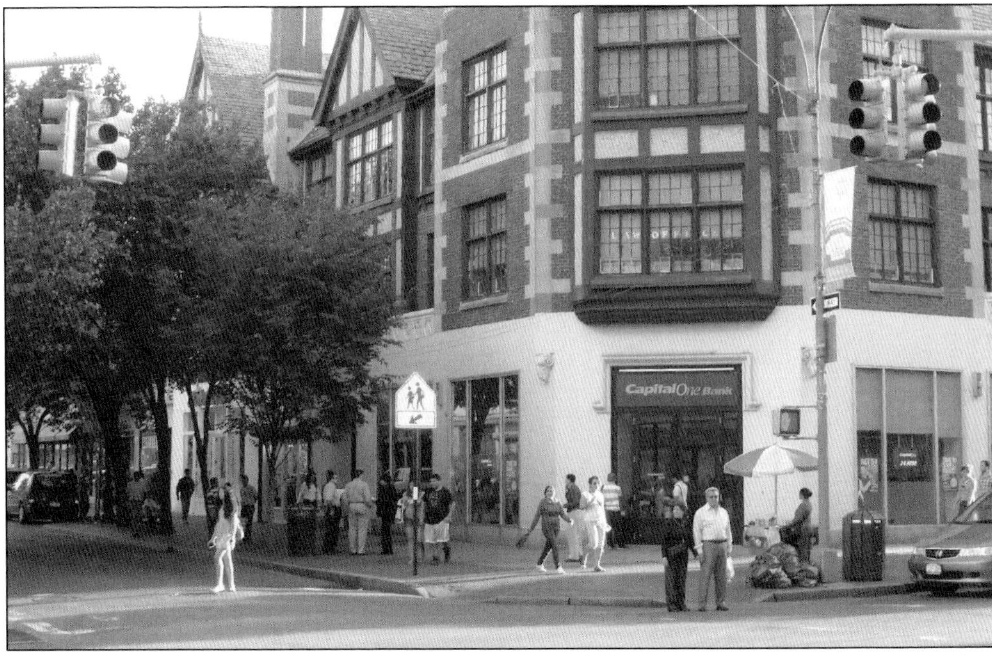

A Modern-day Businesses Section. The Gables, as seen today, located at the corner of Eighty-second Street and Thirty-seventh Avenue, shows another former location of the Queensboro Corporation's headquarters. It now houses a Capital One Bank. Compare this with the image on the bottom of page 59.

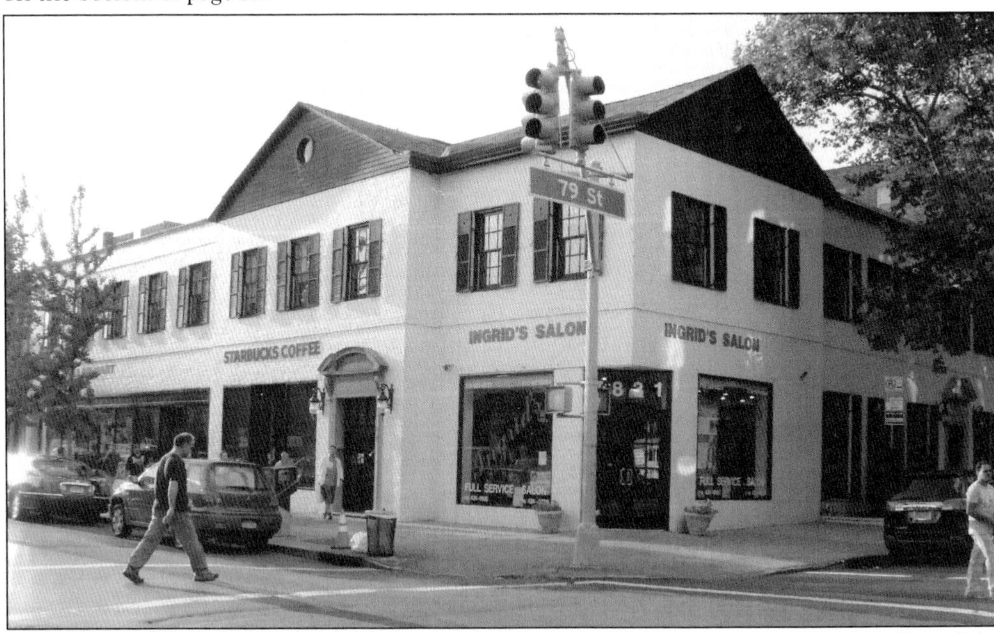

Queensboro Corporation Today. Since the neighborhood's formation, the main office of the Queensboro Corporation occupied several locations. Its final one (designed by Andrew J. Thomas) is seen in this contemporary photograph on the corner of Seventy-ninth Street and Thirty-seventh Avenue. Different businesses, like Starbucks Coffee, Ingrid's Salon, and dental offices, occupy the space that Queensboro once held. Compare this with the image at the top of page 60.

Queensboro Corporation Legacy. The legacy of the agency that created and promoted Jackson Heights remains forever etched in the limestone archway above the former main entrance.

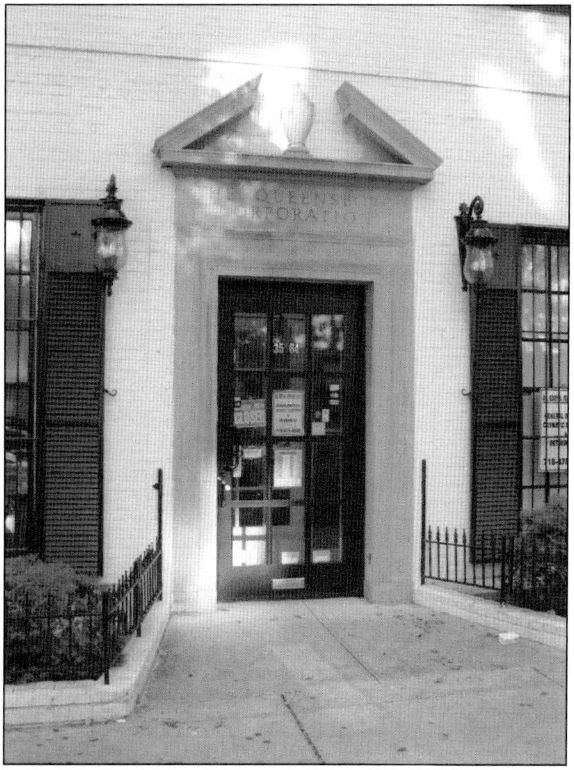

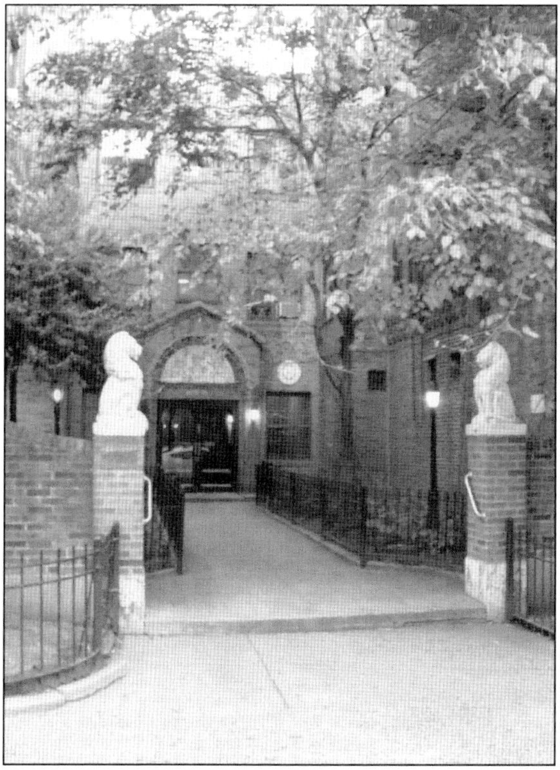

Good Fortune. Without city landmark recognition, Jackson Heights' stately buildings would have been at the mercy of modern developers. Graceful entrances such as this would have been a thing of the past. Note the ever-watchful eyes of a pair of lions.

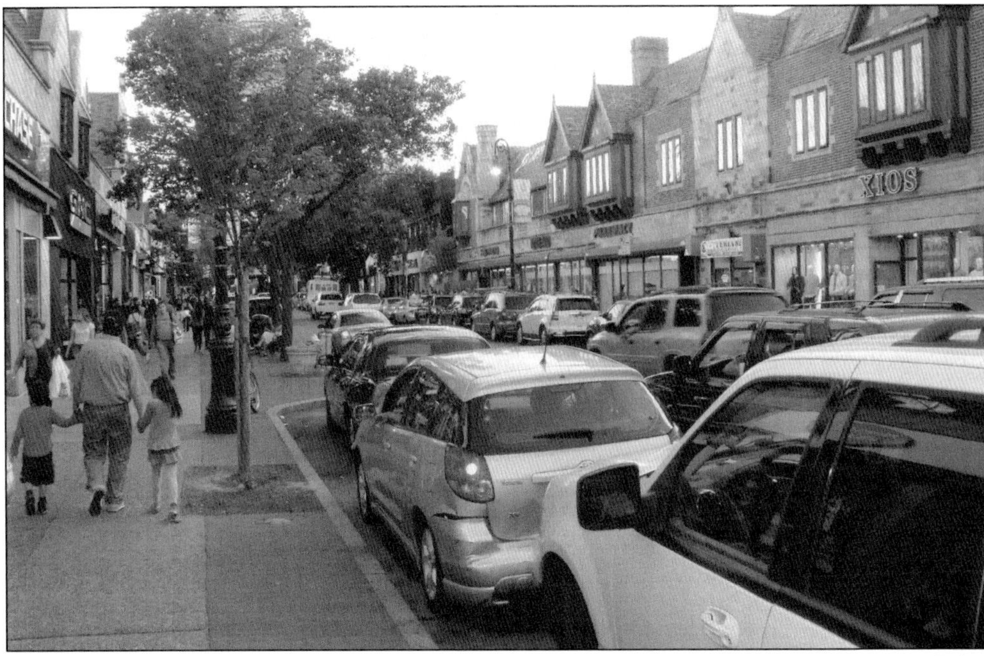

The Gables Today. Far removed from the days of Kresge's five-and-dime, the Gables nevertheless houses active businesses today, both large and small. Shown here are Xios clothing store, a Rite Aid pharmacy, a Chase bank, and a GNC health store. The pedestrian traffic here can be staggering.

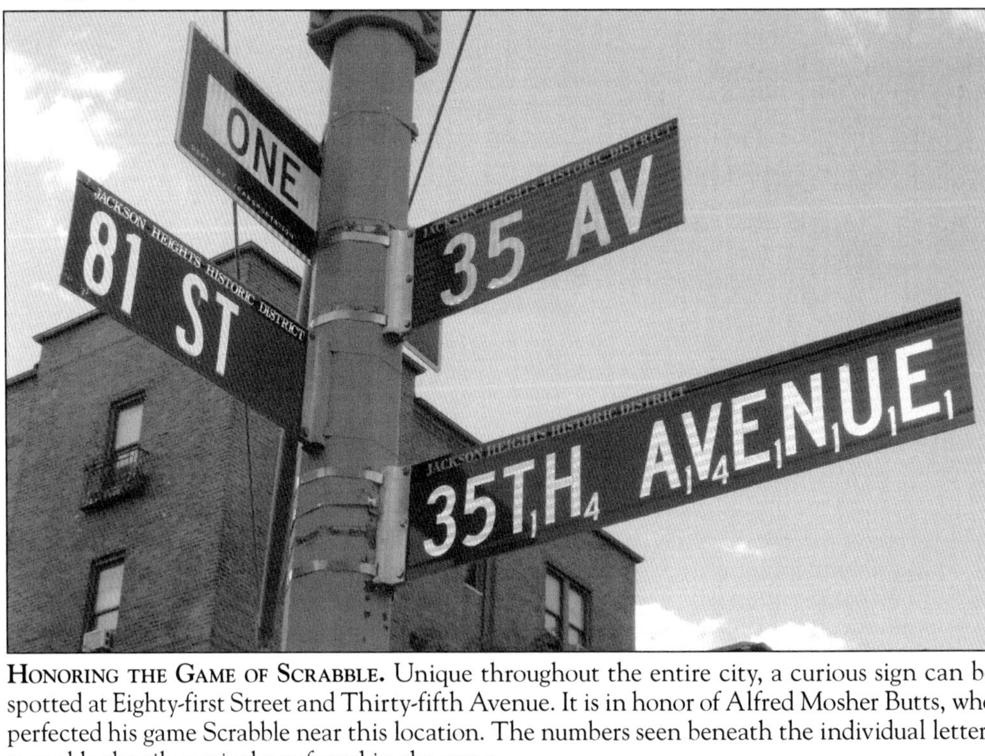

Honoring the Game of Scrabble. Unique throughout the entire city, a curious sign can be spotted at Eighty-first Street and Thirty-fifth Avenue. It is in honor of Alfred Mosher Butts, who perfected his game Scrabble near this location. The numbers seen beneath the individual letters resemble the tile equivalents found in the game.

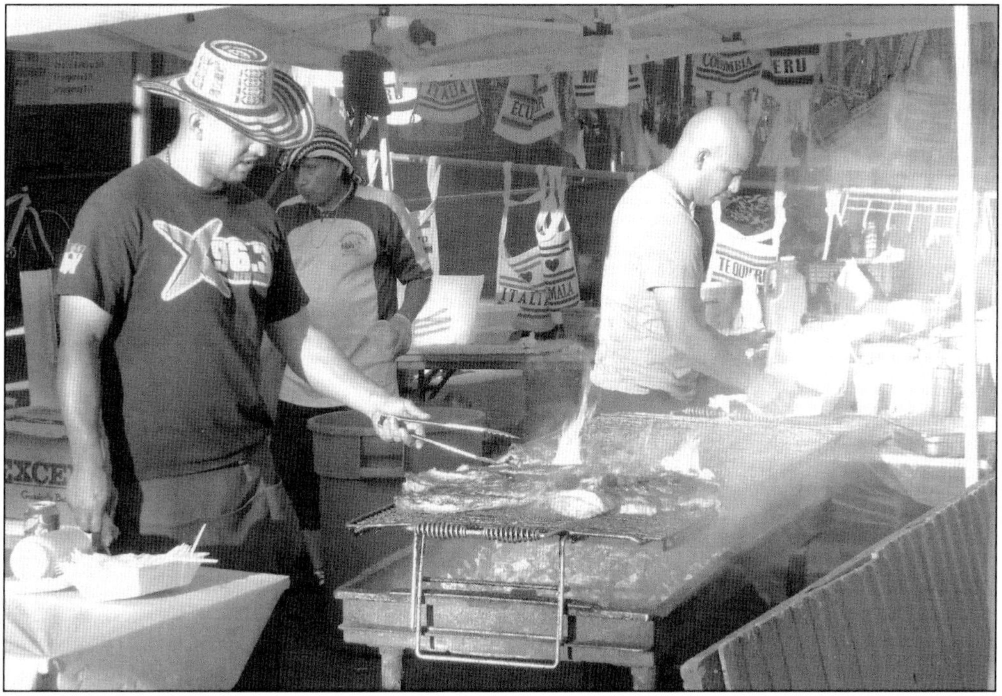

Annual Street Festivals. Street festivals have become common in Jackson Heights, as they celebrate cultures from across the globe with a variety of foods and music. Here, a local restaurant cooks steaks and ribs during an annual summer street festival along Thirty-seventh Avenue.

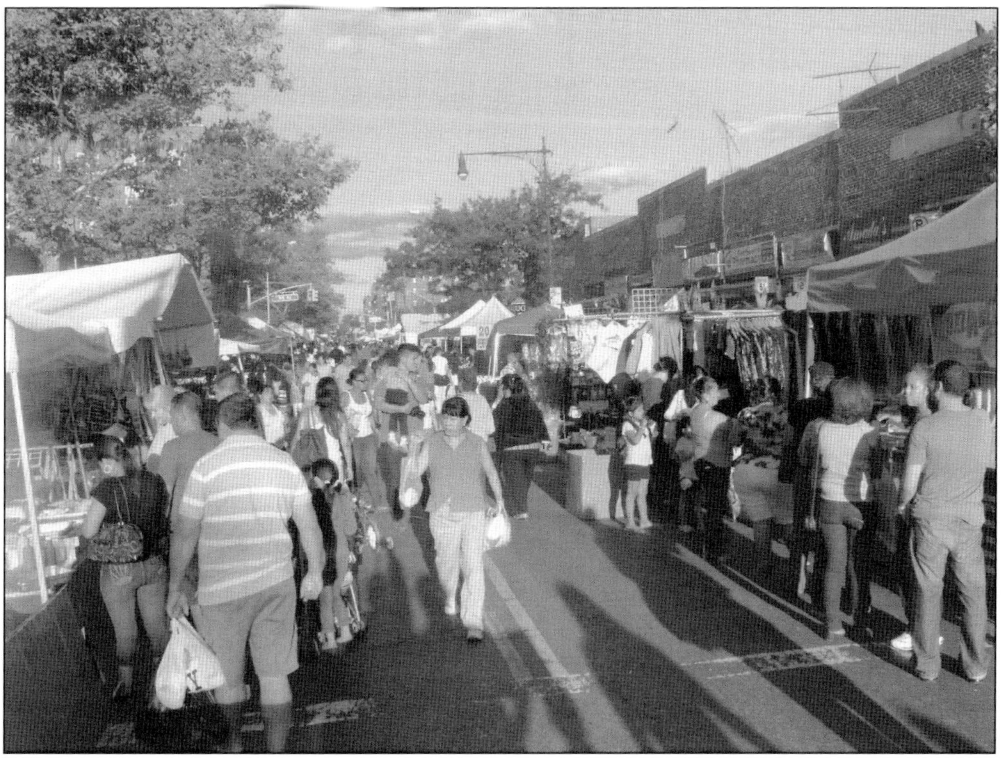

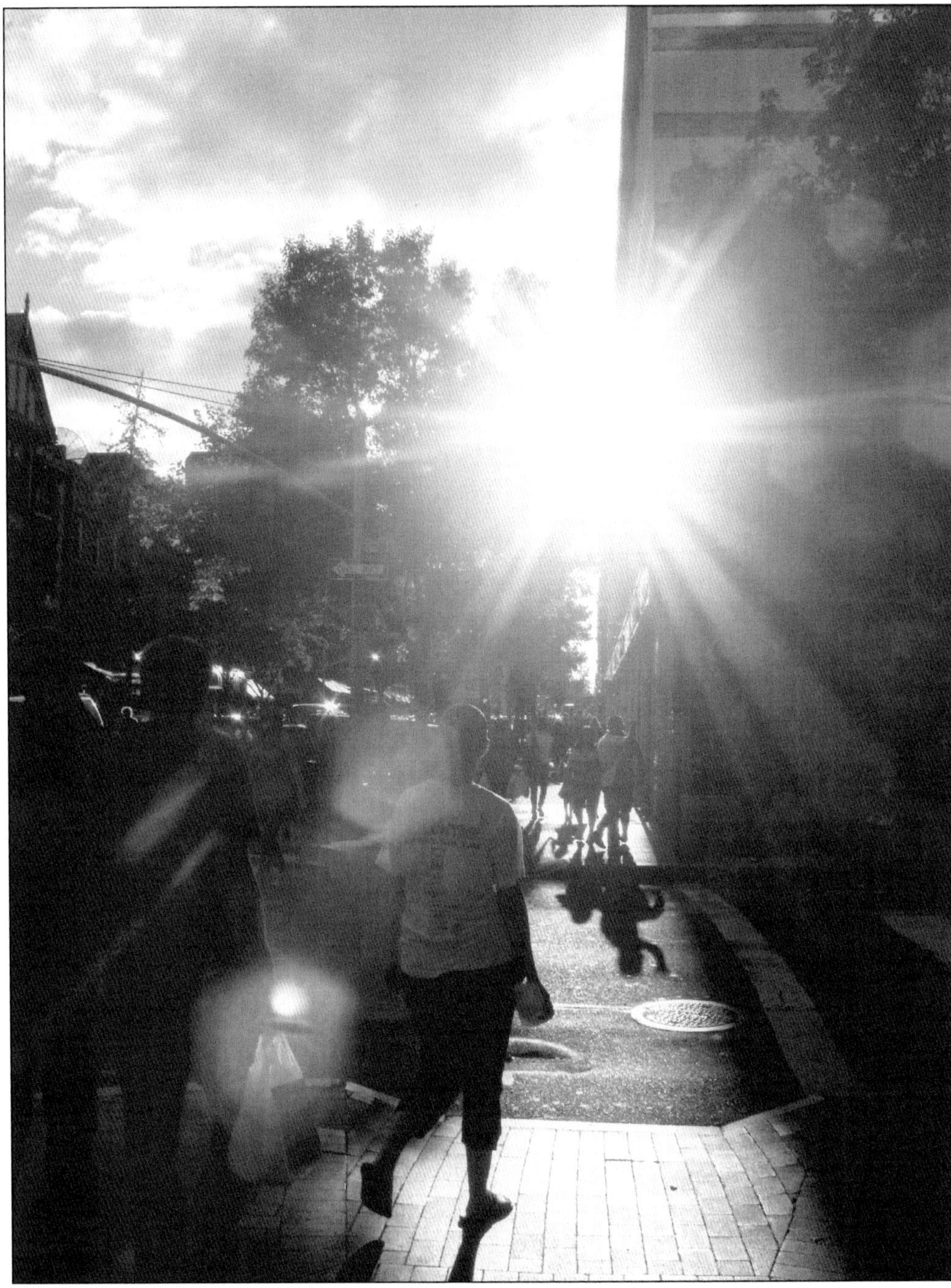

Final Word. "A healthy social life is found only, when in the mirror of each soul the whole community finds its reflection, and when in the whole community the virtue of each one is living."—Rudolph Steiner, social reformer and philosopher (1861–1925).

Bibliography

Brean, Herbert. "A Case of Identity." *Life*, June 29, 1953, 97–107.

Buccellato, James T. *Jackson Heights: 65 Years in Brief*. Self-published.

Copquin, Claudia Gryvatz. *The Neighborhoods of Queens*. New Haven: Yale University Press, 2007.

Hazelton, Henry Isham. *The Boroughs of Brooklyn and Queens, Counties of Nassau and Suffolk, Long Island, New York, 1609–1924, Volume II*. New York: Lewis Historical Publishing, 1925.

Hood, Clifton. *722 Miles: The Building of the Subways and How They Transformed New York*. Baltimore: John Hopkins University Press, 2004.

Jackson, Kenneth, Lisa Keller, and Nancy Flood, eds. *The Encyclopedia of New York City: Second Edition*. New Haven: Yale University Press, 2010.

Karatzas, Daniel. *Jackson Heights, a Garden in the City: The History of America's First Garden and Cooperative Apartment Community*. Jackson Heights, NY: Jackson Heights Beautification Group, 1998.

Kroessler, Jeffrey A. *Lighting the Way: The Centennial History of the Queens Borough Public Library, 1896–1996*. Virginia Beach: Donning Company, 1996.

Plunz, Richard. *A History of Housing in New York City*. New York: Columbia University Press, 1990.

Queens Chamber of Commerce. *Queens Borough, New York City, 1910–1920*. Edited by Walter I. Willis. New York: L.I. Star Publishing, 1920.

queensnyc.com/2012/10/sunnyside-and-jackson-heights-2-of-8-hidden-gems-when-it-comes-to-looking-for-new-digs/

Rickles, Don and David Ritz. *Rickles' Book: A Memoir*. New York: Simon & Schuster, 2007.

Riker, James. *The Annals of Newtown, in Queens County, New York*. New York: D. Fanshaw, 1852.

Sherman, Franklin J. *Building Up Greater Queens Borough: An Estimate of Its Development and the Outlook*. New York: unknown, 1929.

Stern, Robert A.M., Gregory Gilmartin, and Thomas Mellins. *New York 1930: Architecture and Urbanism between the Two World Wars*. New York: Rizzoli, 1987.

www.allamericanwatches.com/page/200980

www.jhbg.org/history/history.html

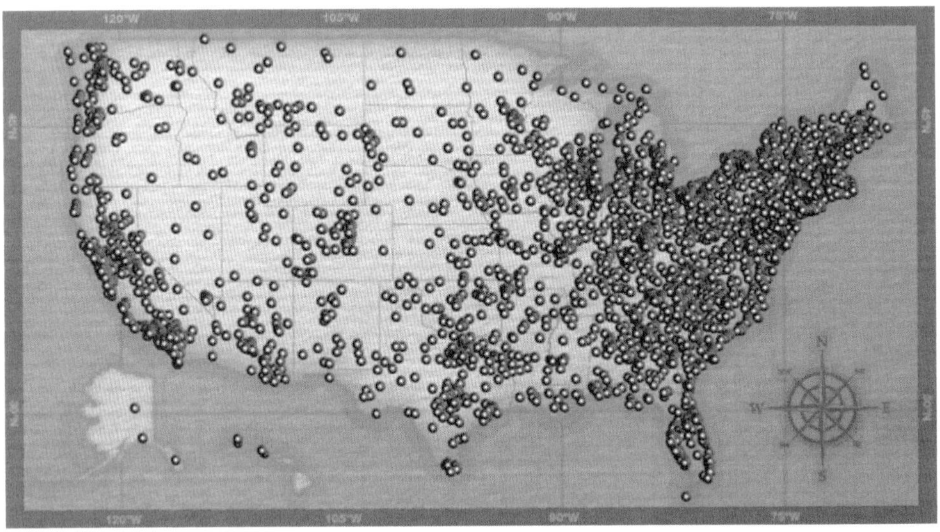